EUROPOLIS

MANCHESTER
1824

Manchester University Press

SERIES EDITORS: *Thomas Christiansen and Emil Kirchner*

PATRIZIA NANZ

EUROPOLIS

Constitutional patriotism
beyond the nation-state

MANCHESTER UNIVERSITY PRESS
Manchester and New York

distributed exclusively in the USA by Palgrave

Copyright © Patrizia Nanz 2006

The right of Patrizia Nanz to be identified as the author of this work has been asserted by her in accordance with the Copyright, Designs and Patents Act 1988.

Published by Manchester University Press
Oxford Road, Manchester M13 9NR, UK
and Room 400, 175 Fifth Avenue, New York, NY 10010, USA
www.manchesteruniversitypress.co.uk

Distributed exclusively in the USA by
Palgrave, 175 Fifth Avenue, New York,
NY 10010, USA

Distributed exclusively in Canada by
UBC Press, University of British Columbia, 2029 West Mall,
Vancouver, BC, Canada V6T 1Z2

British Library Cataloguing-in-Publication Data
A catalogue record for this book is available from the British Library

Library of Congress Cataloging-in-Publication Data applied for

ISBN   0 7190 7387 1 *hardback*
EAN   978 0 7190 7387 8

First published 2006

16 15 14 13 12 11 10 09 08 07 06   10 9 8 7 6 5 4 3 2 1

Edited and typeset in Minion with Lithos
by Frances Hackeson Freelance Publishing Services, Brinscall, Lancs
Printed in Great Britain
by CPI, Bath

CONTENTS

Acknowledgements

The completion of this project was only possible with the support of many sources. Some parts are based on my dissertation research, which was carried out at the European University Institute (Florence) and funded by the Italian Ministry of Foreign Affairs. A stay of several months at the Hanse Institute for Advanced Studies (Delmenhorst) and at the Political Science Department of MIT (Cambridge, MA) allowed me to make revisions that were necessary to transform the dissertation into a book. Seyla Benhabib, Joshua Cohen and Glyn Morgan generously commented on the manuscript during my stay in the United States and encouraged its revision. In its last stages, the book was greatly improved by the valuable insights of John Keane and the late Bernhard Peters, as well as through the helpful advice of two anonymous reviewers and the series editors Grazia Cassara' (Feltrinelli Editore) and Thomas Christiansen. I would like to thank my friends Emma Sinclair-Webb and Xenia von Tippelskirch for providing excellent editorial assistance, as well as Lorraine Frisina for translating the interviews and – together with Martina Piewitt – editing the English text. The last corrections have been made during my stay at the Institute for Advanced Study (Berlin).

Special thanks go to Philippe Schmitter, who supervised my doctoral dissertation and whose encouragement to envisage questions of political science in a 'larger and sometimes unconventional way' has been an enormous inspiration to me. Gianfranco Poggi backed my decision to return to research after years of working in publishing, and guided this work with unyielding commitment. At a critical turning point in this project, I met Charles Sabel at Columbia University, whose hermeneutic insight helped me to translate my initial philosophical intuitions into a political theory of Europe. Peter Wagner provided interesting discussions on social theory and helpful comments during the writing process. Gabriele Rosenthal taught me the art of biographical interviewing during a couple of intense weeks at the Ben Gurion University, Beer Sheva (Israel). I also profited from conversations with Yves Mény, Thomas Risse and Michael Zürn, who all helped to elaborate my theory of the European public sphere to further include an inquiry into the possible emergence of democratic global governance.

I wish to express my appreciation to those who from the beginning of this project have been endless sources of support. I first explored many of the issues treated here during my graduate studies in Frankfurt am Main and at McGill University. In Montreal, Charles Taylor and James Tully introduced me to the discussion surrounding the actual making of the Canadian constitution. The public events at la *Cité libre* in 1994 were an unforgettable experience, which I interpreted through a Humboldtian/Bakhtinian lens of multiple world views and perspectives. During many hours of discussion, Charles Taylor pressed me to articulate my own conception of understanding as mutual translation or 'exploration of difference', while defending his own position in ways that sought to encourage rather than deflect further debate and exchange. Although Carol Feldman and Jerome Bruner argued for a more culturalist idea of Europe, they showed, in important moments, a much appreciated enthusiasm for my project of a 'politics without *demos*'. Jürgen Habermas certainly has had the most profound influence on my thinking. He was both a challenging and understanding mentor during my graduate studies in Frankfurt and encouraged my plans to move from philosophy of language to a theory of the European public sphere. He must have been puzzled by the many biographical detours and the amount of time I took, but to his great credit he never showed it and his sympathy has remained consistent through the years. It is difficult to convey my debt to his scholarship. These four individuals, as well as the late Günther Busch, former head of the Humanities Department of S. Fischer publishing house, have shown me how to live an intellectual life with political passion, curiosity and moral rigour. I feel privileged to have had the opportunity of knowing them.

My particular thanks go to my friends and colleagues who were willing, in the midst of their own busy schedules, to read and comment on drafts: Daniele Archibugi, Jessica Almqvist, Bert van den Brink, Gesa Gordon, Ken Hirschkop, Cathleeen Kantner, Eugenia Siapera, Yves Sintomer, Marianne van der Steeg and Jens Steffek. Their advice was priceless and by no means reflects whatever weaknesses still remain. It is difficult to convey the depth of my gratitude to Oliver Gerstenberg. His encouragement and interest in this project were critical to its completion, while his sharp intelligence challenged me to rethink central aspects of my arguments. For many years and throughout all my various moves, the loyalty of my dear friends has been invaluable to me. To name just a few, Teresa Bartolomei (Lisbon), Roberto Budini Gattai (Florence), Alessandra Columbu (Milan), Paola Fabbri (Frankfurt am Main), Isabelle Ferreras (Brussels), Gesa Gordon (Berlin), Emma Sinclair-Webb (London and Istanbul) and Xenia von Tippelskirch (Paris).

Finally, I wish to acknowledge the invaluable assistance of my family. Thanks are due to Peter for his unconditional support and affection over the past years; to my mother for her help in innumerable ways and for her genuine curiosity about the development of my thoughts; to my father, and Tanja, for encouraging me in all my endeavours; and to my brother Matthias for reminding me that there is life beyond work. *Europolis* is dedicated to the memory of my grandmother, Irma Piva-Piani (1907–91).

(Wär ich wie du. Wärst du wie ich.
Standen wir nicht
unter einem Passat?
Wir sind Fremde.)

(Paul Celan, *Ausgewählte Gedichte*,
Suhrkamp Verlag, Frankfurt
am Main 1968, p. 60.)

What wide difference, therefore, in the sentiments of morals,
must be found between civilized nations and Barbarians,
or between nations whose characters have little in common?
How shall we pretend to fix a standard for judgements of this nature?

(David Hume, *Enquiries concerning Human
Understanding and concerning the
Principles of Morals*, Clarendon Press,
Oxford 1975, p. 333.)

Far from being a peculiar pastime of a narrow set of specialists,
'translation' is woven into the texture of daily life and practiced
daily and hourly by us all. We are all translators; translation is the
common feature in all forms of life, as it is part and parcel of the
'informatics society' modality of being-in-the-world.

(Zygmunt Bauman, *In Search of Politics*,
Polity Press, Cambridge 1999, p. 201.)

PART I

The European public sphere –
and why bother?

1

Introduction

> Reason is, and ought only to be
> the slave of the passions.
> *David Hume*[1]

In modern Western democracies, the public sphere, mediating between political authority and people, is an important source of legitimacy:[2] it is this arena, (analytically) distinct from both state and market, in which a collectivity of citizens may come together as the bearer of 'public opinion', and thus exert some influence over policy making. Unlike American society, where the state plays a minor part in channelling social conflicts, European societies remain, by and large, political regions identifiable by a strong welfare state presence and a nationally organized political system capable of creating social integration.[3] Yet the authority of the single nation-state is gradually being undermined by processes of European integration. The most obvious evidence of this development has been the establishment of the principles of direct effect and the supremacy of Community law over national law.[4]

Phenomena of transnational legalisation point to the need of constitutionalism as an ideal to expose European rule-making to claims of democratic legitimacy.[5] It is important to acknowledge that constitutionalist justification of politics takes place not only in strong institutionalised (democratic and legal) procedures, but also in a decentred public sphere in which citizens deliberate about fundamental questions and ask for normatively legitimate treatment. From such a perspective, I will argue that the idea of European constitutionalism is to ultimately include citizens as constitutional interpreters in an ongoing transnational process of social learning. Seeing that the European Union (EU) is no longer a mere instrument for implementing the will of member states, any bestowal of democratic legitimacy upon it must depend upon the creation of a European public sphere, which can serve as an institutionalized arena for discursive interaction beyond national boundaries. If the European Community[6] is to re-invent itself on the basis of European-wide political mobilization and citizen identification, the roles of transnational dialogue and transnational citizenship practices are indispensable.

In this book, I present a vision of Europe as a *plébiscite de tous les jours*[7] – a European public sphere as a multiplicity of continuous and overlapping civic dialogues conducted across cultural and national boundaries that lead to the mutual formation and change of individual perspectives. At the heart of this argument is a dialogical conception of politics and the self which I explore through the lens of translation theory.[8]

In their emotions, alliances and political loyalties, selves are not coherent in the sense of conforming to some simple model of consistency. Within any political community there is always contestation arising not only from conflicting – particularly economic – interests, but also from competing ethical perspectives, world views or outlooks, and cultural identities. In my view, the self and politics are analogous arenas of conflicting moral tendencies, divided aims and socio-cultural ambivalence. Selves and politics are part of every person's experience, just as ideological contention is part of political reasoning, particularly under conditions of uncertainty and the indeterminacy of knowledge. While we still have diverse life stories unfolding in a variety of socio-cultural contexts and amid different conceptions of the good, misunderstandings and conflicts will not come to an end. Rather they are the very motivation for an ongoing mutual (self-)clarification, for the resolution of ambiguity, and for political deliberation. Rationality is a bond between persons, but it is not a very powerful one. In a conflict where passionate loyalties exist on both sides, it is only a commitment to engage in the 'mutual exploration of difference' which enables the participants to find the 'best' or the most 'just' solution to a common problem, thereby generating dialogical solidarity across ethical, cultural and national boundaries.

Quite apart from the substantive conceptions of justice under discussion, the specific forms of argument and negotiation, and the arenas in which these 'epistemic struggles' are to be fought out are themselves often subject to dispute. Such procedural issues are at stake in current debates about European political integration. They beg the questions: what are the conditions under which it might be possible to construct a political democracy on the scale of Europe as a whole? What are the normative and empirical presuppositions for a European constitutional patriotism – that is, a common European identity based on a conscious affirmation of political and constitutional principles – and for a European-wide public sphere – that is, an institutionalized arena for transnational political participation and for the intercultural formation of collective identities? In order to tackle these questions, we have to inquire into a conceptual paradigm of democratic deliberation under conditions of persisting national, cultural and ethical pluralism. With the constant deepening of EU competences, the Union's institutions increasingly require a degree of direct or substantive legitimacy alongside the procedural legitimacy provided by EU treaties, and the indirect legitimacy derived from the member states. The arguments surrounding the extended role of politics and the aims and scope of collective and political action raise issues that, if pressed far enough, lead us away from political science and into the realms of philosophy.

The arguments that I draw from these realms are relevant for two principal reasons: they suggest, first of all, that in order to bring into existence institution-alized forums for political participation beyond the limits of the nation-state, the practice of European constitutional dialogue – understood as a form of self-determination of the European people – should have priority over a simple declaration of principles. Only through regular argumentation and engagement in dialogue with our fellow citizens can we foster loyalty to the institutions of Europe (a 'situated' European constitutional patriotism). In fact, the idea of a European constitutional dialogue is very suited to the EU's constitutionalism that has been an essentially open-ended process of deliberation and political struggle. The EU constitution does not emanate from scratch, but rather through the incremental forging of a constitutional structure with roots in European law, in common national constitutional traditions, and in international law. Its constitutionalism therefore fits the notion of a constitution as an ongoing project much better than national constitutions understood as written texts. Accordingly, European constitutional patriotism refers to a commitment to the EU's constitutionalism and its underlying ideals, not to a particular constitution. This would, in fact, allow citizens to have a critical stance towards the Constitutional Treaty,[9] depending on whether they believe (or not) that the Treaty embodies constitutional ideals. The idea is that constitutional dialogue calls for the perpetual expansion and amendment of the constitution.

Second, I also contend that popular respect for the establishment of transnational citizenship practices will chiefly derive from the customary use of those practices. Social legitimacy in the new Europe, in other words, arises from gradually acquired familiarity with transnational political participation. Much will depend on whether the political process at the European level will provide citizens with sufficient opportunities and incentives to engage with constitutional ideals. European constitutional patriotism will only develop if constitutional ideals are the focal points of political and legal contestation that are meaningfully connected to citizens' political action. Given equality of access and of respect for different voices, there is a chance (however small) that a kind of 'case law' will develop within democratic politics which will serve to legitimize the creeping constitutionalism that already characterizes juridical practices and the activities of European expert groups (comitology) – constitutionalism understood as a transnational (rather than post-national) dialogue, linking various deliberative spaces across Europe, and allowing for mutual reflective learning.[10]

This account of politics conceives of 'deliberation' as a dialogical exchange of public reasons for the purpose of resolving common problems that makes participants answerable and accountable to one another. According to this definition, deliberation is not so much a form of discourse or argumentation aiming at reaching a consensual understanding, but a joint, cooperative activity of mutual translation and justification of viewpoints in an ongoing process of pragmatic experimentation, in the search for positive-sum outcomes. By promoting continuous intercultural translation or inter-societal learning, this kind of citizenship practice could produce a European political community which is not based on a *demos* or a common cultural heritage, but on the shared pursuit of the most just and efficient solutions to social problems or the best interpretations of constitutional principles. Or, in other words, a polity based on a 'situated constitutional patriotism' that goes well beyond the nation-state.

There is clearly a risk that, in emphasizing the ongoing exploration of difference as a means to expand the horizons of citizens, we will end up with an idea of politics as an unending struggle between different world views. The obvious challenge to such an idea would be to question whether it is compatible with the existence of (legitimate, which is today non-coercive) social and political integration. I will argue, however, that the radical cultural and ethical pluralism of situated constitutional patriotism is counterbalanced by the 'interpretative charity' or 'dialogical solidarity' that deliberation is intended to produce. And that this (substantial) mutual perspective-taking is a necessary condition for political cohabitation (i.e. the tolerance of different ethical perspectives), as well as the political justification of principles (e.g. when specifying the principle of tolerance in a given moral or legal conflict). Justificatory discourses presuppose the exploration of difference so as to avoid cutting off our experience of the social world and to include the disclosure of hitherto undiscovered perspectives, social pathologies and the likes.

At present, Europe is an emerging post-national normative order, but one which is unlikely to become a new, integrated super-state. Rather, it is a deliberative and decision-making space, sustained by a set of evolving institutions, in which the question of statehood and the boundaries of political community are continually contested. In fact, the EU is a particular kind of polity, which is not based on pre-existing solidarities, but on mutually agreed projects and cooperative enterprises. This book is not about the EU's multi-level system, but rather about what democracy could mean for a pluralistic polity at a meta-level. Disputes about just and fair political procedures and institutions for Europe may continue indefinitely. To affirm the permanence of contestation and struggle about the meaning of principles and rights within an ordered collaborative setting is not to envisage or celebrate a world without stability, standards or clear decision-making. Rather it is to treat rules and laws as an open space for constant interpretation in political deliberation, as opposed to instruments of closure. Nonetheless, it should be underlined that, with *Europolis: Constitutional Patriotism beyond the Nation-State,* I offer a conceptual paradigm of democratic deliberation (that is perhaps utopian by nature), not a political programme.

Although I agree with Stuart Hampshire's paraphrasing of Hume's dictum that in 'moral and political philosophy one is looking for premises from which to infer conclusions already and independently accepted because of one's feelings and sympathies',[11] this project aims not only to articulate my intuition about the usefulness of a theory of translation for a pluralistic approach to politics, but also to see whether there is evidence for this theory 'out there' in contemporary Europe. I wanted to be sure that what brought me to hold this particular and contingent view on politics and the self was not simply my own personal experience. As children we discover the world through the eyes of the many different persons we encounter and relate to. Because of this we learn to switch perspectives, learning that total mutual understanding (or *ungebrochene Intersubjektivität* in German) or transparency is never possible, but that to endeavour to explore the differences between people is nonetheless worthwhile. I have perhaps been particularly curious about this issue for reasons to do with my rather ambivalent sense of national and cultural belonging.

During my graduate studies in Frankfurt and Montreal, I began to think about the Humboldtian and Bakhtinian idea of the plurality of languages as a plurality of ways of seeing the world, as well as the idea of the possibility of translation between languages or vocabularies. However, I realised that, ultimately, most political theorists (ranging from the liberal to the communitarian to the procedural-deliberative) are wary of the disruption of politics provoked by difference and heterogeneity. They confine politics to the juridical, administrative or regulative tasks of containing plurality and stabilizing the people by building consensus or consolidating communities and identities. By contrast, I wanted to argue that plurality could be an asset to the epistemic struggle of politics. Multiple interpretations of the social world and of potential solutions to problems could be explored within an open field of discovery. This kind of constructivist view of the political community has no a priori or pre-given (cultural) boundaries. When I started to develop these ideas as a theory of the public sphere, I ran into the debate on European integration, where most participants are convinced of the impossibility of a European public sphere precisely because it would have to cross national and cultural boundaries. I immediately understood that I wanted to extend the theory of mutual translation to this debate, thereby contributing to political theory of transnational democracy. Under conditions of societal denationalization my personal experiences of national/cultural ambivalence and constant mutual learning seem to be both widely shared and deeply at odds with conventional political theory. Unknown by many political theorists but common to everyday practice, the process of constant mutual translation of perspectives, world views or outlooks has become more prominent.

The larger aim of *Europolis*, then, is to extend the idea of constitutional dialogue within society itself to encompass not just existing socio-political units, but also new, transnational governance arenas that are (conceived of here as) sites for mutual learning. The idea of a European public sphere as a multiplicity of ongoing cross-cultural civic dialogues can serve as a conceptual tool for current research on new forms of European governance arrangements. They stand for a move beyond both territorial and functional integration and provide forums for the recombination of conflicting views on issues concerning society as a whole (e.g. foodstuff regulation, product safety, environmental standards and risk regu-lation in general). If we conceptualize the public sphere as a communicative net-work where different publics partially overlap, the emerging character of the EU as a multi-level system of policy-making can be seen as offering the opportunity for the creation of new communities of political action. Such a 'pluricentric' view of European politics should, of course, explore whether these new modes of gov-ernance, as for example the Open Method of Coordination (e.g. operating in the areas of employment, pensions, or social exclusion policy), ensure the account-ability of democratic decision-making bodies.

This book is divided into three parts. In Part I, I will outline the main argu-ments (and the normative implications) of the main two contemporary demo-cratic theories of European integration with respect to the role they do or do not assign to the European public sphere. I will also discuss the false dichotomy of global markets and national democracy that economic liberalism and social demo-cratic theories create (Chapter 2). First, I will show how the market-dominance view leads to an understanding of EU institutions as a de-politicized regulatory branch of the Member States. Next, I shall reconstruct in greater detail a promi-nent thesis in the literature on European integration – namely, the *demos*-thesis as argued by Claus Offe, Fritz Scharpf and Dieter Grimm. Finally, I will briefly sketch an alternative, deliberative vision of a denationalized polity as can be found in the EU.

Part II is the core of this project. It is here that I propose my own dialogical or 'interdiscursive' version of the theory of deliberative democracy. Chapter 3 revis-its the concept of the public sphere, whose absence in the EU has been lamented by most integration theorists, reformulating the Habermasian conceptualization in terms of the transnational and pluricultural polity of the EU. Instead of simply aiming to contain pluralism, my conception of the public sphere actively values the everyday exploration of difference between strangers with heterogeneous cul-tural/ethical and national backgrounds. Chapter 4 discusses the political *problematique* of socio-cultural pluralism from the perspective of multiculturalism. I propose a dialogical concept of culture as constantly (re)produced and negoti-ated with other cultures in public discourse. Chapter 5 shows that we can derive an idea of continuous intercultural translation or 'multicultural literacy' from the philosophy of language. In Chapter 6 I will look at the political implications of theories of translation and mutual comprehension in order to broaden and deepen discussion of the possible emergence of a new polity in the EU. It is in this chapter that I will spell out the idea of mutual translation as a form of political delibera-tion or as a constitutional dialogue understood as the exploration of different interpretations of principles. I will show that with the addition of the concept of translation, the idea of constitutional patriotism becomes, at the same time, both more constructivist and more 'situated': democratic deliberation is not seen as sociologically naturalized (by the boundaries of a common culture/language or *demos*), but as situated in dialogical interaction, creating an always more densely differentiated network of contexts within which the constitutional project is critically interpreted and becomes potentially inclusive to new members of a political community.

Finally, in Part III of this book, I will consider whether the idea of such a situated constitutional patriotism beyond the nation-state is simply an 'armchair' theory or one that is supported by empirical evidence about peoples' sense of belonging under conditions of Europeanization. In exploring this question, we must deem those who live and work in-between nations, cultures and languages as knowledgeable 'political theorists' on the matter. The increasing mobility of Europeans has certainly produced transnational spaces of professional and everyday life experience that transform peoples' sense of belonging. After briefly presenting the material, setting and methodology of my exploratory research (Chapter 7), I will interpret the life stories of migrants from different socio-cultural backgrounds through a systematic analysis of empirical data, tentatively relating it to previous discussions of theory (Chapter 8). This chapter analyzes peoples' collective identities and their understanding of citizenship in reference to the EU. I will show that in contemporary Europe there is a host of empirical evidence in support of the idea of an emergent intercultural dialogue. For the people, European identity is not a matter of convergence but of 'interdiscursivity': they display a pastiche of self-understandings and a multilayered idea of citizenship, both of which serve as a basis for their engagement in transnational citizenship practices.

I conclude that we should be cautious not to reify the concept of European identity or an 'imagined community' on the basis of a set of common values or a fixed legacy. Rather, the core of European identity must be found in the growing reflexivity within European collective identities. It is open for difference and permanent contestation, and has no need to exclude the 'other' for its own stabilization. For the development of a 'situated' transnational constitutional patriotism it is crucial that the nature of the political process at the European level provides citizens with opportunities and incentives to engage in transnational citizenship practices.

Notes

1 D. Hume, *A Treatise of Human Nature*, in: D. Hume, *The Philosophical Works*, vol. 2, Scientia Verlag, Aalen 1964, p. 195.

2 Legitimacy can be understood as the general compliance of a population with decisions of a political order that goes beyond coercion or the contingent representation of interests. Normatively, democratic legitimacy results from a rational agreement among free and equal citizens.

3 See: A. Touraine, 'European Sociologists between Economic Globalization and Cultural Fragmentation', in: T. Boje, B. van Steenbergen and S. Walby (eds.), *European Societies: Fusion or Fiction?*, Routledge, London/New York 1999, pp. 249–262.

4 '*Direct effect* means that provisions of Community law must be applied by the national courts of the member states without prior transformation into national law through the national parliament, the principle of *supremacy* signifies that a directly effective provision of Community law always prevails over a conflicting provision of national law' (U. K. Preuss, 'Citizenship in the European Union: a Paradigm for Transnational Democracy?', in: D.

Archibugi, D. Held and M. Köhler (eds.), *Re-imagining Political Community: Studies in Cosmopolitan Democracy*, Polity Press, Cambridge 1998, p. 138).

5 The *telos* of constitutionalism is to establish the internal relation between the rule of law and democratic forms of political will-formation, that is 'the conditions under which one can legally institutionalise the forms of communication necessary for legitimate law-making' (J. Habermas, 'On the Internal Relation between the Rule of Law and Democracy', in: *European Journal of Philosophy* 3:1, 1995, p. 16).

6 The terms European Union and European Community are used interchangeably here.

7 i.e. a 'daily plebiscite' (E. Renan, 'Qu'est-ce que une nation?', in: E. Renan, *Oeuvres complètes*, vol. 1, Calmann Lévy, Paris 1947, p. 904).

8 That is, the Humboldtian concept of an 'unshared' dimension of mutual understanding and intersubjectivity coined by Habermas as 'gebrochene Intersubjektivität'.

9 Much will have to be said about the seemingly failed process of ratifying the Constitutional Treaty and the options for addressing the resulting political crisis in the EU, but this is not the place to do it (for a bibliography on this topic see: www.unizar.es/euroconstitucion/Treaties/Treaty_Const_Rat_Bibliography.htm). Suffice it to say that the process of ratifying the Constitutional Treaty – which broke down after the French and Dutch referendums in May and June 2005 – was an important step towards constitutional politics. That is to say, popular input for the constitutional nature of the European legal order already in place. The failure of the ratification process was not least due to the gap between the political elite and the citizens of Europe. Moreover, the fact that for the European constitution each country's voting taking place at a national level is undesirable, because the primacy of national problems (e.g. reservations about Chirac's government) can obstruct the view of the problems posed by the acceptance or rejection of the European constitution. From my theoretical perspective, a pan-European referendum after an extended period of public debate on the significance and meaning of Europe would be crucial to help creating a lively transnational dialogue on the EU's constitutional ideals.

10 'Learning' is a weaker notion than 'consensus' or 'convergence of viewpoints', but is certainly stronger than a mere compromise between the exogenous preferences or outlooks of actors ('tit for tat'). For a similar view on constitutionalism see J. Tully, *Strange Multiplicity: Constitutionalism in an Age of Diversity*, Cambridge University Press, Cambridge 1995.

11 S. Hampshire, *Justice is Conflict*, Princeton University Press, Princeton 2000, p. xiii.

2

Against the mainstream: two ways of conceptualising European political integration

There is a well-established strand of normative research on the European Union (EU) carried out by political and legal theorists. This debate is linked to the controversy about the legitimacy deficit of a 'supranational' organisation that is gradually acquiring some characteristics of a state. The only common denominator of these approaches is that they explore whether the EU has been established in accordance with democratic principles and of constitutionalism (or the rule of law). They agree that the EU, regardless of whether the Constitutional Treaty will be ratified by the member states or not, already has 'constitutional law', namely in its 'thin' definition of a body of law which constitutes and differentiates the main organs of government and their powers, and which specifies the main rights and obligations connecting the citizenry to these organs of governments. However, there are many sceptical voices which question the political identity and authority claims of the EU and therefore the legitimacy of dignifying the EU with a (political) constitutional status. The debate has become bogged down in the apparently irreconcilable mutual opposition of two positions. On the one hand, there is the view that an EU constitutional democracy is neither possible nor necessary, a perspective which arises principally from the tradition of economic liberalism, on the other hand, there is the view of those I will call the *demos*-theorists, according to whom a European (political) constitution is necessary, but not possible.

In the following I will focus on some ways of conceptualizing European political integration with respect to the role they do or do not assign to the public sphere. I will show that theories based either on economic liberalism or social democracy leave us with a false dichotomy[1] which opposes global markets to national democracy. In the second part of this chapter I shall reconstruct in more detail the (social democratic) *demos*-thesis, as argued by Claus Offe, Fritz Scharpf and Dieter Grimm.

Europe as a market: economic liberals

At the core of the 'libertarian' view, exemplified by the tradition of economic lib-eralism, is the idea that the private liberties of the market citizen – self-ownership, security of property and the obligation of contract – are conceptually prior to political liberties. Most theorists in this tradition take a strong elitist stance of which we can trace roots back to sceptical commentators on popular democracy such as Edmund Burke and Joseph Schumpeter.[2] According to this view, the only function of a constitution is to circumscribe a set of 'private rights', insulating them from the vicissitudes of pluralist politics, placing them beyond the reach of majorities and establishing them as legal principles to be applied by the courts. This liberal-individualist theory views politics as the aggregation of the individual preferences of self-interested actors. The political process of opinion- and will-formation is determined by the competition of collectivities acting strategically and trying to maintain or acquire positions of power. Accordingly, public delib-eration among citizens (and the idea of a public sphere) drops out altogether: citizens need policy makers who are ultimately accountable to them but they do not need to participate in public discourse on policy issues. The citizen's main role is to choose periodically which among competing teams of potential office-holders will exercise public authority. And if they are dissatisfied with their ac-tions, they can vote them out at the next election. From this perspective, an important criterion of good public discourse is its transparency:[3] The media should reveal what citizens need to know about the working of their government, the parties that aggregate and represent their interests, and the office-holders they have elected. Ideally, journalists should play the role of dispassionate experts. Public discourse is understood as a free marketplace of ideas, designed to produce wise decisions by accountable representatives organized in political parties. In the lib-eral model it is assumed that there is no such thing as the common good above and beyond the sum or the trajectory of all the various individual goods, and so private interests are the only legitimate basis of political discourse. Politics con-sists of bargaining and seeking compromises that satisfy as many private interests as possible. This view in the end assumes that meaning can be reduced to un-equivocal symbols – prices – which only need to be publicized to guide the co-ordination of action.

   The vision of the EU suggested by this approach – represented for example by Ernst-Joachim Mestmäcker – is quite straightforward. While democratic politics remains bound to nation-states, the economic rights and liberties of the market citizen are the true constitution of the EU.[4] This vision claims a purely utilitarian or functionalist legitimation for European economic law on the grounds that these rules are market-enhancing. From this perspective, it is the task of the EU to imple-ment and protect a system of open markets and undistorted competition, whereas *political rights* remain vested in the member states which retain those legislative powers *that are compatible with open markets*. By a different line of argument, Giandomenico Majone comes to similar conclusions: the EU is primarily a 'regulatory state', committed to the definition and enforcement of rules promoting (economic) efficiency. Such a view leads to an understanding of the EU institutions as a (de-politicized) regulatory branch of the Member States as a defence against 'democracy' identified with purely strategic bargaining, preference-aggregation and the majority principle. The chain binding law and democratic politics is thus broken. European law has its own, democracy-independent, utilitarian substitute legitimation: if a rule is market-enhancing, then it is legitimate. The very goal of the European Community is to separate economics from politics as far as possible. Under such a system, there is obviously no need for a constitutional project aimed at the extension of citizenship from the national to the Community level.[5]

Neither is there any conceptual space for the notion of a public sphere in such an approach. Indeed, the notion is deliberately excluded.[6] The European democratic deficit, Majone argues, is actually 'democratically legitimized'. In fact, the legitimacy of the EU should not be assessed by standards of the nation-state. His whole argument depends on a sharp distinction between efficiency-oriented and distribution-oriented standards of legitimacy. The former are geared towards the correction of market failures and must be handed over to independent expertocratic agencies, whereas the former belong to the 'political' process of bargaining among groups with divergent preferences and majoritarianism. Decisions involving significant redistribution of resources from one group to another cannot, according to Majone, be legitimately delegated to independent experts, but must be taken by elected officials or experts and administrators directly responsible to elected officials. In contrast, efficiency-oriented standards are geared towards the correction of market failures and towards the increase of the efficiency of market transactions. Indeed, a precondition for the accountability of regulatory (as opposed to distributive) decision making is that decisions be taken in the greatest possible insulation from the real-world pressures of pluralist power politics. Majone assumes that it is possible to identify (predominately) efficiency-oriented decisions and policy-areas, with regard to which a 'delegation' to independent institutions is democratically justifiable. Accordingly, the task of European law is to 'constitutionalize' the legal basis of this independence. Since depoliticization is a precondition of accountability, the democratic deficit is, as Majone claims, 'democratically justified' at a deeper level, that is, as a legitimate way of respecting the normative differences between the efficiency-oriented and the distribution-oriented realm.

However, it has been shown, both theoretically and empirically, that it is difficult to separate regulatory and distributive policies: any regulation of competitive practices will generate winners and losers among the competitors involved, the liberalization of monopoly services may have benefited consumers, but it has also destroyed many thousands of jobs, there are 'spill over' effects of economic and monetary integration on employment and social policy.[7] Regulatory policies have distributive consequences. And in fact, although most European policy has so far been oriented towards the creation of markets and the regulation of competition and of product standards, it is increasingly oriented also towards environmental and consumer protection. By the logic of the *Wirtschaftsverfassung* – according to which policy outcomes should be determined by the interest in cost-avoidance of the median producer (state) – it cannot explain why the EU is successfully managing to achieve not only an integrated market by eliminating obstacles to internal trade, but also to protect public health and safety, thereby aiming to avoid regulatory races to the bottom. The political institutions of the EU are now such that in many, if not all, regulatory areas 'high' outcomes are possible.[8] Policy areas that seemed intractable ten years ago – such as transport, immigration, asylum and education – are no longer so. The neoliberal credo that there could be an 'economic integration without political integration'[9] has been surpassed by reality.

The '*demos*-thesis': social democrats

The social democratic position fears above all that the emergent form of transnational regulatory governance will endanger the achievements of the redistributive welfare state. In contrast to 'economic constitutionalism', it is concerned with safeguarding the priority of politics over markets. The nub of this approach is the argument that democratic politics – in the strong sense of solidaristic redistribution and of reciprocal justification between free and equal citizens – cannot be established on a European level. The argument runs like this: democratic self-government – understood as the capacity to solve problems through collective action and will-formation – presupposes a high degree of cultural homogeneity within the society that wants to constitute itself as a political unit. Without a collective identity citizens would not be prepared to treat their fellow citizens' interests in regard to particular issues as their own. Political will-formation is thus conceived as people reasoning together to promote a common good that is more than the mere sum of individual preferences.

The *demos*-theorists claim that politics presupposes trust and solidarity among strangers, and that trust and solidarity in turn presuppose a culturally integrated homogenous political community or *demos*. Trust is defined as the passive dimension of the socio-cultural resources of democratic politics, i.e. the absence of fear and the belief that all the other citizens of the polity are willing to respect the same duties.[10] Trust is thus the moral basis of democracy without which a citizenry would not accept its risks. Solidarity, on the other hand, means the active dimension of the socio-cultural resources of democracy and the welfare state, i.e. an outlook that does not view distributive justice with indifference but believes that there are duties toward other citizens. Solidarity is the moral basis of the welfare state without which citizens would not be willing to accept sacrifices imposed in the name of the collectivity by redistributive policies. These two 'horizontal' convictions are the socio-cultural resources for the effective functioning of state power (a 'vertical' phenomenon).

The argument, then, is that trust and solidarity, the two fundamental socio-cultural resources of democratic politics, are generated from a belief in 'our' essential sameness, a *Gemeinschaftsglaube* (Max Weber) which is based on pre-existing commonalities of history, language, culture and ethnicity. Only if that belief in a 'thick' collective identity is taken for granted will majority rule lose its threatening character, and interpersonal and inter-regional redistributive measures that would not otherwise be acceptable, will be legitimated. European integration would therefore presuppose a European people (*Staatsvolk*) as a cultural and cognitive frame of reference. Given the historical, cultural, ethnic and linguistic diversity of its member states, there is no question for the protagonists of this argument that the European Union is very far from having achieved the 'thick' collective identity that we have come to take for granted in national democracies. And in its absence, institutional reforms will not greatly accelerate the formation of a European people. By this view, public deliberation can take place only within pre-established *demos*. Most authors who are sceptical about the normative viability and the empirical possibility of a European public sphere implicitly presuppose a substantialist (or 'holistic') idea of the public as a culturally integrated homogenous political community or *demos* with a shared collective identity, a common language and media system.[11]

To sum up, the central argument is that there must be a pre-established *demos* before constitutional democracy can possibly begin to operate. And since for the time being a homogeneous *demos* only exists at the national level, European competencies have to be narrowly defined, and should continue to depend on democratically accountable national governments in the Council of Ministers. I will call this argument the *demos*-thesis.

The *demos*-thesis is clearly more relevant than economic liberalism if we want to look for a normatively substantive theory of democracy in Europe, and I will therefore give it some more detailed consideration. The fear of those who argue the *demos*-thesis with respect to European integration – often with the support of social democrats – is that the current processes of denationalization, i.e. the increasing socio-cultural heterogeneity of the polity that comes with the opening of national boundaries, will erode the socio-cultural sources of democratic legitimacy and social integration without producing a supranational alternative.

Open dialogue presupposes closed boundaries

Claus Offe has recently argued that since political resources (legitimacy and efficiency) get lost through denationalization, the processes of European integration should be reversed. In his path-breaking 'Demokratie und Wohlfahrtsstaat: eine europäische Regimeform unter dem Streß der europäischen Integration' (1998) he discusses the structural differences between the European 'would-be polity' and the nation-state, and the implications of these differences for democracy and the welfare state. In the following I will briefly reconstruct Offe's argument.

Offe argues, first of all, that mutual recognition between strangers and the very possibility of the self-constitution of a society as a polity means self-constitution as a *demos*. He defines '*demos*' as a 'Subjekt-Objekt eines willentlich gegründeten Herrschaftsverbandes'.[12] It is at the same time the subject of a constitutional democracy and the object of the constitutional act through which a people defines itself. Offe asserts that self-constitution as a *demos* presupposes a socio-cultural substratum of commonalities and that these commonalities are defined in reference to space and time. By 'space' he means territorially-defined constituencies such as the nation-state. Territorial boundaries are 'decision points' for the common good/distributive justice.[13] By 'time' Offe means to refer to a shared sense of history. He goes on to argue that trust as the moral basis for democracy (tolerance of risks) and solidarity as the moral basis for the welfare state (acceptance of the sacrifices imposed in the name of the collectivity by redistributive policies) can only exist among strangers who share these commonalities, i.e. the social norms of a *demos*. The smaller and more homogenous the group of beneficiaries of social policies, he argues, the more easily the resources for social democracy, and in particular the potentials of solidarity, can be mobilized.[14]

Offe's second step is to describe the implications of the *demos*-thesis for denationalization, and in particular EU integration. He claims that with denationalization, the normative nexus between the socio-cultural resources of democratic politics and a presupposed homogenous *demos* is structurally endangered. Accordingly, no extension of trust and solidarity beyond the nation-state is possible. Offe argues that democracy and the welfare state are only possible within national boundaries:

> In a nation-state mode of socialization … actors regard each other as they do themselves, acknowledging that they all participate in a community of rights that is authoritative and stably established.[15]

Offe explains the danger to the normative nexus between the socio-cultural resources of democratic politics and a presupposed homogenous *demos* by claiming that there is a constitutional unbalancing of positive and negative integration. Negative integration, i.e. the removal of trade barriers, leads to a spillover of the logic of markets (individual interest) into the logic of solidaristic democracy (public interest). Offe thereby criticizes negative integration in a 'formal Marxist' manner as a reification of social and moral resources which undermines the presuppositions of the welfare state and leads to economic liberalism. European integration reverses the cumulative process of extension of liberal, democratic and social rights described by T. H. Marshall.[16] Positive integration, i.e. the creation of a unitary regulatory system for trade and social policies, represents a spillover of bureaucratic rationality into democratic politics. Offe therefore criticizes positive integration in a 'formal Weberian' manner as a political heteronomy (through non-democratic European institutions) which undermines the presuppositions of democratic legitimation:

> The choice is between the plague of negative economic third-party effects of volunteerism and the cholera of a political heteronomy on the part of European institutions, against whose sovereignty claims there is no democratic cure.[17]

He concludes that both types of European integration erode the socio-moral presuppositions of democratic politics without being able to generate them in other ways, *et tertium non datur*. He can therefore interpret any further constitutionalization of Europe only as a deeply destructive process for social democracy.

Offe explains his claim that there can be no extension of trust and solidarity beyond the nation-state with an empirically-based null hypothesis: the common cultural roots of the different EU member states are not strong enough to generate the full status of European citizen and the Europe-wide solidarity which would be necessary for democratic politics at the European level.[18] Therefore trust and solidarity cannot be extended beyond the nation-state. Denationalization erodes the mutual moral commitment among citizens. Consequently Offe argues that we should reverse the process of European integration if we want to regain the *acquis national* in regard to the socio-cultural presuppositions of democracy and the welfare state, as well as its political resources (legitimacy and efficiency).

In '"Homogeneity" and Constitutional Democracy: Coping with Identity Conflicts through Group Rights' (1998), Offe claims that territorial and cultural boundaries are pivotal pre-political conditions for democracy. He argues that democracy cannot be brought into being by democratic means. He identifies four 'democratic impossibilities', that is, 'matters which, by their very logic, cannot be resolved in democratic ways':[19] first, there must be a *pouvoir constituant* 'prior to and unconstrained by the democratic principles which govern in a democratic society once established … the initial framework in which democratically legitimated power is to be created is not enacted democratically'.[20] Second, it is 'democratically impossible for the people to decide or (re)define who belongs to the people (as opposed to who is to be enfranchised within an existing people)'.[21] Third, 'territorial borders cannot be changed in obviously democratic ways'.[22] Fourth, with respect to democratic agenda-setting, 'the citizenry of a democracy cannot decide on the issues the citizens are to decide on'.[23]

In the light of what Offe calls 'reflexive homogeneity',[24] democratic constitutionalism risks receding into a decisionism *à la* Carl Schmitt. Offe claims that a political community has to be 'homogeneous' in the sense that its citizens have to be tied together 'through an understanding of the communality of their fate'[25] which is fostered through 'national unity'.[26] Such a decisive nationalism is formulated as a response to the devastating consequences of de-nationalization for contemporary democracies and the modern welfare state.

To sum up, we can say that for Offe there are two principal reasons why social democrats should worry about European integration. In the first essay we considered, he argues that democratic politics requires trust and mutual solidarity in order for minorities to accept majority decisions and for majorities to be willing not to violate the interests of minorities. In the second essay, he argues that democracy depends on the idea of popular sovereignty, but that democracy cannot itself determine who the people are and how the boundaries of a political community should be drawn. Only where a group of individuals share a national identity can we say that these two presuppositions of democracy are fulfilled. National identity provides a moral basis for democracy in the form of shared social norms and practices (which generate trust and solidarity), and constitutes a *demos* with common territorial claims and common allegiances.

Offe's approach can be understood as a 'reflexive' version of modernization theory, now resurfacing with a new communitarian twist: the socio-cultural substratum of a homogenous *demos* generates trust and solidarity and thus provides the glue with which society is bound together. This theory of social integration echoes Tönnies's idea of a 'socio-psychological community' in that it takes for granted that cultural homogeneity/cohesion exists in national societies. From a sociological point of view, however, the idea of a homogenous constituency or community was always a constitutive myth rather than an accurate depiction of collective identity, even at the level of nation-states. National identities have never been either unitary or unified, even before the reality of post-war population movements, transnational capitalism, global communication and the explosion of mass consumption.

Moreover, Offe's argument is plausible only if we accept that solidarity and trust are parasitic upon pre-existing commonalities (e.g. territory and history) which are 'out there' in some extra-discursive sense, and that the socio-cultural resources or background convictions of a national society are static, i.e. given with the '*Gemeinschaftsglaube*' of a *demos*. Offe in fact gives no argument in support of these assumptions. He simply posits the 'fact' that trust and solidarity between strangers presuppose a shared sense of belonging to a *demos*. Further, as I will argue in Part II of the book, a less substantialist, more constructivist understanding of the socio-cultural resources of democratic politics is rather more convincing. As we will see in Part III, this kind of dialogical view is supported by the empirical evidence in contemporary Europe.

Loss of we-identity undermines the possibility of politics

Fritz Scharpf has claimed that effective European policy is limited to certain areas of relatively low political salience in which its legitimacy is not in doubt.[27] He assumes that European governance will erode the achievements of the welfare state by moving from an aggregative model (of individual interests) to a deliberative model of democracy, where all citizens are involved in forming a collective will, particularly when it concerns issues of redistribution of resources among citizens. The implementation of the welfare state should therefore be left to the nation-state which alone is capable of legitimizing social policies through majority rule.[28]

The question Scharpf addresses, then, is that of the normative presuppositions of democratic legitimacy with respect to majority decisions, in particular those concerning distributive justice. In the following I shall briefly reconstruct Scharpf's argument.

Scharpf's first step is to argue that deliberative democracy is not about the aggregation of individual interests but about collective action oriented towards public interest. In a legitimate democracy citizens have a moral duty to obey decisions taken in the name of the collectivity, even if in doing so they act against their own individual interests. Scharpf goes on to claim that (social democratic) deliberative democracy presupposes a 'we-identity'. Since the public interest can override individual self-interest, democracy 'logically' (!) presupposes 'the existence or implies the creation of a collective identity'.[29] Without a we-identity citizens would not be prepared to obey majority decisions when these go against their individual preferences.[30] In other words, only when the belief in a 'thick' collective identity can be taken for granted can we rely upon majority rule to legitimize measures of interpersonal and inter-regional redistribution that would otherwise not be acceptable. In Scharpf's view, the equality which is a criterion for distributive justice is 'clearly tied to membership status'. Thus, democratic politics 'presupposes boundary rules that define whose welfare is to be counted in the aggregation and whose resource position is to be equalized with regard to which reference group'.[31] For Scharpf, 'psychologically and thus empirically' (!), collective identities are given 'only at the level of primary groups' and presuppose 'pre-existing similarities or commonalities'.[32] Besides this substratum of socio-cultural commonalities (we might call this a 'thick' *demos*-thesis), a we-identity also presupposes an institutional infrastructure and common space for political discourse.[33]

Scharpf therefore argues that the we-identity of a homogeneous *demos* is a necessary requirement for social democracy in order to ensure that the people are public-interest-oriented and thus to guarantee the possibility of redistributive policies. A collective identity that is based on pre-existing commonalities (given at the national level) provides shared criteria of justice and a set of social norms, and thus generates a solidaristic bond between the members of the relevant collectivity.

The second part of Scharpf's argument involves the description of the implications of this *demos*-thesis for EU integration. He discusses the normative preconditions as well as the effectiveness of political choices at the national and European level, beginning by distinguishing between two dimensions of democratic legitimacy: input-oriented authenticity (government *by* the people), i.e. political choices are legitimate because they reflect the will of the people, and output-oriented effectiveness (government *for* the people), that is, political choices are legitimate because they effectively promote the common welfare of a constituency:

> Even if a democratic polity can be assumed, majority decision-making must be legitimated either in an 'input oriented' manner, through the genuine assent of its members, or, in an 'output oriented' manner, through its efficient service to the common welfare of its members.[34]

Scharpf agrees with the sentence of the Bundesverfassungsgericht that the democratic legitimacy of a European polity would presuppose the existence of a European *demos* (Staatsvolk) which is in fact lacking.[35] From the input-oriented frame of reference, an original European legitimation presupposes Europe-wide political communication and opinion-formation, which there obviously is not. Scharpf therefore agrees with Dieter Grimm that institution building and the creation of a constitution cannot in themselves assure the political identity and solidarity on which legitimate governance must be based. If we are looking for input-legitimacy at the European level, in other words, we will find that there are three problems with respect to the accountability of EU office-holders to a European constituency: the lack of a pre-existing sense of collective identity, the lack of a Europe-wide policy discourse, and the lack of a Europe-wide institutional infrastructure.[36]

At the national and transnational level, input-oriented arguments about legitimacy are supplemented by output-oriented arguments which insist on the institutional capacity for effective problem-solving (and the presence of institutional safeguards against the abuse of public power). Output-oriented legitimacy presupposes the existence of an identifiable constituency with a 'thin' we-identity and thus allows, in principle, for the coexistence of multiple collective identities. But although there is in principle no reason why governance at the European level should not be supported by output-oriented legitimacy arguments, Scharpf argues that the European capacity for effective problem-solving is doubtful,[37] because of the 'locational competition' (*Standortkonkurrenz*) between the highly industrial and the less developed member states. Particularly social and environmental policies would, at the European level, be characterized by the conflicting interests of the single member states instead of being coordinated by collective interest. In order to solve the problems of a constituency such as the European Union effectively, office-holders would have to identify the public interest of the citizens of all member states, which again is impossible without a pre-existing collective identity among the would-be European citizenry. Without a shared we-identity, European citizens would not be willing to accept the sacrifices imposed in the name of a European collective good via measures of inter-regional redistribution. Scharpf thus asserts that the effectiveness of political choices would be best assured by elite-led national policy discourses that, on the one hand, are conducted in awareness of the constraints imposed by supranational law (EU law, GATT rules etc.) and on the other, are reflexive, that is, willing to take into account the interests of the other nation-states involved. European government, he suggests, should therefore be confined to the maintenance of a capacity for judicial law-making that safeguards the democratic legitimacy of the European multi-level polity precisely by assuring the reflexivity of national policy choices.[38] He thus is in favour of enlarging the scope of national policies and ends up assuming a sort of 'reflexive nationalism'.

So, Scharpf distinguishes between two dimensions of democratic legitimacy: input-oriented authenticity (government by the people) and output-oriented effectiveness (government for the people). His argument focuses on the latter, which carries presuppositions with respect to the requirement for a pre-existing collective identity which are weaker than Offe's moral preconditions of democracy (trust and solidarity). At the same time Scharpf has a less substantialistic, but more ambiguous view of the *demos*: whereas Offe excludes the formation of a postnational identity (Habermas) which would expand trust and solidarity to strangers beyond the boundaries of a pre-existing *demos*, Scharpf argues that the

> construction of a collective identity above the level of primary groups ... is facilitated by pre-existing similarities or commonalities that have a quality of 'obviousness' – such as common kinship and race or common locality, language, religion, culture, or history.[39]

He goes on to claim that the nation-state has successfully managed to create collective identities above the level of primary groups. However, by embracing this mildly constructivist view on identity-formation, Scharpf contradicts his own argument. Since collective identities do not totally rely on (although they are 'facilitated' by) pre-existing commonalities, but are to a certain extent constructed (for instance at the nation-state level), he surely cannot argue against the possibility of constructing we-identities at a supranational level.

No European public sphere, no European constitution

Dieter Grimm argues that Europe-wide integration of democracy is illegitimate because the prerequisites for legitimate will-formation on the part of Union citizens have up to now been absent. In his famous article 'Does Europe Need a Constitution?' (1995), he warns the federalists, who after the Maastricht Treaty expected a European Constitution to provide the solution to Europe's democracy problem, that the creation of a European constitution would only mediate a fictitious legitimation for a European federal state since, as yet, no European people exists as its legitimating basis. Therefore, the legitimate sources of EU political authority, he claims, must be the member states and their respective national governments.

Grimm begins by arguing that a constitution goes back to an act attributed to the people, it is 'the expression of a society's self-determination as to the form and objectives of a political unity'.[40] He goes on to claim that a society that wants to constitute itself as a political unit requires a collective identity based on

> an awareness of belonging together that can support majority decisions and solidarity efforts, and for it to have the capacity to communicate about its goals and problems discursively.[41]

Moreover, he argues that a constitutional state has to draw on certain social prerequisites, in particular intermediate structures of deliberation (associations, parties, communication media), that it cannot itself guarantee[42] and that public deliberation presupposes a common language which carries 'linguistically mediated experience and interpretation of the world'.[43]

Grimm's normative concept of democratic legitimacy is a deliberative one, which is to say that it derives from a consensus among people who communicate about their social goals and problems, and negotiate about their interests. However, his ambiguous, slightly substantialist, 'communitarian' definition of the people (which is ultimately based on a common language) undermines this constructivist argument for 'democratic legitimacy through communication'. Consequently his argument that the constitutional state guarantees social integration in the legally abstract form of political participation is undermined by his idea that the constitution has to draw on social presuppositions, which he ultimately bases in the collective identity of the people as mediated through a common language. Even though Grimm stresses that the people are not to be understood as a pre-given unity or a homogeneous *Volksgemeinschaft* à la Carl Schmitt, he claims that the constituency of a democratic polity presupposes socio-cultural prerequisites carried by a common language. Thus, he implicitly assumes that the possibility of a public sphere and political discourse depends on a common language, romantically understood as expressing a common world view, which somehow provides the glue for the divergent social views and interests to be found in a modern polity. I will discuss this argument in more detail in Chapter 3.

Grimm also describes the implications of his normative assumptions for EU integration. He asserts first of all that there are at present no European people with a common collective identity. He is also pessimistic about the possibility that a transnational discourse (for example in the form of a Europe-wide party system or European public sphere) would develop a European people because there is no lingua franca to mediate a common interpretation of the world. Thus, Grimm's Euroscepticism is in effect empirically based: since there is, as yet, no European people as the legitimating basis for a European federal state, there should also be no European constitution. The perspective from which he normatively justifies the requirements for democratic will-formation, however, prejudices his empirical evaluation of the present circumstances.

Grimm also argues that as long as there are no mediating structures between people and institutions (such as a Europe-wide networked civil society, a European public sphere or a common political culture) supranational decision processes would in fact accelerate existing tendencies towards the autonomization and oligarchization of bureaucratized politics, tendencies which are already eroding the democratic substance of the nation-state. Only the functional elites share a common language and can thus deliberate about political choices. This argument adds a linguistic 'twist' to Offe's 'formal Weberian' argument about bureaucratic political heteronomy. In the end it is Grimm's 'communitarian' view on language that prevents him from putting forward a coherent, deliberative theory of democracy which would allow him to argue that a constitution could be founded without presupposing a common language (or fostering a 'situated constitutional patriotism' beyond the nation-state, see Chapter 6).

In conclusion, we can say that whereas Offe focuses his argument on the moral resources of democracy (bonds of trust and solidarity) and prepolitical homogeneity, thereby putting forward a 'strong' *demos*-thesis, Scharpf's argument is more concerned with the effectiveness of political choices and the definition of the common good in a pluralistic society, and thus amounts to a 'weak' *demos*-thesis. Both, however, have a substantialistic view of democratic politics based on the presupposed we-identity of a homogenous *demos*. Although Grimm adopts a deliberative theory of democratic legitimacy, in the end this falls back into a substantialistic view which relies on a common language to form a socio-cultural substratum for public communication and is necessarily confined to a specific community of people.

This work aims to move beyond the two dilemmas which the contemporary European constitutional debate seems to pose: on the one hand, we have the view arising from the tradition of economic liberalism that separates European economic law from the idea of democracy, claims a democracy-independent utilitarian or functionalist substitute legitimation for European economic law (if a rule is market-enhancing then it is legitimate), and finally argues that European economic law *is* the true constitution of the EU. On the other hand, we have the view – mainly sustained by social democrats – that for both normative and functional reasons assumes the shelter of the nation-state as a guarantor of collective identity and of effectiveness, concluding that the basic decisions about the European Community should be left with the member states where they can be democratically warranted.

Ways out? A discursive model of politics and its implication for Europe

There is, however, a growing trend in the literature of democratic theory to deconstruct the notion of *demos* and to base conceptualizations of democracy on weaker, communicative presuppositions.[44] Instead of presupposing that democratic legitimation requires a certain (pre-political) homogeneity of the constituency of a polity, this view argues that legitimation is instead generated through deliberation among free and equal citizens. Jürgen Habermas's proceduralist theory of deliberative democracy formulates an idea of democratic constitutionalism which fully accounts for the universalist core of this idea and detaches it from the particularism of any specific national (political) culture. In this view, democratic legitimacy is ultimately the communicative power of the public as a collective body.[45] And it is the democratic procedure for the production of law itself which is the only source of legitimacy of coercive law:

> The ethical-political self-understanding of citizens in a democratic community must not be taken as an historical-cultural a priori that makes democratic will-formation possible, but rather as the flowing contents of a circulatory process that is generated through the legal institutionalisation of citizens' communication. This is precisely how national identities were formed in modern Europe. Therefore it is to be expected that the political institutions to be created by a European constitution would have an inducing effect.[46]

From this perspective, there is no a priori reason why Europe, which has for some years been integrating economically, administratively and to some extent socially, cannot subsequently create the communicative context necessary for *political* integration with the core being formed by a political public sphere.

As I will argue in Part III, the boundaries of identity, interest and the public good are constantly transformed within the deliberative process. If we wish to move beyond the two dilemmas, which the contemporary European constitutional debate seems to express, then we need to explicitly spell out the idea of a legitimacy-conferring deliberative politics that is on the one hand independent of any pre-established political ethos of national communities, and on the other hand strong enough to provide a counterpoint to market-based conceptions of European constitutionalism. My own dialogical vision tries to exceed conventional models of European integration insofar as it is based on a theory of ongoing translation (Chapter 5). According to this theory, the mutual recognition of strangers is created through dialogue (which generates its own justificatory presuppositions), and socio-cultural heterogeneity or plurality is seen as an asset for constitutional dialogue defined in terms of the mutual exploration of difference: transnational arenas for deliberative dialogical problem-solving may transform the actor's perspectives from conflict to collaboration in a shared transnational constitutional project, thereby transforming diversity into a resource for the development of innovative perspectives (inter-societal learning). In this view, people's participation in normative public dialogue and non-state regulatory processes of deliberation achieves social cohesion and generates dialogical solidarity. There is, in fact, a close link between theories of the public sphere and democratic theory more generally. The latter focuses on accountability and responsiveness in the decision-making process, and the former on the role of public deliberation in facilitating or hindering this process.

Notes

1 See O. Gerstenberg, 'Law's Polyarchy: A Comment on Cohen and Sabel' in: O. Gerstenberg and C. Joerges (eds.), *Private Governance, Democratic Constitutionalism and Supranationalism*, European Communities, Brussels 1998, pp. 31–48.

2 For a particularly clear contemporary statement of this position, see R. Epstein, *Simple Rules for a Complex World*, Harvard University Press, Cambridge, MA, 1995.

3 See also: M. Marx Ferree, W. Gamson, J. Gerhards and D. Rucht, 'Four Models of the Public Sphere in Modern Democracies', in: *Theory and Society* 31:3, 2003, p. 291.

4 E.-J. Mestmäcker, 'On the Legitimacy of European Law', in: *RabelsZ*, 58, 1994, p. 615.

5 See also: E. U. Petersmann, 'Constitutionalism, Constitutional Law and European Integration', in E. U. Petersmann (ed.), *Constitutional Problems of European Integration*, Special Issue 46, Aussenwirtschaft, 1991, p. 247.

6 G. Majone, 'Europe's "Democratic Deficit": The Question of Standards', in: *European Law Journal* 4:1, 1998, pp. 5–28.

7 See, for example A. Heritier and S. Schmidt, 'After Liberalization: Public-Interest Services and Employment in the Utilities', in: F. Scharpf and V. Schmidt (eds.), *Work and Welfare in the Open Economy*, vol. 2, Oxford University Press, Oxford 2000, pp. 554–596.

8 V. Eichener, *Das Entscheidungssystem der Europäischen Union: Institutionelle Analyse und demokratietheoretische Bewertung*, Leske & Budrich, Opladen 2000.

9 Majone, 'Europe's "Democratic Deficit"': The Question of Standards', p. 17.

10 C. Offe, 'Demokratie und Wohlfahrtsstaat: Eine europäische Regimeform unter dem Stress der europäischen Integration?', in: W. Streek (ed.), *Internationale Wirtschaft, nationale*

Demokratie: Herausforderungen für die Demokratietheorie, Campus Verlag, Frankfurt am Main/New York 1998, pp. 99–136.

11 See authors as different as: P. Kielmansegg, 'Integration und Demokratie', in: M. Jachtenfuchs and B. Kohler-Koch (eds.), *Europäische Integration*, Leske & Budrich, Opladen 1996, pp. 47–71; A. Smith, 'National Identities and the Idea of European Unity', in: *International Affairs* 68:1, 1992, pp. 55–76; D. Grimm, 'Does Europe need a Constitution?', in: *European Law Journal* 1:3, 1995, p. 291; F. Scharpf, 'Demokratie in der transnationalen Politik', in: W. Streek (ed.), *Internationale Wirtschaft, nationale Demokratie: Herausforderungen für die Demokratietheorie*, Campus Verlag, Frankfurt am Main/New York 1998, pp. 151–174; J. Gerhards, 'Europäisierung von Ökonomie und Politik und die Trägheit der Entstehung einer europäischen Öffentlichkeit' , in: M. Bach (ed.), *Die Europäisierung nationaler Gesellschaften: Sonderheft 40 der Kölner Zeitschrift für Soziologie und Sozialpsychologie*, Westdeutscher Verlag, Wiesbaden 2000, pp. 277–305; see also: Gerhards, 'Das Öffentlichkeitsdefizit der EU im Horizont normativer Öffentlichkeitstheorien', in: H. Kälble, M. Kirsch and A. Schmid-Gernig (eds.), *Transnationale Öffentlichkeiten und Identitäten im 20. Jahrhundert*, Campus Verlag, Frankfurt am Main/New York 2002, pp. 135–158; Offe, 'Demokratie und Wohlfahrtsstaat', pp. 99–136.

12 *Ibid.*, p.100.

13 *Ibid.*, p. 102.

14 *Ibid.*, p. 133.

15 ' … in … einem nationalstaatlichen Modus der Vergesellschaftung, in dem sich Akteure gegenseitig als "ihresgleichen", vor allem als Teilnehmer einer für alle maßgeblichen und dauerhaft feststehenden Rechtsgemeinschaft anerkennen' (*Ibid.*, p. 134). Translation provided by Lorraine Frisina.

16 *Ibid.*, p. 111.

17 'Die Wahl ist zwischen der Pest negativer ökonomischer Drittwirkungen des Voluntarismus und der Cholera einer politischen Fremdbestimmung seitens europäischer Institutionen, gegen deren Souveränitätsanspruch aus der Sicht der Nationalstaaten kein demokratisches Kraut gewachsen ist' (*Ibid.*, p. 111). Translation provided by Lorraine Frisina.

18 'Die meisten Europäer befinden sich in der Sicht der meisten anderen Europäer nicht im Status von "unseresgleichen"' (*Ibid.*, p. 120).

19 C. Offe, '"Homogeneity" and Constitutional Democracy: Coping with Identity Conflicts through Group Rights', in: *The Journal of Political Philosophy* 6:2, 1998, p. 115.

20 *Ibid.*, pp. 115–116.

21 *Ibid.*, p. 116.

22 *Ibid.*, p. 117.

23 *Ibid.*, p. 118.

24 *Ibid.*, p. 119.

25 *Ibid.*, p. 119.

26 *Ibid.*, p. 140.

27 See: Scharpf, 'Demokratie in der transnationalen Politik', pp. 151–174; F. Scharpf, *Governing in Europe: Effective and Democratic?*, Oxford University Press, Oxford 1999.

28 Scharpf, 'Demokratie in der transnationalen Politik', pp. 151–174; Scharpf, *Governing in Europe*, p. 203.

29 F. Scharpf, *Games Real Actors Play: Actor-Centered Institutionalism in Policy Research*, Westview Press, New York 1997, p. 162.

30 'Notwendige Voraussetzung der demokratischen Legitimität ist also offenbar eine "Wir-Identität" im Sinne von Norbert Elias (1987), welche es auch der unterlegenen Minderheit ermöglicht, das Mehrheitsvotum nicht als Fremdherrschaft, sondern als kollektive Selbstbestimmung zu verstehen' (Scharpf, 'Demokratie in der transnationalen Politik', p. 154).

31 *Ibid.*, p. 162. See also: 'Demokratie ist auf kollektive Selbstbestimmung gerichtet und setzt … eine Unterscheidung von Zugehörigen und Fremden erlaubende "Wir-Identität" voraus'

(*ibid.*, p. 164).

32 Scharpf, *Games Real Actors Play*, p. 162.

33 'Eine solche Wir-Identität … aber bedarf … der sozio-kulturellen Unterstützung und einer strukturellen Infrastruktur, die politische Kommunikation über wichtige Optionen des Politischen Handelns und der Einlösung politischer Verantwortlichkeit erst ermöglichen' (Scharpf, 'Demokratie in der transnationlen Politik', pp. 154–155).

34 'Auch wenn ein demokratisches Gemeinwesen vorausgesetzt werden kann, müssen Mehr-heitsentscheidungen entweder – "input-orientiert"- durch die unverfälschte Zustimmung der Mitglieder oder – "output-orientiert" – durch ihre effektive Gemeinwohldienlichkeit legitimiert werden' (*ibid.*, p. 164). Translation provided by Lorraine Frisina.

35 *Ibid.*, p. 154.

36 Scharpf, *Governing in Europe*, p. 187.

37 *Ibid.*, p. 189.

38 *Ibid.*, p. 204.

39 Scharpf, *Games Real Actors Play*, p. 162.

40 Grimm, 'Does Europe need a Constitution?', p. 291.

41 *Ibid.*, p. 297.

42 *Ibid.*, p. 288.

43 *Ibid.*, p. 295.

44 See for example: J. Habermas, 'Remarks on Dieter Grimm's "Does Europe need a Constitu-tion?"', in: *European Law Journal* 1:3, 1995, pp. 303–307; J. Habermas, *Between Facts and Norms: Contributions to a Discourse Theory of Law and Democracy*, MIT Press, Cambridge, MA, 1996.

45 This communicative power 'springs from the interactions between legally institutionalized will-formation and culturally mobilized publics. The latter, for their part, find a basis in the associations of a civil society quite distinct from both the state and economy alike' (J. Habermas, 'Three Normative Models of Democracy', in: S. Benhabib (ed.), *Democracy and Difference: Contesting the Boundaries of the Political*, Princeton University Press, Princeton 1996, p. 29).

46 Habermas, 'Remarks on Dieter Grimm's "Does Europe need a Constitution?"', pp. 306–307.

PART II

The multiple voices of Europe:
theoretical perspectives

In the second part of the book, I will consider European (political) integration from a normative point of view. It is the core of this project, as it aims at proposing my own dialogical or interdiscursive version of the theory of deliberative democracy. Chapter 3 revisits the concept of the public sphere, whose absence has long been lamented by the *demos*-theorists, and reformulates the Habermasian conception in terms of the transnational and pluricultural polity of the EU. In Chapter 4, I shall discuss the political problematique of socio-cultural pluralism from the perspective of multiculturalism or multinationalism. More specifically, I will criticize the main positions of this debate and propose a dialogical concept of cultures that are constantly (re)produced and negotiated with other cultures in public discourse. Chapter 5 shows that the idea of a continuous intercultural translation or 'multicultural literacy' is rooted in theories of language: every act of mutual comprehension is about translating the idiolect of the other with 'interpretative charity' in order to see the world form the perspective of the other. Finally, I will spell out this idea of mutual intercultural translation as a form of political deliberation or constitutional dialogue (Chapter 6). Seen as such, the idea of 'constitutional patriotism' becomes, at the same time, both more constructivist and 'situated'. There are, in principle, no boundaries to extending this to new citizens who become interpreters of constitutional principles. Accordingly, a 'reasonably radicalized pluralism' within deliberative democracy becomes an asset to rather than an obstacle for (local, regional, national and transnational) politics.

3

Toward a dialogical theory of the public sphere

As seen in Chapter 2, many theorists of European integration, in particular social democrats and constitutionalists are almost unanimous in their lament of a 'democratic deficit'[1] and the absence of a political community (defined by a shared European identity as a basis for solidarity) in the EU. Before addressing the question of whether (and how) public discourse across lines of national and cultural (not to mention linguistic) difference is possible, it seems important to re-examine the available concepts of the public sphere, their usefulness and shortcomings in the analysis of today's decentred and multicultural societies and, in particular, of the heterogeneous polity of the new Europe. We need to consider the possibility of a concept of the public sphere that might correspond to the irreducible (social and cultural) diversity of collectivities on the one hand, and to the transnational interconnections of power on the other.

In this chapter, I shall begin by discussing Habermas's influential concept of the public sphere, which I take to be an indispensable starting point for social scientists who remain committed to theorizing the limits of democracy, but who want to challenge the current nostalgia for the nation. I shall then go on to analyze the resulting debate in political theory and the many critiques which have been directed at Habermas's arguments, showing that these criticisms form the basis for a reconceptualization of the public sphere that should make it more suitable for depicting the complexities of public life both at the national and transnational levels. Finally, I shall outline an 'interdiscursive'[2] concept of the public sphere based on Mikhail Bakhtin's dialogical theory of understanding, which helps to elucidate how the notions of identity and citizenship can function in a post-national epoch.

The idea of the public sphere

Put simply, the 'public sphere'[3] is a social space in which members of a society discuss matters of common interest and form opinions about those matters. The participants clarify and negotiate their interests and goals, express social demands and potentially decide upon collective action. They exchange convictions and value-judgements, and may articulate a collective identity from a set of self-understandings.[4] Public communication takes place through a variety of media (e.g. newspapers, books, television, the internet), as well as face-to-face encounters: for example, in informal conversations in freely accessible settings (such as bars and cafés, train compartments, street corners, etc.) or in the institutionalized setting of voluntary associations (such as social movements, political parties, interest groups, citizen's initiatives etc.).[5] The public sphere is important not only because it is where public opinion is formed, but also because it enables the (re)production of public culture and the integration of society in a non-coercive fashion.[6]

As a concept, the 'public sphere' has many advantages. It invokes 'identity', but does so with more emphasis on its discursive 'constructedness'. It stresses the possibility of collective action rather than the nature or characteristics of individuals. Unlike 'community', which suggests a fairly homogenous collectivity and often connotes consensus, the notion of the public sphere can accommodate a plurality of perspectives while emphasizing the open-ended interaction between cultural and social identities. Unlike 'culture', it hints at the existence of a site of interaction with other cultures and classes and stresses internal differences as well as a continuing self-formation, as opposed to a given body of practices that distinguish one cultural group from another.

Habermas's conception of the public sphere

The concept of the public sphere finds its most sophisticated elaboration in Habermas's 1962 monograph, *Strukturwandel der Öffentlichkeit: Untersuchungen zu einer Kategorie der bürgerlichen Gesellschaft*.[7] In this work, he enquires into the historical and social conditions under which a rational-critical debate about public affairs can provide a legitimate basis for political action. He approaches this question by exploring the particular historical moment at which certain possibilities for human emancipation were unlocked, possibilities which – as developed in the idea of 'communicatively-generated rationality' – were to become the leitmotif of his life's work. *Strukturwandel der Öffentlichkeit* should be read as a critical response to the political pessimism of the first generation of the Frankfurt School, although it too belongs to the tradition of critical theory. In this book, we find a historically grounded, immanent critique of the institutions of the bourgeois public sphere in England, France and Germany, an enquiry both into history and normative ideals. Habermas seeks to go beyond the changing realities of bourgeois political life to recover a setting for public reason and for the accompanying legitimacy claims of formal democracy. In the following paragraphs, I shall briefly recapitulate his idea of the public sphere, which stresses its openness to popular participation, as well as the quality or form of rational-critical discourse.

Habermas argues that, historically speaking, the growth of a distinctive political public occurred in the later eighteenth century with the demarcation of a boundary between state and society, the widening of political participation and the crystallization of citizenship ideals. By analyzing the institutions that made bourgeois democracy genuinely radical in its day, Habermas tries to show that debate in the public sphere was, at least in principle, based on rational-critical argumentation in which the best argument was meant to prevail, rather than the outcome of disputes predetermined by the social identity of proponents or opponents. The discourse of the public sphere, he argues, 'bracketed' status differences,[8] making them irrelevant for the purpose of discourse itself. Citizens entered into the bourgeois public sphere on the basis of the autonomy it afforded them, both socio-psychologically and economically, by their private lives and non-state civil relations. Habermas concludes that the basis of the bourgeois public sphere is a clear distinction between public good and private interest and the participation of citizens in defining public policy through reasoned exchange.

Habermas's account of the eighteenth century as the golden age of the public sphere is followed by an account of its progressive decline in the twentieth century, when the boundaries between state and society began to disappear with the development of welfare state capitalism, and rational-critical debate gave way to the consumerism of mass culture. He argues that the media that once provided an exemplary arena for rational-critical debate have become yet another domain for cultural consumption, and that the bourgeois public sphere has collapsed into a sham world of image creation and opinion management. No longer believing that either the public sphere or the socialist transformation of civil society could underpin the development and the recognition of a truly general interest, Habermas gradually turned away from the attempt to provide a historically specific grounding for democracy, moving instead towards the idea of grounding consensual will-formation in a universal human capacity for communication. In his path-breaking *Theorie des kommunikativen Handelns* (1981), he shifts his attention from the institutional construction of a public sphere as the basis for democratic will-formation to the validity claims universally implicit in all speech. In the latter, he finds the basis for a progressive rationalization of communication and the capacity for non-instrumental interpersonal relationships. Public agreement is now grounded in the intersubjectivity of speech. Communicative action provides an alternative to money and power as a basis for social integration.[9] As I shall later explain, the public sphere remains an ideal (and the locus of democratic practice) for Habermas, but in his later conception it becomes a contingent product of communicative action rather than its basis.

Further developments of the public sphere concept

In the 1960s and 1970s *The Transformation of the Public Sphere* was read more for its account of the degeneration of the bourgeois public sphere than as an analysis of this sphere's constitution and emancipatory potential. It was written in the context of a flourishing post-war political sociology that focused on the conditions of Western democratization and especially on the impact of public communication (and the formation of public opinion) on democratic political systems.[10] Since the late 1980s and 1990s, democratization is once again on the world agenda. The belated English translation of Habermas's book on the public sphere arrived in 1989, during the bicentennial of the French Revolution but, more pertinently, at the beginning of the transformation of Central and Eastern Europe. At a time when political theorists and sociologists had 'rediscovered' civil society,[11] it was not surprising that it sparked an international revival of interest in the public sphere. But this time the reaction (and the critique) focused on the normativity of Habermas's account of the political public sphere.

In the same period, the vigorous 'liberal versus communitarian' debate in American (and later also European) political theory provided another approach to the public sphere and the cultural differences negotiated therein. Public discourse plays a rather different legitimating role in liberal and civic-republican models of democracy. Briefly, the liberal-individualist or Lockean theory views politics as the aggregation of the individual preferences of self-interested actors. The political process of opinion- and will-formation is determined by the competition of collectivities acting strategically and trying to maintain or acquire positions of power. According to this view, public deliberation, insofar as it is pertinent to the generation of a shared conception of the public good,[12] drops out altogether. Political discourse consists of bargaining and seeking compromises that satisfy as many private interests as possible. As a result, this model cannot accommodate instances of public discourse in which there are no clearly identifiable interests. Furthermore, the liberal-individualistic view seems incapable of taking into account the fact that actors' views can be altered in the process of public debate, and that citizens frequently see themselves as part of a political collectivity and do not vote on the basis of individual interests alone.

In contemporary liberalism (e.g. John Rawls, Ronald Dworkin) this model of politics, with its division between the private and the public realm, is seen in more legal terms: political discourse serves to interpret the principles of justice in a pluralistic community of law. Discourse has to be based on 'conversational constraints', most importantly neutrality and fairness, so as to resolve the problem of the mutual coexistence of disagreeing groups. By identifying normative premises that all participants find reasonable, these differences can be bridged.[13] This neutral conception of an overall juridical framework for political deliberation is too weak to allow for a wider and more dynamic account of the public sphere that is able to generate social integration.[14] Liberalism does not offer a deep account of mutual understanding of cultural/ethical differences and learning in situations of conflict.

By contrast, the civic-republican or Rousseauian model – currently represented in the work of communitarians like Charles Taylor, Michael Walzer, Alasdair MacIntyre and Benjamin Barber – defines democratic politics as collective self-rule. Political will-formation is thus conceived as people reasoning together to

promote a common good that is more than merely the sum of individual preferences. The common good is seen as a substantive conception of the good life,
which defines the community's way of life. Thus, in the republican view, public
discourse can be carried out only by a 'pre-given', substantively integrated ethical-
cultural community in which solidarity prevails. The idea is that private interests
are revised as they are transcended in the course of the debate. Accordingly, in the
civic-republican conception (and especially in its recent communitarian version),
the public sphere, with its basis in civil society, acquires a strategic significance. It
is seen as a medium of democratic decision-making itself – that is, a collection of
common spaces or forums, in which citizens exchange ideas and achieve a 'common mind'.[15]

Here the paradigm of political discourse is not competitive bargaining, but
dialogue aimed at fostering mutual understanding. The citizens engaged in public discussion see themselves as belonging to a community (conceived as being a
relatively homogeneous group with a shared cultural background). According to
the civic-republican model, public discourse not only leads to the formation of
public opinion but also to a shared self-understanding of the collectivity. This
conception of the public sphere, which is implicit in most (eurosceptical) social
democratic literature on European integration, focuses on its function of social
integration and the reproduction of a political culture or a national identity. It
allows us to analyze a public space where citizens clarify and articulate their interests, preferences and identities. But, when it frames all public communication
within a single, all-encompassing 'we', the civic-republican model of democracy
comes close to ruling out claims of self or group interest and (social and cultural)
differences. It cannot accommodate situations in which there is a persistent diversity of opinions or worldviews that refuse to converge on a consensus or cultural
understanding, and where fair bargaining processes provide an appropriate mode
of political will-formation. More importantly, the communitarian conception of
public discourse as dialogue has difficulties in dealing with the plurality of competing publics and the resulting fragmentation of complex modern societies.

As a protagonist in the 'liberal versus communitarian' debate, Habermas developed a model of 'deliberative democracy',[16] reintroducing the concept of the
public sphere into his theory. His proceduralist view of politics takes elements
from both the liberal view and the civic-republican view and invests the democratic process with normative connotations stronger than those of the former
model but weaker than those of the latter. In agreement with republicanism it
places the process of political opinion- and will-formation at its centre, but conceives the liberal principles of the constitutional state as a consistent answer to the
question of how the demanding communicative forms of democratic opinion
and will-formation can be institutionalized.[17]

In his recent writings, Habermas attempts to reintroduce social complexity
and contingency into the normative framework of constitutional democracy. In
*Faktizität und Geltung: Beiträge zur Diskurstheorie des Rechts und des demokratischen
Rechtsstaats* (1992), Habermas's most systematic treatment of democratic theory,

social life is seen as so complex that it is impossible for democracy to organize society or for actors to control their acts. In order to overcome the resulting deficit in social integration, powerful institutions are necessary. For Habermas, it is law that performs this integrative function, and therefore decision-making and institutions must be oriented to the making of law. His account of the rule of law in modern constitutional states provides a 'two track' (*zweigleisig*) solution to the problem of complexity: political decision making in institutions must be open to the 'weak public'[18] (as the bearer of public opinion) and yet structured in such a way as to be effective. Parliament (or equivalent decision-making 'strong publics') provides an institutional focus for a broader, decentred communication dispersed across the public sphere and, potentially, involving all citizens.[19] In other words: according to his 'two-track model', law and political decisions are legitimate if institutionalized decision-making procedures are (1) open to inputs from an informal and vibrant public sphere and (2) appropriately structured by formal institutions to ensure effective implementation. Thus, the 'moment' of deliberation does not reside primarily with the judiciary nor with the body of elected representatives, but is spread throughout a vast communicative network. Habermas's deliberative theory of democracy is normative in the sense that the legitimacy of governing (at the nation-state and European level) is seen as dependent upon the institutionalization of an overarching, unifying public sphere.

Habermas argues that in modern societies, where the boundaries between the political system and the public sphere are blurred, political *power* (the ability to make binding decisions and execute government decisions) is found mainly at the centre, whereas *influence* (through the formation of public opinion) extends throughout society. The many mediations of institutional influence, as well as the complexity of public spheres are perhaps the reasons why Habermas turns to the idea of 'subjectless' communication in the informal public sphere. He ultimately interprets public opinion as 'anonymous' (since it is not located in any particular group of individuals) and as 'decentred' within the network of communication itself. Habermas, therefore, turns away from arguing for the formation of a general will – which would have to be indicated by empirical majorities or discovered by representative bodies – concentrating instead on 'discursive structures' that link the public with formal institutions (by creating channels of public influence).[20] And he concludes with a view of the civic public as dissolved into an impersonal 'structure of communication'.

Thirty years after the publication of *Strukturwandel der Öffentlichkeit*, Habermas, in the foreword to its new edition, defines the concept of public sphere as 'denoting all those conditions of communication under which there can come into being a discursive formation of opinion and will on the part of a public composed of the citizens of a state'.[21]

Rethinking the public sphere

In the following section, I hope to show how a 'constructive' critique of Habermas's various conceptions of the public sphere can open the way for an 'interdiscursive' or 'dialogical' model that is better suited to depicting the complex and variegated reality of public life in Europe today.[22] As we have seen, Habermas's early historical analysis is less concerned with the political dimensions of the public sphere (already achieved) than with the strong liberal ideal of the reasoning public. This has several consequences for his early conception of the public sphere: it assumes that (a) it is exclusively based on rational-critical discourse, which (b) takes place in a unitary public realm. Furthermore, it assumes (c) that it is possible for interlocutors to debate 'as if' they were social equals, and (d) that discourse in the public sphere should be limited to discussion about the common good, excluding 'private' interests and issues. All these assumptions have been subjected to a concerted critique that now follows in brief.

(a) By underlining the conception of critical-rational discourse, Habermas neglects the extent to which public communication does not consist in argumentation aiming at consensus, but also involves questions of individual interest, social and cultural recognition, power, prestige, etc. Participation in public debates is not simply a matter of formulating contents, but also of being able to speak 'in one's own voice'; thereby simultaneously enacting one's socio-cultural identity through specific expressive modes or rhetorical features.[23] Accordingly, in order to appropriately analyze the public sphere, other forms of public communication (e.g. identity narratives, story-telling, bargaining, etc.) must also be considered.[24]

(b) By subsuming all forms of public sphere into the liberal model, Habermas effectively assumes a single authoritative public sphere. In his early conception he, therefore, misses the extent to which the public sphere has, from its inception, involved a multiplicity of competing publics.[25] The public sphere has always involved contested meanings, fragmentation and conflict.[26] In history, members of subordinate social groups (women, workers, peasants, blacks, etc.) have constituted 'subaltern counterpublics'[27] in order to create alternative discourses parallel or opposed to official public spheres. In this sense, social movements also challenge the agenda of official public discourses, bringing new issues (e.g. the environment) to the fore.

(c) Habermas's conception of the public sphere stresses its role in the formation of political will, thereby de-emphasizing its role in the formation and enactment of social identities. As a result, he sees social and cultural identity as something people leave behind when they engage in public discourse. Bourgeois civil society, however, was not quite the neutral context for the emergence of rational political discourse that Habermas's historical account might suggest.[28] Public spheres are culturally specific institutions in which participants occupy precise cultural and social positions. The 'bracketing' of social inequalities usually works to the advantage of dominant social groups and tends to silence the subalterns. Thus Habermas's conception of the public sphere cannot account for domination (whether gender, race or class-based repression) nor exclusion from the public sphere.[29]

(d) Feminist critique has shown how modern political thought (and especially the public/private dichotomy) is highly gendered,[30] something which was especially true in the heyday of liberal bourgeois society.[31] The rhetoric of domestic privacy seeks to exclude certain issues (e.g. abortion, sexual violence) from public debate by personalizing them. Since the boundaries between the public and the private are culturally and historically defined (and permeable as such), it is more appropriate to analyze many forms of public discourse as ongoing negotiations and contestation of what counts as 'public' and 'private'.[32]

Habermas's later conception of the public sphere has received far less attention from social scientists. His normative theory of the 1990s stresses the procedural, as opposed to the substantive, definition of a democratic public sphere. As already discussed, he shifts from reconstructing the formation of a general will to analyzing 'discursive structures' that link the public with formal institutions by creating channels of public influence. His revised model of the public sphere can be characterized as a communicative network formed by different actors who engage in contestation over particular aspects of social and political life.[33] Contrary to his earlier model, this formulation places no restrictions on what may become a topic for deliberation and, what is more, it can accommodate a plurality of publics. While the bourgeois conception of the public sphere promoted the general (or weak) public of lay persons engaged in the formation of public opinion, Habermas's later conception can far better account for the involvement in decision-making of specialized (or strong) publics. Nevertheless, even this more comprehensive model of the public sphere still tells us very little about culturally mobilized (weak) publics and the way in which their popular sovereignty 'retreats into democratic procedures'.[34] Such an interpretation of the political content of popular sovereignty (described as 'anonymous' and 'intersubjectively dissolved')[35] is altogether too minimal to preserve the radical elements of participatory democracy which he looked for in *Strukturwandel der Öffentlichkeit*.[36] More relevantly, and for many of the same reasons, his recent reworking of the concept of the public sphere seems too abstract to be useful as a tool for an adequate empirical analysis of how public opinion, collective identity and political culture are formed in a decentred and socio-culturally heterogeneous polity.

As Habermas himself points out,

> [A] public sphere that functions politically requires more than the institutional guarantees of the constitutional state; it also needs the supportive spirit of cultural traditions and pattern of socialization, of the political culture, of a populace accustomed to freedom.[37]

His procedural theory of constitutional democracy can account only for the first condition. Thus, it seems important to rethink the concept of the public sphere so as to account for the second condition – namely, cultural and political identity formation in complex late-capitalist societies.[38] It is from this kind of perspective that I shall attempt to 'constructively' criticize his revised conception of the public sphere.

(a) Focusing on legislative politics, Habermas's recent reformulation of his conception of the public sphere still gives pride of place to critical-rational discourse (i.e. argumentation aiming at consensus), thereby neglecting other forms of communication.[39] Precisely because he emphasizes a certain type of discursive interaction, he tends to see the public sphere as an essentially neutral network of overlapping sub-publics which is equally hospitable to any form of socio-cultural expression. Yet a clearly defined, transparent language does not exist.[40] All utterances are situated in specific cultural and social-historical contexts and are framed by their respective expressive modes or 'speech genres'.[41]

(b) While accommodating a multiplicity of public arenas, Habermas's revised conception of the public sphere still presupposes a single, overarching public sphere under the umbrella of a common liberal political culture and a shared constitutional identity. As we will see in more detail in Chapter 4, his idea of 'constitutional patriotism' refers to a kind of post-national identity whose normative reference point is the democratic constitution rather than the nation-state, its territory or a dominant cultural tradition. Seen from such a 'constructivist' perspective, which is, of course, much better suited to our multicultural societies than the 'holistic' conception which prevails in some of the literature on European integration, European identity is conceived as an overarching normative ideal which transcends national and socio-cultural identities.[42] We could radicalize Habermas's definition of the public sphere as a communicative network of public arenas, by visualizing a criss-crossing and overlapping of publics via Wittgenstein's metaphor of 'family resemblances'.[43] In this manner, the communicative network of public discourses would have no threads of a pre-given (political) culture or collective identity enmeshed within it. Thus, as I intend to show in what follows, post-national identities, rather than an overarching normative ideal, become *inter*cultural: they are 'interdiscursively' constructed in the sense that they are formed in an ongoing dialogical interaction *between* cultural or national discourses or 'voices' (Bakhtin).

(c) Habermas's theory of democracy underestimates the role of cultural conflicts in contemporary multicultural societies and the power relations involved therein. For the theorists of deliberative democracy, the plurality of specialized and competing publics is democratic only if they are embedded within a single, all-encompassing open civic public sphere. They fear that pluralism, leading to conflicting values and interests, could cause the public sphere to collapse into a dogfight between competing publics.[44] This approach, however, cannot account for the fact that conflict resolution in situations of fundamental cultural heterogeneity requires not so much consent and agreement based on a shared political culture, but interpretation and learning, and above all the capacity (and the willingness) to dialogically explore and negotiate social and cultural differences. It is, therefore, important to give a theoretical account of the learning processes[45] which can take place in interactions between publics with diverging socio-cultural positions. These need not lead to convergence, but certainly towards a breaking down of boundaries or a loosening of 'old landmarks' that can open up new perspectives on common problems.[46] I will try to develop the idea of a democratic politics which reasonably radicalizes pluralism: according to such an approach, deliberation seeks to foster a pervasive level of comfort with heterogeneity to be treated as difference within the normative context of constitutional dialogue (Chapter 6).

(d) Habermas's 'two-track model' of deliberative democracy, where institu-tionalized decision-making processes must be open to inputs from informal (or weak) publics, does not seem adequate in the gradual transformation of con-temporary decentred and heterogeneous polities: the proliferation of decision-making bodies within the governing system (described in the literature on 'governance')[47] poses considerable problems for his conception of the division of political labour between an informal public and the formal institutions that regu-late the flow of influence among powerful, non-governmental agents. This is par-ticularly true of the EU's multi-level governance system,[48] which includes communitarian institutions, as well as nongovernmental (supranational, national and subnational) policy-making bodies.[49] The horizontal networks linking these different publics constitute transnational policy communities which deliberate on specific issues (e.g. migration, the environment). Yet, if we conceptualize the public sphere as a communicative network where different publics partially over-lap ('family resemblances'), an emerging characteristic of the EU as a multi-level system of policy-making can also be seen as offering the chance for the creation of new communities of political action (or strong and hybrid publics). According to such a 'pluricentric' view of European politics, we should, of course, explore new institutional arrangements which can ensure the accountability of democratic decision-making bodies.[50]

Toward an interdiscursive model of the public sphere

A lively political and academic debate has recently emerged about the normative viability and empirical possibility of a European public sphere. Yet, there is little agreement in the literature as to whether there exists a transnational public sphere in Europe. The empirical assessment depends on the (diverging) conceptions of the public sphere. Most authors who deny even the possibility of an emerging European public sphere implicitly presuppose a substantialist (or 'holistic') idea of the public as a culturally integrated homogenous political community or *demos* with a shared collective identity, a common language and media system. For Jürgen Gerhards, for example, there would be a European public sphere if (and only if) national publics would address European issues and take a European rather than national perspective on these issues.[51] Not only are such views idealizing the uni-tary nature of national publics, but there is also no reason why the empirical pos-sibility of the European public sphere should be measured on the normative basis of the national public sphere:[52] the EU is very unlikely to develop into a tradi-tional nation-state writ large. And the development of a 'European perspective' might not depend on a converging process of the member-states' perspectives, but rather on the recognition of divergent (national) perspectives as legitimate *within* European politics.

As historical analyses of the public sphere show,[53] there has never been a single authoritative public sphere in which citizens formed *a* public opinion or *a* com-mon collective identity. Even at the level of nation-states, the idea of the socially and culturally integrated community was always a constitutive myth rather than a sociologically accurate depiction of collective identities. This is even truer of contemporary heterogeneous societies where political complexities, socio-economic inequalities and cultural pluralism make the public sphere a realm of, at best, loosely connected and fragmented discourses in which many groups of individuals enact collective identities and negotiate political will.[54] Starting from the actual plurality of publics, it has become clear that a (pre-existing) community along national or cultural lines is itself not a necessary requirement for the constitution of a transnational (or intercultural) European public sphere. How then can we conceptualize a notion of 'the public sphere' which neither draws on the idea of a cultural homogeneity among citizens, nor withdraws into a purely procedural conception of the public sphere as an anonymous, unsituated network of communicative forms?

In the following, I shall outline an *interdiscursive model of the public sphere* which supposes, in contrast not only to social democratic (eurosceptical) or *demos* views, but also to more discourse-theoretical ones, the *pervasiveness of ambiguity* or indeterminacy. According to such an approach, the very (ethical/cultural) differences which obstruct understanding in the demos view, and which are to be contained by 'constitutional patriotism' in the discourse-theoretical view, are the engine of understanding to be achieved through practices of mutual translation in a world of pervasive ambiguity. Instead of simply containing or limiting pluralism, my conception of the public sphere actively values the everyday life exploration of difference between strangers with heterogeneous cultural/ethical backgrounds. The associated dialogical conception of citizenship can account for the struggle that most of us experience living under conditions of radical pluralism and points to an image of a European political identity with multiple voices and innumerable perspective on common social problems.

I propose to conceptualize the European public sphere as a pluralistic social realm of a variety of (sometimes) overlapping or contending publics engaged in a transnational (intercultural) dialogue and citizenship practices. Accordingly, European identity can be imagined as produced by an ongoing process of struggle between different socio-cultural and national[55] perspectives or discursive 'voices', such as can be heard in the official discourse of the EU, the discourse of social scientists, the (mainly nationally-organized) media discourse of intellectuals and opinion leaders, the informal discourse of people in everyday life and so on. Social researchers can thus deconstruct existing (official) representations and reveal ideological assumptions in the construction of a 'new Europe'. The positive value of analyzing European identity through its invention 'from above' (the top-down approach) lies in displaying the variegated dissemination through which we construct the field of meanings associated with it.[56] But social research can also generate new understandings of how people in contemporary Europe appropriate these different ideologies when formulating collective identifications on a supranational level (the bottom-up approach). This is, in fact, the aim of my empirical case study, as developed in Part III.

Interdiscursivity proceeds from the idea that there is a constant interchange between the discourses of different publics and, accordingly, that all public discourse is intrinsically 'multi-voiced'. Thus, such an approach underscores the *process* of negotiation and conflict in the creation of European identity and the power relations involved therein. It does not make any claims about the cohesiveness of public discourse. Rather, the present approach takes the question of the possible existence of an additional 'superpublic' – comprising more limited sub-publics – as an empirical one. In terms of communicative standards, depending on the socio-cultural context and speech situation, it also includes forms of discourse other than argumentation (e.g. narratives). Such an approach assumes that a concept of the public sphere should be normative only to the extent that it helps to expose 'interdiscursive asymmetries' caused by hegemonic discourses (the suppression of subaltern counter-publics, exclusion of voices, etc.).[57] More radically than Habermas's concept, the interdiscursive approach stresses the plurality of *unshared* socio-cultural perspectives[58] (within and between publics) and the possible disagreement (or misunderstanding) between these perspectives. Moreover, it suggests the possibility of an ideally symmetrical dialogical exploration of cultural and ideological *differences* (rather than similarities), i.e. a mutual perspective-taking that provides the basis for the ongoing negotiation of an *inter*cultural collective identity and transnational (rather than postnational) political culture. This conception of the public sphere, unlike the universalizing ideal of a single, overarching public, is seen as the task, as yet unfulfilled, of a 'conversation we have to open up' among the multitude of socio-cultural and national collectivities or 'voices'.

How is it possible for members of different publics to communicate across lines of socio-cultural and national diversity? Nancy Fraser argues that the intercultural communication involved in a pluralistic public sphere

> requires multicultural literacy, but that … can be acquired through practice. In fact, the possibilities expand once we acknowledge the complexity of cultural identities. Pace reductive, essentialist conceptions, cultural identities are woven of many different strands, and some of these strands may become common to people whose identities otherwise diverge, even when it is the divergences that are most salient.[59]

These 'common strands' – warranting the commensurability of discourses – are the constantly (re)generated and negotiated collective (self-) understandings which are produced in public communication and which, in turn, become the cultural framework for everyday life experiences.[60] And the reality of post-war population movements, transnational capitalism, global telecommunication and the explosion of mass consumption make the development of theories of cultural translation or multicultural literacy all the more pressing.[61]

The contemporary phenomena of multiple affiliations and the mixing of elements from different cultures render the ambivalent nature of collective identity strikingly evident. Constantly moving between different symbolic worlds, a growing number of people define themselves in terms of multiple bonds of national belonging and feel at ease with subjectivities that embrace plural and fluid socio-cultural identities. In line with this perspective, my case study will analyze migrants as 'prototypical cases' of the decentred self in modern societies (see Part III): by negotiating their ambivalent national belonging in their daily life, the multiple identities of their (individual) selves become manifest.[62] Seen as such, one can argue that multiculturalism does not only mean a difference *between* cultures, but also difference *within* cultures and, thus, *within* every self. Paradoxically, cultural difference has become the basis for an exaggeration of difference and, with it, the assertion of the incommensurability of cultures.[63] Against a 'multiculturalism based on difference', which risks the compartmentalization of cultural or ethnic groups by emphasizing their mutual distinctness, an interdiscursive approach emphasizes the *processes* involved in the creation of culture and identity.[64] As I shall argue in Chapter 4, it follows that a 'critical' multiculturalism does not require the politics of authenticity or of affirmative action, which emphasize 'fundamentalist' cultural self-definitions among national or cultural minorities, but rather of identity based on an *inter*cultural 'pastiche'. Starting from the assumption that culture is always sited and negotiated,[65] a 'critical' politics of multiculturalism argues for the possibility of new, positive identity-fusions, transcending fragmentation, but at the same time recognizing the differential interest that (disadvantaged) social groups have in sustaining boundaries. Its necessary task is to envisage policies where cultural or national collectivities engage in reflexive self-critical distancing from their own discourses, and hence come to recognize the potential validity of other discourses. What emerges as a response to this task is the conflictual model of translation.

As I will argue in more detail below (Chapter 5) the question of translation or 'multicultural literacy' draws on arguments from the philosophy of language. We will see that Donald Davidson argues that understanding within a language is always itself a continuing translation of the idiolects of speakers, and thus translation between languages is, in fact, only an extension of what native speakers do all the time when trying to make sense of one another's meanings.[66] In a similar vein, Mikhail Bakhtin has argued that language is radically interdiscursive or 'dialogical'[67] – that is, that all utterances are part of an open-ended dialogue where meanings (for instance what we mean by 'Europe') are negotiated in the interaction between the discourses arising from the speakers' different socio-cultural and ideological positions. Communication across lines of socio-cultural and national difference or 'multicultural literacy' is possible precisely because in public discourse cultural identities and selfhood are enacted liminally, on the boundaries of self and other, of identity and difference.[68] If the exploration of ambiguity (and misunderstanding) in the continuing clarification of meaning is a necessary precondition for understanding (and self-understanding), and if, therefore, national languages include a plurality of different sub-languages or speech genres, then we can argue that the linguistic and socio-cultural diversity of Europe is not something qualitatively different from the diversity, which already exists within national communities.[69]

For the creation of a European public sphere, the diversity of languages is, of course, a serious practical (not normative) problem.[70] With some notable exceptions, European nation-states have tended in the past to impose a single dominant language within their territory; however, there has never been an absolute coincidence between linguistic and political borders: historically speaking, territories have always been linguistically 'divided', hosting different sub-languages or 'speech genres' and languages have also been 'shared' amongst bordering nation-states.[71] At one time, however, the European elite were educated to be multilingual and to master ancient languages. Moreover, linguistic heterogeneity became institutionalized in Europe in the form of mutual processes of (diplomatic, technological, trade, literary etc.) translation from one language to another. Today, it has been shown that the ascendancy of English as a lingua franca in the domain of work and consumption allows Europeans to better communicate across national borders.[72] To master several languages (at least English as a second language) means not being excluded from the contemporary world of transnational communication. At present in Europe there can be no question of imposing one single language for the public use; but, at the same time, there is also a 'universalised regime of translation'.[73] In fact, as Umberto Eco has claimed, 'translation' is the common language of Europe.[74] The future of Europe as a 'community of citizens' therefore depends upon whether the mass of citizens will have access to this common language – namely, the practices of translations.

As already discussed, a public (defined as a collectivity of persons connected by continuous processes of communication over particular aspects of social and political life) can, in principle, extend beyond national borders. As we will see shortly (in Chapter 5), transnational (or intercultural) communication requires, however, two necessary conditions: first, participants of public debates must presuppose that their different cultural/national perspectives on a certain issue are not incommensurable (i.e. that mutual understanding or translation is possible); and second, they must recognize each other as legitimate speakers within a (shared) public sphere whose statements are taken seriously.[75] In pluralistic societies, and particularly in the variegated public life of the European polity, public communication depends on the commitment to a cognitive openness vis-à-vis the views of diverging addressees with the telos of cooperative problem-solving. This second condition can be measured empirically, for example through a qualitative analysis of media discourses which explores whether other Europeans fellows are accepted as legitimate contributors to national debates of common concern (e.g. the BSE scandal) and, more importantly, through the observation of a transnational dialogue as an exploration of different viewpoints that sets in motion a process of reflective inter-societal learning.[76] There are, of course, various degrees of 'transnationalness' that is, more or less intense interactions between national (regional, local) public spheres with more or less *substantial* inclusiveness or perspective-taking.[77]

The emergence of a substantive transnational (political) public sphere in Europe does not depend least upon its institutional arrangements.[78] However, the conception of an interdiscursive public sphere is capable of extrapolating from real elements and tendencies in contemporary multi-level governance. For example, at the EU level, one may take the Open Method of Coordination (OMC), which institutionalizes arenas of political deliberation with the aim to generate a European-wide collective will-formation. The OMC is defined by the Lisbon European Council as a new form of policy coordination, which occupies an intermediate place between intergovernmental cooperation and supranational integration.[79] This new governance mechanism aims to coordinate the actions of several member states in a given policy domain (e.g. employment, pension, environment, immigration) and to create conditions for mutual learning (e.g. through benchmarking performances and comparing best practices) that hopefully will induce some degree of voluntary policy convergence while permitting substantial national diversity in methods and the timing of specific policy initiatives.[80] By fostering extended deliberation amongst stakeholders over the nature of problems and their best-fit solutions, the OMC may be seen as a source of transnational public discourses across a variety of issues:[81] deliberative policy-making produces a pool of arguments underlying EU guidelines and reignites debate about member state policy orientation. These (transnationally) shared arguments guide political deliberation about different national policy choices from within and, in doing so, contribute to the emergence of a European public sphere in which the policy choices of several member states (published, for example, within national media) are exposed to 'transnational' public scrutiny. The result of this 'transnationalization' is not the harmonization of national publics or the emergence of a distinct public sphere at the European level (e.g. via European media) – but a criss-crossing of public communication about the same issues or problems. Accordingly, the exploration of different national/cultural viewpoints may lead to a significant rise in (critical) opinion-formation or, more generally, set in motion a process of *reflective inter-societal learning*. What follows, is *the idea of a dialogical solidarity among strangers that stresses the process of cooperative enquiry – the search of best policy practices or the most just solution.*

Participation in a transnational public sphere is, in fact, part of the process by which individual and collective identities are made and remade. The interdiscursive model of the public sphere enables us to form an analytical conception of 'European citizenship' as a vantage-point which allows us to rethink transnational modes of civic engagement and democratic exchange between various forms of publics and policy-making bodies,[82] and of 'European identity' as a form of intercultural (or 'pastiche') consciousness without falling into the trap of Euro-nationalism[83] in any form. The European project has a past which is not perceived in the same way by different regions and different social groups. By listening to the different accounts given and stories told by others, and by recounting their own narratives in exchange, participants in a European (constitutional) public dialogue come to see their discourses and histories as woven together from a multiplicity of 'voices'. Such a public culture is neither unified nor purely expressive of constitutional principles (see Chapter 6). Rather its focus is that of an 'imagined community' of citizens which is reflexively engaged with others in public communication:[84] through intercultural dialogue citizens learn to resist uncritical identification with a 'closed' national memory and recognise both the advantaged and disadvantaged predicaments of others. This vision of a European culture could help to foster social integration by forging new transnational communities of political action founded upon the assumption of the inalienable right of individuals to choose to participate in public arenas, irrespective of nation or culture. At the same time, a 'pastiche' European culture, where national and cultural margins are analytically conceived as battlegrounds for contesting discourses or 'voices', would undermine the idea of a 'fortress Europe' with sealed cultural boundaries.

Notes

1 While the decisions of EU institutions have a direct effect on citizens, the predominant form of legitimation available today is a highly indirect one derived from (democratically elected) national governments, rather than from the collectivity of European citizens.

2 In using the term 'interdiscursive' I intend to stress the possibility of talking across lines of socio-cultural and national diversity, i.e. the possibility of translation between discourses (without ironing out their differences).

3 In German 'Öffentlichkeit' means both the public sphere and the public as a collectivity of persons connected by continuous processes of communication.

4 It is difficult to keep the issue-related debates prominent in processes of political will-formation entirely separate from identity formation. In this sense the political and the cultural aspect of public discourse are inextricably linked (see for instance the 'identity politics' common to new social movements).

5 Thus, the 'public sphere' refers both to (a) the forums in which a public, that is a group of citizens, is engaged in discourse about society and its rules and (b) the universe of these discourses themselves.

6 See also: J. Habermas, *Theory of Communicative Action*, vol. 2, Polity Press (new edition), Cambridge 1991, p. 317: 'The institutional core of the public sphere comprises communicative networks amplified by a cultural complex, a press and, later, mass media; they make it possible for a public of art-enjoying private persons to participate in the reproduction of culture, and for a public of citizens of the state to participate in the social integration mediated by public opinion.'

7 Luchterhand Verlag, Neuwied (new edition: Suhrkamp Verlag, Frankfurt am Main 1990). See also the English translation: J. Habermas, *The Structural Transformation of the Public Sphere*, MIT Press, Cambridge, MA, 1989.

8 Of course only elites were admitted to the bourgeois public sphere; however, these elites were of different statuses: in coffee houses master craftsmen might debate with landed gentry, in Parliament the nobility mixed with commoners, etc.

9 J. Habermas, *Theorie des kommunikativen Handelns*, vol. 2, Suhrkamp Verlag, Frankfurt am Main 1981 (see English translation: *Theory of Communicative Action*, 1991).

10 For example E. Katz and P. Lazarsfeld, *Personal Influence: The Part Played by People in the Flow of Mass Communication*, Free Press, Glencoe (Il.) 1955; K. Deutsch, *Nationalism and Social Communication*, MIT Press, Cambridge, MA, 1953; H. Blumer, 'The Mass, the Public, and Public Opinion', in: B. Berelson and M. Janowitz (eds.), *Reader in Public Opinion and Communication*, Free Press, Glencoe (Il.) 1953; Raymond Williams, *Culture and Society 1780–1950*, Chatto & Windus, London 1958.

11 See: J. Cohen and A. Arato, *Civil Society and Political Theory*, MIT Press, Cambridge, MA, 1992; J. Keane, *Democracy and Civil Society*, Verso, London 1988; J. Keane, *Global Civil Society?*, Cambridge University Press, Cambridge 2003; C. Taylor, 'Modes of Civil Society', in: *Public Culture* 3:1, 1990, pp. 95–118; M. Walzer, 'The Idea of Civil Society: A Path to Social

Reconstruction', in: *Dissent* 38, 1991, pp. 293–304 ; J. Alexander, 'The Return to Civil Society', in: *Contemporary Sociology* 22, 1993, pp. 797–803; A. Seligman, *The Idea of Civil Society*, Princeton University Press, Princeton 1992; R. Putnam, *Making Democracy Work: Civic
Traditions in Modern Italy*, Princeton University Press, Princeton 1993.

12 In the liberal model it is assumed that there is no such thing as the common good above
    and beyond the sum or the trajectory of all the various individual goods, and so private
    interests are the legitimate basis of political discourse.

13 See for instance B. Ackerman, 'Why Dialogue?', in: *Journal of Philosophy* 68:1, 1989, pp. 5–
    22. John Rawls's normative idea of an 'overlapping consensus' is too complex to be sum-
    marized here. Roughly, it means the justification (through public discourse) of a shared
    political conception through its embedding in the different and even opposing reasonable
    moral doctrines of citizens. Therefore the 'overlapping consensus' is not a moral compro-
    mise, but an agreement about a common political framework for deliberation (see: J. Rawls,
    'The Domain of the Political and the Overlapping Consensus', in: *New York Law Review*
    64:2, 1989, pp. 233–255).

14 The liberalist model, in its juridical conception of public discourse, seems very much influ-
    enced by the 'American way' of politics, where judicial battles are more and more preva-
    lent.

15 See C. Taylor, 'Liberal Politics and the Public Sphere', in: C. Taylor, *Philosophical Arguments*,
    Harvard University Press, Cambridge, MA, 1995, pp. 257–287.

16 Habermas adopts Joshua Cohen's definition of the notion of 'deliberative democracy' as
    'rooted in the intuitive ideal of a democratic association in which the justification of the
    terms and conditions of association proceeds through public argument and reasoning,
    among equal citizens. Citizens in such an order share a commitment to the resolution of
    problems of collective choice through public reasoning and regard their basic institutions
    as legitimate in so far as they establish the framework for free public deliberation' (see: J.
    Cohen, 'Deliberation and Democratic Legitimacy', in: A. Hamlin and P. Pettit (eds.), *The
    Good Polity: Normative Analysis of the State*, Basil Blackwell, Oxford 1989, p. 21). The idea
    of 'deliberative democracy' has been further developed by other theorists: S. Benhabib,
    'Toward a Deliberative Model of Democratic Legitimacy', in: S. Benhabib (ed.), *Democracy
    and Difference: Contesting the Boundaries of the Political*, Princeton University Press,
    Princeton 1996, pp. 67–94; J. Fishkin, *Democracy and Deliberation: New Directions for Demo-
    cratic Reform*, Yale University Press, New Haven, CT, 1991; J. Bohman, *Public Deliberation:
    Pluralism, Complexity, and Democracy*, MIT Press, Cambridge, MA, 1996. For the concept
    of a 'deliberative public sphere' see: B. Peters, 'Deliberative Öffentlichkeit', in: L. Wingert
    and K. Günther (eds.), *Die Öffentlichkeit der Vernunft und die Vernunft der Öffentlichkeit:
    Festschrift für Jürgen Habermas*, Suhrkamp Verlag, Frankfurt am Main 2001, pp. 655–677.

17 'Discourse theory brings a third idea into play: the procedures and communicative pre-
    suppositions of democratic opinion- and will-formation function as the most important
    sources for the discursive rationalization of the decisions of an administration constrained
    by laws and statute. Rationalization means more than mere legitimation but less than the
    constitution of political power' (see: J. Habermas, 'Three Normative Models of Democ-
    racy', in: S. Benhabib (ed.), *Democracy and Difference: Contesting the Boundaries of the Po-
    litical*, Princeton University Press, Princeton 1996, p. 28).

18 Habermas adopts Nancy Fraser's terminology of 'weak publics' whose 'deliberative prac-
    tice consists exclusively in opinion formation and does not encompass decision making'
    (see N. Fraser, 'Rethinking the Public Sphere: A Contribution to the Critique of Actually
    Existing Democracy', in: C. Calhoun (ed.), *Habermas and the Public Sphere*, MIT Press,
    Cambridge, MA, 1992, p. 134). Fraser argues that, with the achievement of parliamentary
    sovereignty, the line separating civil society and the state is blurred. A sovereign parlia-
    ment functions as a public sphere within the state. She calls it a 'strong public' because it is
    empowered to translate public opinion into authoritative decisions.

19 See: J. Habermas, *Between Facts and Norms: Contributions to a Discourse Theory of Law and*

Democracy, MIT Press, Cambridge, MA, 1996, pp. 307–308.

20 For this 'structuralist approach' (as Habermas calls it) see his *Between Facts and Norms*, p. 185.

21 See: J. Habermas, 'Further Reflections on the Public Sphere', in: Calhoun (ed.), *Habermas and the Public Sphere*, p. 446.

22 This re-examination is based on the political principle that to deconstruct a concept does not mean one should do without what was valued or desirable in the original notion.

23 Habermas focuses on its 'problem solving function' and neglects its role as a source of (self)understanding to which C. Calhoun refers as the 'world-disclosing' function (see: 'Introduction', in: Calhoun (ed.), *Habermas and the Public Sphere*, p. 34).

24 See for instance: I. Young, 'Communication and the Other: Beyond Deliberative Democracy', in: Benhabib (ed.), *Democracy and Difference*, pp. 120–135. Johnson criticizes Habermas for not considering bargaining: J. Johnson, 'Is Talk Really Cheap? Prompting Conversation Between Critical Theory and Rational Choice', in: *American Political Science Review* 87:1, 1993, pp. 74–86.

25 Since Oskar Negt and Alexander Kluge's pioneering critique of Habermas, theorists have sought to pluralize and multiply the concept of the public sphere (O. Negt and A. Kluge, *Öffentlichkeit und Erfahrung*, Suhrkamp Verlag, Frankfurt am Main 1972).

26 Habermas cannot for instance account for 'the plebeian public sphere' associated with the Jacobin phase of the French Revolution or other popular radical traditions (like the emancipatory impulses in of the English working class studied by E. P. Thompson). See: G. Eley, 'Nations, Publics, and the Political Cultures: Placing Habermas in the Nineteenth Century', and K. Baker, 'Defining the Public Sphere in Eighteenth Century France: Variations on a Theme by Habermas', pp. 181–211, both in: Calhoun (ed.), *Habermas and the Public Sphere*, pp. 289–339.

27 'Subaltern counterpublic' is Nancy Fraser's term (see her 'Rethinking the Public Sphere', in: Calhoun (ed.), *Habermas and the Public Sphere*, p. 123; and 'Politics, Culture, and the Public Sphere: Toward a Postmodern Conception', in: L. Nicholson and S. Seidman (eds.), *Social Postmodernism: Beyond Identity Politics*, Cambridge University Press, Cambridge 1995, p. 291).

28 As Geoff Eley points out, the bourgeois public sphere can also be seen as a new 'hegemonic' mode of political domination (see: G. Eley, 'Nations, Publics, and the Political Cultures: Placing Habermas in the Nineteenth Century', in: Calhoun (ed.), *Habermas and the Public Sphere*, p. 325).

29 See: N. Fraser, 'Politics, Culture, and the Public Sphere', in: Nicholson and Seidman (eds.), *Social Postmodernism: Beyond Identity Politics*, pp. 287–312.

30 Since 1968 feminists have systematically politicized 'private issues' in order to transform the private/public distinction in terms of family, sexuality, and subjectivity.

31 Joan Landes has shown how in the context of the French Revolution women were silenced through a highly gendered bourgeois male discourse. The separation between the masculine realm of public activity and the feminine realm of the private sphere of the household has systematically excluded women from political participation and civil rights (see: J. Landes, *Women and the Public Sphere in the Age of French Revolution*, Cornell University Press, Ithaca 1988). See also K. Peiss, 'Going Public: Women in Nineteenth Century Cultural History', in: *American Literary History* 3:4, 1991, pp. 817–828.

32 For greater discussion regarding notions of the public and private, see for instance the debates on 'identity politics' as can be found in Fraser, 'Politics, Culture, and the Public Sphere', in: Nicholson and Seidman (eds.), *Social Postmodernism: Beyond Identity Politics*, pp. 287–312.

33 See: J. Habermas, *Between Facts and Norms*, MIT Press, Cambridge, MA, 1996, p. 360.

34 Habermas, 'Three Normative Models of Democracy', in: Benhabib (ed.), *Democracy and Difference*, p. 28.

35 See: Habermas, *Between Facts and Norms*, p. 486.

36 See: Bohman, *Public Deliberation*.

37 Habermas, 'Further Reflections on the Public Sphere', in: Calhoun (ed.), *Habermas and the Public Sphere*, p. 453.

38 Whether in complex societies such a common liberal political culture, capable of holding together different subcultures and lifestyles, exists is, of course, an empirical question.

39 See also: Young, 'Communication and the Other', in: Benhabib (ed.), *Democracy and Difference*, pp. 120–135.

40 This argument has been convincingly made by D. Davidson, 'A Nice Derangement of Epitaphs', in: E. LePore (ed.), *Truth and Interpretation: Perspectives on the Philosophy of Donald Davidson*, Blackwell, Oxford 1986, pp. 433–446.

41 Speech genres are forms of utterances specific to socio-historical contexts, which both constrain and facilitate communication (see: M. Bakhtin, 'The Problem of Speech Genres', in: Bakhtin, *Speech Genres and Other Late Essays*, University of Texas Press, Austin 1986, pp. 60–102). The analysis of these 'sub languages' becomes important when we want to investigate the enactment of social and cultural identities in public life.

42 As opposed to Dieter Grimm's 'cultural fundamentalist' argument that a European identity is precondition for a more developed European Union and a European constitution, Habermas is in favour of creating a European constitution which – in his view – would then foster postnational collective identifications (see: J. Habermas, 'Remarks on Dieter Grimm's "Does Europe need a Constitution?"', in: *European Law Journal* 1:3, 1995, pp. 303–307 and also his *Facts and Norms*, p. 507).

43 'I can think of no better expression to characterise these similarities than "family resemblances"; for the various resemblances between members of a family: build, features, colour of eyes, gait, temperament, etc. etc. … One might as well say: "Something runs trough the whole thread – namely the continuous overlapping of those fibres."' (L. Wittgenstein, *Philosophical Investigations*, Blackwell, Oxford 1967, § 67.)

44 See for instance: Bohman, *Public Deliberation*.

45 The idea of 'learning' is thereby weaker than a 'search for consensus', but certainly stronger than a mere compromise ('tit for tat') of exogenous preferences of social actors.

46 B. Parekh, *Rethinking Multiculturalism: Cultural Diversity and Political Theory*, Macmillan, London 2000.

47 Contemporary political authority (including its agenda-setting and legislative, participatory and implementatory aspects) is divided into semi-autonomous, specialized segments or sectors with procedural or issue-specific publics (i.e. experts, NGOs or other associations), which function as policy communities (see for instance: J. Gerhards, 'Politische Öffentlichkeit: Ein system- und akteurtheoretischer Bestimmungsversuch', in: F. Neidhardt (ed.), *Öffentlichkeit, öffentliche Meinung, soziale Bewegungen*, Westdeutscher Verlag, Opladen 1994, pp. 77–105).

48 See for example: K. Eder, K. U. Hellman and H. J. Trenz, 'Regieren in Europa jenseits öffentlicher Legitimation: Eine Untersuchung zur Rolle von politischer Öffentlichkeit in Europa', in: *Politische Vierteljahresschriften*, Sonderheft 39, 1998, pp. 321–344.

49 Such nongovernmental publics are policy communities of experts, agencies, corporations, lobbies, NGOs, and other associations.

50 Of course, there are many important questions which I cannot address further in this work: What democratic arrangements are best suited to institutionalizing coordination among different (strong and hybrid) decision-making publics, including their various co-implicated (weak) publics? What kind of arrangements best ensure the accountability of policy-forming communities to the collectivity of citizens? Charles Sabel and Oliver Gerstenberg, for instance, propose procedures which they call 'direct-deliberative polyarchy'. Within a framework of differential democratic problem-solving, issue-specific publics are seen as self-managing institutions and thus as potential sites of direct or quasi direct democracy (see: O. Gerstenberg and C. Sabel, 'Directly-Deliberative Polyarchy: An Institutional Ideal for Europe?', in: R. Dehousee and C. Joerge (eds.) *Good Governance and Administration in*

Europe's Integrated Market, Oxford University Press, Oxford 2002. See also the propositions made in P. C. Schmitter, *How to Democratize the European Union ... and Why Bother?*, Rowman & Littlefield, Lanham 2000).

51 J. Gerhards, 'Westeuropäische Integration und die Schwierigkeiten der Entstehung einer europäischen Öffentlichkeit', in: *Zeitschrift für* Soziologie 22:2, 1993, p. 99; see also: J. Gerhards, 'Das Öffentlichkeitsdefizit der EU im Horizont normativer Öffentlichkeitstheorien', in: H. Kälble, M. Kirsch and A. Schmid-Gernig (eds.), *Transnationale Öffentlichkeiten und Identitäten im 20. Jahrhundert*, Campus Verlag, Frankfurt/New York 2002, pp. 135–158.

52 See also: C. Kantner, 'Öffentliche politische Kommunikation in der Europäischen Union. Eine hermeneutisch-pragmatische Perspektive', in: A. Klein and R. Koopmans (eds.), *Bürgerschaft, Öffentlichkeit und Demokratie in Europa*, Leske & Budrich, Opladen 2002 and M. van de Steeg, 'Bedingungen für die Entstehungen von Öffentlichkeit in der EU', in: Klein and Koopmans (eds.), *Bürgerschaft, Öffentlichkeit und Demokratie in Europa*.

53 See for example: Eley, 'Nations, Publics, and the Political Cultures', and Baker, 'Defining the Public Sphere in Eighteenth Century France', pp. 181–211, both in: Calhoun (ed.), *Habermas and the Public Sphere*, pp. 289–339

54 The fact that within nation-states we find a multiplicity of publics that intersect, makes transnational public discourse conceivable in principle. From this perspective, a transnational public sphere is not only possible, but its internal plurality would differ from the national one only in degree and not in nature. The hope that there can be an institutionalized public sphere where people debate across lines of socio-cultural and national differences gains some plausibility if we consider the actual plurality of publics within a nation which, in turn, may interact with the many different publics of other nations.

55 National identities are, of course, neither unified nor unitary and cannot but be seen simply as 'other' in relation to what is outside their borders. Instead, the 'other' always emerges forcefully within a national public discourse (e.g. the voices of outsiders, immigrants, etc.). See: P. Gilroy, *The Black Atlantic: Modernity and Double Consciousness*, Harvard University Press, Cambridge, MA, 1993.

56 See, for example, C. Shore, *Building Europe: The Cultural Politics of European Integration*, Routledge, London/New York 2000 and M. Sassatelli, 'Imagined Europe: The Shaping of a European Cultural Identity through EU Cultural Policy', in: *European Journal of Social Theory* 5:4, 2002, pp. 435–451.

57 This would require a political sociology of public life in which multiple but unequal publics interact. Using the concept of the public sphere as a critical tool, political scientists could thus expose the limits of democracy as it exists today and explore new forms of democratic exchange within the context of the multilevel structure of EU decision-making.

58 Bakhtin argues that we share meaning only partially and that what we share is in any case not as interesting as what we do not share. We cannot learn or progress from shared meaning. From the same perspective, he claims that doubt is a precondition for the co-pursuit of truth, disagreement a precondition of mutual understanding .

59 Fraser, 'Rethinking the Public Sphere', in: Calhoun (ed.), *Habermas and the Public Sphere*, p. 127.

60 As we will see in Part III, the increasing mobility of people within Europe has produced 'transnational spaces' of professional and everyday life experience that transform the individual's sense of belonging.

61 As Z. Bauman puts it – without specifying the presuppositions of this claim – 'Far from being a peculiar pastime of a narrow set of specialists, "translation" is woven into the texture of daily life and practised daily and hourly by us all. We are all translators; *translation is the common feature in all forms of life,* as it is part and parcel of the 'informatics society' modality of being-in-the-world' (Z. Bauman, *In Search of Politics*, Polity Press, Cambridge 1999, p. 201).

62 I have elaborated this point in my essay 'In-between Nations: Ambivalence and the Making of European Identity', in: B. Stråth (ed.), *Europe and the Other and Europe as the Other*, Peter Lang Verlag, Brussels 2000, pp. 279–309. As we will see in Part III, I take the *inter*cultural identity of migrants (which I shall analyze through a series of in-depth interviews) as the basis for an interdiscursive conception of identity-formation.

63 See: P. Werbner and T. Modood (eds.), *Debating Cultural Hybridity: Multi-Cultural Identities and the Politics of Anti-Racism*, Zed Books, London 1997, and P. Werbner and T. Modood (eds.), *The Politics of Multiculturalism in the New Europe: Racism, Identity and Community*, Zed Books, London 1997.

64 See for instance: T. Turner, 'Anthropology and Multiculturalism: What is Anthropology that Multiculturalists Should be Mindful of It?', in: *Cultural Anthropology* 8:4, 1993, pp. 411–429.

65 That is, culture can be understood properly only as the historically negotiated creation of more or less coherent symbolic and social worlds.

66 Davidson argues that understanding requires the exploration of ambiguity in the continuing clarification of meaning between the speakers. In this sense, misunderstanding is a precondition for understanding (see: 'A Nice Derangement of Epitaphs', in: LePore (ed.), *Truth and Interpretation*, pp. 433–446).

67 'Any understanding is imbued with response and necessarily elicits it in one form or another: the listener becomes the speaker. A passive understanding of meaning of perceived speech is only an abstract aspect of the actual whole of actively responsive understanding, which is then actualized in a subsequent response that is actually articulated.' (see: Bakhtin, 'The Problem of Speech Genres', p. 68).

68 I developed this argument in: P. Nanz, 'Vielstimmige Lebenswelt', in: *Deutsche Zeitschrift für Philosophie* 2, 2003, pp. 199–212. See also: Bakhtin, 'The Problem of Speech Genres', pp. 60–102

69 The difference is only a matter of degree, not of nature.

70 A. de Swann has rightly insisted on the importance and difficulties of the idea of common European linguistic policy, without which there can be no European democracy: A. de Swann, *Words of the World: The Global Language System*, Polity Press, Cambridge 2001; see also F. Coulmas (ed.), *A Language Policy for the European Community: Prospects and Quandaries*, Mouton de Gruyter, Berlin 1991.

71 See: D. Baggioni, *Langues et nations en Europe*, Payot, Paris 1997 and D. Laitin, 'The Cultural Identities of a European State', in *Politics and Society* 25:3, 1997, pp. 277–302.

72 P. Schlesinger, 'The Babel of Europe? An Essay on Networks and Communicative Spaces', in D. Castiglione and C. Longman (eds.), *Public Discourses of Law and Politics in Multicultural Societies*, Oxford, Hart Publishing, forthcoming.

73 E. Balibar, 'Europe as Borderland, lecture presented in Human Geography', University of Nijmegen, 10 November 2004, p. 35 [on file with the author].

74 U. Eco, *The Search for the Perfect Language*, Blackwell, Oxford 1995.

75 Nationalist reactions (e.g. '*The* Spanish do not know what the rule of law means') deny this legitimacy and treat perspectives from other member states as observations of outsiders.

76 This qualitative dimension of discourse – the substantial quality of reciprocal to-and-fro in dialogue – is not captured by the research design of the current project 'Transnationale Öffentlichkeit und die Strukturierung politischer Kommunikation in Europa. Abschlußbericht an die DFG' (ED 25/13–1) by K. Eder, C. Kantner and H.-J. Trenz Humboldt-University, Berlin 2004. Their quantitative content-analytical concept of a transnational public sphere focuses on the degree of commonality with which an issue is discussed across borders in various national spheres.

77 For a convincing empirical analysis of the degree of 'transnationalness' of the European public sphere see the current research project by B. Peters and H. Wessler at the University of Bremen, 'The Transnationalization of Public Spheres and its Impact on Political Systems: The Case of the EU' (B 3 within the Sonderforschungsbereich 'Staatlichkeit im Wandel',

see: www.sfb597.uni-bremen.de).

78 As to the difficulties see: B. Peters, 'Nationale und transnationale Öffentlichkeit – Eine Problemskizze', in: C. Honegger, S. Hradil and F. Traxler (eds.), *Grenzenlose Gesellschaft?*, Leske+Budrich, Opladen 1999, p. 661–673 and B. Peters, S. Sifft, A. Wimmel, M. Brüggemann and K. Kleinen-Von Königslöw, 'National and Transnational Public Spheres: The Case of the EU', in: *European Review* 13:1, 2005, pp. 139–160.

79 Council of the European Union, *The Ongoing Experience of the Open Coordination Method*, Note of the Portuguese Presidency of the Union, 9088/00, 13 June 2000.

80 The OMC is commonly described as a process working in four stages: first, the EU ministers agree on policy goals in the policy area concerned; second, the guidelines are translated by member states into national and regional policies with specific targets; third, the ministers agree on benchmarks and indicators in order to measure and to compare best practice within the EU and worldwide; fourth, through evaluation and monitoring, member states' performance is assessed, relative to each other and to their declared goals. For a positive evaluation of the OMC see: F. Scharpf, 'European Governance: Common Concerns vs. The Challenge of Diversity', MPIfG Working Papers 01/6, Cologne 2001.

81 For an empirical assessment see: C. De la Porte and P. Nanz, 'Open Method of Coordination – a Deliberative and Democratic Mode of Governance?', in: *Journal of European Public Policy* 11:2, 2004, pp. 267–288.

82 The EU as a multilevel governance system provides a context for what Heater refers to as 'multiple citizenship': individuals will increasingly have multiple sites through which to exercise their obligations and rights and these would include the neighborhood, the associations of civil society, local, regional and federal government and regional bodies such as enhanced the EU (see: D. Heater, *What is citizenship?*, Polity Press, Cambridge 1999, pp. 126–134).

83 It is in this sense that I understand the revolutionary credo of Frantz Fanon: 'National consciousness, which is not nationalism, is the only thing which will give us an international dimension' (F. Fanon, *The Wretched of the Earth*, Penguin, Harmondsworth 1967, p. 199). The ambivalent, *inter*cultural and thus anti-nationalist nation-space becomes the arena for a new *inter*national culture.

84 See also: P. Markell, 'Making Affect Safe for Democracy? On "Constitutional Patriotism"', in: *Political Theory* 28, 2000, pp. 38–63.

4

Multiculturalism: the exploration of difference

Once a teacher asked: 'Where do you come from?' I did not reply. I said: 'The main thing is that I'm a human being.' She laughed [and said to me] 'Yes, I know that you're a human being, but where do you come from?' I said that I come from Turkey, but I don't feel Turkish. I also don't feel German. I went on and [the teacher then] said 'You must not say that.' I [then] said, 'I am international.' She said, 'You must never say that! Either you're Turkish or German or Italian or whatever.' So if I were to say that I am international, would that be bad? [To be] so mixed?

Ali[1]

In Europe, the continuous change in the cultural and ethnic mixtures of nation-states has been conceptually frozen and politically defined as the historical essence of the people (a *demos*), the ontological centre around which the nation-state has been identified. What is often taken as the essence of a national culture, however, is in fact the accumulation of innumerable ingredients over countless years. As a rule, (national) cultures are made up of many different, far more specific cultures (regional, ethnic, religious, etc.).[2] In this sense, virtually every society is 'multicultural'. And, because of increasing international mobility, the populations of many countries are becoming even more diverse, leading to shifts in national cultures and identities. Contemporary societies are increasingly plural (think of new ethnic or cultural diasporas as well as new 'localisms') and at the same time more porous and open to international migration. It is not that societies which previously were homogenous have suddenly become highly pluralistic. It is simply that the character of pluralism has changed. On the one hand, cultural differences within societies are greater than they used to be because immigrant cultures have – both in size and political organization – become more visible; on the other hand, there has been an increasing tendency to stress the importance of cultural belonging as a prerequisite for leading a good life. There has been a deep historical shift in the understanding of plurality, which has given the idea of 'multiculturality' a new meaning.[3]

The political system of the EU faces socio-cultural pluralism on two levels, affecting inter-state as well as intra-state conditions. The EU consists of many national societies which, for two reasons in particular, can themselves be regarded as multicultural. First of all, the so-called nation-states – although they often base the legitimacy of their political institutions upon a presumed national identity[4] or *demos* – comprise many varieties of long-resident ethnic, linguistic and religious groups. Indeed there has been a resurgence of different groups which have long existed within particular states but who now seek to gain political, social and economic power (e.g. the Basques, the Corsicans, the Scots). We could call these societies 'multi-nation states'. Within them, several nations (e.g. historical communities occupying a given territory, sharing a distinct language and history) co-exist, jostling for the status of a self-governing people (e.g. in Spain, France, the United Kingdom). Even as the legitimacy of nation-states within their own territorial contexts is under threat, the idea of the nation – on an ever smaller scale – is everywhere flourishing. Secondly, trans-border population movements have meant that many of the states of contemporary Europe have become 'multi-ethnic'. There have been mass labour migrations and refugee flows since 1945 which have accelerated and become more complex since the late 1980s.[5] Here the aim is to adequately 'integrate' individuals and families from different ethnic or cultural groups within a political community. A state is multicultural if its members either belong to different nations (a multi-nation state), or have emigrated from a different nation (a multi-ethnic state).[6] Most member states of the EU experience both sorts of cultural pluralism.

What we identified in the previous chapter on normative theories of European integration as nostalgia for a culturally integrated, 'homogenous' nation (the '*demos*-thesis') represents a fear not only of the loss of the sovereignty of the nation-state, but also of socio-cultural heterogeneity within the nation-state. The possibility of a flourishing ethical/cultural pluralism is associated with the threat of social fragmentation.[7] Multiculturalism prompts political theory to rethink its central concepts (e.g. legitimacy, solidarity, citizenship) along similar lines as the question of a transnational political integration of the EU member states. A multicultural society, on the national as well as the European level, may be defined as one in which political legitimacy is not based upon the idea of the homogeneity of its inhabitants (the *demos*-thesis), whether this presumed homogeneity be linguistic, religious, cultural or ancestral (racial/ethnic).[8] From a normative point of view, the socio-cultural boundaries of an association of free and equal members of a political and legal system are wholly contingent and unrelated to these essentializing categories.

How, then, can we conceive of democracy – understood as political self-government – under conditions of denationalization and socio-cultural heterogeneity ('transnationalization' and multiculturalism)? Can the universalistic idea of a postnational 'constitutional patriotism'[9] adapt to the challenge of ethical/cultural pluralism? What is the relation between the pluralism on which socio-cultural practices are based, the unifying or integrating political culture of a polity

– generated through the production of shared meanings in dialogical encounters – and universal constitutional principles?

In what follows, I will first briefly present the questions that multiculturalism poses for liberal political theory. I will then outline the position of some influential authors in the contemporary debate (Taylor, Waldron, Kymlicka and Habermas). By pointing to the limits of these theories, I will prepare the grounds for the idea of a 'situated' constitutional patriotism based on an exploration of difference (through mutual translation) in political deliberation (Chapters 5 and 6). To anticipate my conclusion: if we see politics as a field of epistemic struggle – a field in which comprehensive doctrines, world views and self-understandings meet and challenge each other – the plurality of social/ethical practices and senses of belonging, rather than a threat, can be understood as a source of 'social capital'; of innovative interpretations for a constitutional dialogue among ethical/cultural or national groups and publics. The normative notion of deliberative democracy as an open, public field of linguistic-epistemic contention gains support from a constitutional patriotism contextualized or situated in a plurality of differentiated sites of dialogical practices.

Liberal democratic principles centre around the idea of an ethically/culturally neutral legal order that assures everyone equal rights.[10] To be compatible with these principles, state policies should therefore be based on the idea that all citizens should be treated equally. Historically, attempts to increase democracy have generally involved making citizenship rights available to ever wider circles of the population, for example to the working (property-less) class and to women. In recent times, citizenship for both indigenous and immigrant minorities has been seen as the key to greater equality. However, the growing cultural diversity of polities challenges contemporary liberal political theory (as elaborated by Rawls, Dworkin, Ackerman and others), in which the needs and autonomy of *individual* citizens, understood as the bearers of inalienable individual rights, are high on the agenda.[11] In order to work out a conception of political justice that the plurality of 'incompatible, yet reasonable doctrines' (Rawls) might all endorse, liberals distinguish the public point of view (political concept) from the many non-public points of view (ethical/cultural concepts or comprehensive doctrines). The liberal policy of equal dignity is based on the principle of political justice conceived as fairness (which is assumed to be shared by all citizens irrespective of their comprehensive doctrines), but cannot respect and foster all personal and cultural/ethical notions of what is valuable in life.

Multiculturalist critics stress the significance of collective identities for self and politics. They argue that the population of a political community actually consists of people belonging to a variety of social and cultural groups, with specific needs, interests and values, but that liberal citizenship tends to 'homogenize' political identity: all citizens are supposed to have equal rights as citizens, whatever their economic or social positions might be. Members of indigenous minorities, immigrants and women have often claimed that formal political equality may maintain or provoke unequal outcomes in that it does not, in and of itself, overcome racism, economic disadvantage or social exclusion.[12] Equality as citizens may, there-fore, be insufficient to achieve real empowerment and change. Multiculturalists deny the universalistic, self-emancipatory challenge of modernism, founded on the assumption of the inalienable right of individuals to choose, irrespective of their ethnic or national culture. The vigorous debate about multiculturalism cen-tres on the question of whether these different and distinct groups should be rec-ognized as such, and equal rights accorded to each individual member; or whether group diversity should be actively encouraged through institutionalized group or collective rights.

Against this background, the question of multiculturalism must be under-stood as a question of how a liberal-democratic political system deals with cul-tural/ethical heterogeneity without negatively affecting its own universalistic ideals of individual well-being and public justice. Accordingly, the following questions emerge: is there a possible path between the Scylla of universalism and the Charybdis of differentialism? How is a just society possible under conditions of deep doctrinal conflict (ethical, sub- and transnational or intercultural) with no prospect of resolution? What might be the structure and content of a conception of dialogue that can generate shared meanings – and, for that matter, shared in-terpretations of constitutional essentials – across lines of ethical/cultural compre-hensive doctrines or 'vocabularies'?

Charles Taylor: the politics of recognition

In his influential essay 'The politics of recognition', Charles Taylor writes in a thor-oughly communitarian spirit, making much of the social and cultural situatedness of individuality and, particularly, the need for cultural authenticity.[13] Yet perhaps his most interesting contribution to the debate over multiculturalism concerns his conclusion that it is the very logic of liberal ideas of justice and rights which motivates liberal states to take seriously claims for collective rights to political self-government by national (and ethnic) minorities. He sees liberal ideas on the equal worth of individuals as central to securing recognition in modern society. However, increasing cultural diversity and the emergence of multiculturalism lead to potentially contradictory discourses on two levels. On the one hand, the poli-tics of universalism means emphasizing the equal dignity of individuals through the equalization of rights and entitlements (the principle of equal citizenship). On the other hand, the modern notion of identity has given rise to a politics of difference that is based upon the recognition of the unique identity of a certain individual or group, and their distinctness from everyone else. The politics of universalism require norms of non-discrimination which are 'blind' to difference, while the politics of difference require special rights and treatment for certain groups.

Taylor sees human relations, including expectations regarding justice and rights, primarily in terms of recognition: 'Our identity is partly shaped by recog-nition or its absence, often by the *mis*recognition of others'.[14] His identity model starts from the Hegelian idea that identity is constructed dialogically, through a process of mutual recognition. Participants recognize each other as both equal in their human dignity and separate in their individual uniqueness or cultural distinctiveness). In this sense, we define our identity in dialogue with, sometimes in struggle against, the identities our 'significant others' want to recognize in us.[15] Taylor therefore sees serious tensions between the notion of equal respect for (recognition of) the dignity of every human being (which is central to most liberal theories of justice and rights) and the notion of equal respect for (recognition of) concrete traits or, as Taylor calls it, respect for difference. The idea of respect for forming and defining one's own identity has, in recent times, often been radicalized into the principle that every personal and cultural identity should be accorded equal respect or recognition. This is where the two notions of respect come into conflict.

The claims of individual rights and the protection of collective identities seem irreconcilable, but Taylor sets out to bridge the gulf, using the example of Québéc's claim for special rights for the French language and culture. He stresses that the politics of equal dignity and the politics of difference presuppose each other, even though they do not combine easily.[16] His aim is to show how rights-based liberalism can be related to a 'politics of consideration' of cultural diversity, which is supposed to compensate for the costs of equalizing universalism. Taylor argues that one can distinguish the fundamental rights (e.g. rights to life, liberty, free speech) which should never be infringed, from rights that are important, but that can be revoked or restricted for reasons of public policy (e.g. the compulsory use of French language for commercial signs, compulsory French education for all immigrant and non-Francophone children). If need be, a state may actively advance specific conceptions of the good life:

> A society with strong collective goals can be liberal, provided it is also capable of respecting diversity, especially when dealing with those who do not share its common goals.[17]

On this basis, the Québécois are justified in demanding special measures (such as priority for the French language in schools and public life) in order to secure the 'survival' of their collective identity, as long as they maintain fundamental liberal rights, and provide protection for minorities.

Taylor's theory of the self contains some genuine insights into the psychological effects of the misrecognition produced by racism, colonialism and cultural imperialism.[18] However, his *politics of recognition* is theoretically and politically problematic for the following reasons:

(a) Culture is a legitimate, even necessary terrain of struggle, a site of injustice in its own right. But not all forms of misrecognition are equally pernicious, and the ones which are deeply imbued with economic inequality cannot be remedied by cultural recognition alone. Identity politics hypostatizes culture and treats misrecognition as a free-floating cultural harm or a psychic deformation – quite apart from both institutionalized norms and social status – and, accordingly, tends to reduce economic inequalities to a simple expression of cultural injustice. To

frame political claim-making in terms of 'recognition' risks marginalizing or dis-
placing claims for egalitarian redistribution.[19] And since Taylor's notion of collective identity privileges the cultural and ethical dimension, it cannot account for
the full complexity of social identity which would have enabled him to address
both questions of access to power and of the misdistribution of wealth. If so, the
politics of recognition cannot be integrated with either a politics of participatory
parity in a pluralist social life (see point d) or a politics of economic redistribution. Instead, as Habermas points out, we should submit claims of recognition to
democratic processes of public justification and thus foster political deliberation
across cultural and social cleavages.

(b) As concerns the *politics of difference*, Taylor's approach tends to essentialize
group identities. It emphasizes the collective dimensions of individual identity
(ethnicity, religion, gender, etc.), while de-emphasizing its personal dimension
(intelligence, wit, charm, etc.), as well as its autonomy with respect to the various
collective dimensions. Taylor tends to explain respect for difference too strongly
in terms of respect for ethical communities, group cultures etc. and not sufficiently in terms of the value of communal and cultural belonging as an essential
prerequisite for individual well-being. Similarly, the *politics of recognition* conflates
the originality of nations or cultures with the authenticity of persons. Although
the concepts and practices made available by society, religion and so on are fundamental components of its constitution, the latter nonetheless requires each individual to position the self within the collective dimension and often to fight
against the forces of convention (cultural traditions, organized religion, gender
roles, etc.). Taylor's argument in defence of collective goals (e.g. the survival of
certain societies or cultures through indefinite future generations), therefore risks
violating the principle of respect for the autonomy not only of contemporary but
also of future individuals.[20] In this sense, his approach in the end cannot but undermine the individualistic core of rights liberalism which he seeks to preserve.
The *politics of recognition* cannot accommodate the ambivalence between group
identities in cultural life and individual identities. Individual identities are still
the non-negotiable principle behind liberal ideas of achievement, mobility and
justice.

Moreover, in practical terms, if group rights are institutionalized that should
imply certain mechanisms for determining and registering group membership.
But many people assigned to a national or ethnic group may not accept this as
their principle source of political identity. Stressing the need to safeguard a collective identity (e.g. the Francophone Canadians) puts moral pressure on individual
members to conform to given cultural groups (e.g. by sending their children to a
French school). Cultural dissidence (e.g. sending them to English-speaking schools)
and experimentation (e.g. exploring intragroup divisions of gender or class) are
discouraged.[21] The risk implied by a *politics of recognition* is the imposition of a
single, simplified group-identity which denies the complexity of people's lives,
the multiplicity of their identifications and the cross-pulls of their various affiliations. Taylor's approach cannot account for the complex process by which identities,

both individual and collective, develop – the politics of cultural identification – and the struggles within groups for the authority and power to represent them.

(c) Taylor criticizes the *politics of difference* for prematurely judging every culture favourably and, in doing so, implicitly invoking the standards by which we judge all cultures. This, Taylor argues, paradoxically, is an ethnocentric (or at least condescending) position in the sense that it makes everyone else the same. He emphasizes instead, that recognition means more than mere acknowledgement of existence. It presupposes a 'fusion of horizons' (Gadamer) that generates new vocabularies of comparison. Using these, we can judge the worth of a culture and the fact that our own culture is transformed in this dialogical process.[22] But, ironically, the *politics of recognition* tends to deny its own dialogical premises. If identity is constructed in interaction with another subject, why should misrecognized people (e.g. Francophone Canadians) be protected so that they can construct their identity on their own? And, if identities should be recognized as equal in political dialogue, why does Taylor present minority positions as an imposition from the 'outside': 'The challenge is to deal with their sense of marginalization without compromising our basic political principles'.[23] Members of minority groups should, rather, be conceived as participants in a political community whose constitutional principles are always exposed to new interpretations. In the long run this 'politics of cultural preservation' undermines the universalistic core of liberalism, since it fails to recognize that collective goals have to be intersubjectively justified in light of other 'collective' rights. Moreover, in practical terms, it might encourage separatism and group cleavages. It seeks to exempt 'authentic' collective self-representation from all possible challenges in a pluralist public sphere and, thus, scarcely fosters social interaction across differences. Instead, the increasingly heterogeneous ethical grounding of deliberative practices in today's public discourses make the constant (re)negotiation/translation of shared constitutional principles all the more pressing.

(d) Taylor elaborates his idea of the *politics of recognition* around the case of a multi-nation state, Québéc, where a Francophone majority holding power at the provincial level is confronted by an Anglophone majority holding power at the federal level. He does not, however, suggest a general mechanism which would secure protection and equal rights for a *range* of minorities (in Québéc, the indigenous peoples and immigrant minorities) and empower them politically. It seems as if in his view a local or regional society is justified in protecting the cultural identity of its majority population (within a local community or region) against the hegemony of the majority culture of a society in a broader territory in which it is located (the nation-state or transnational polity) as long as such a society respects its respective minorities. But just as members of the cultural majority of a society need the social forms which are essential to their self-understanding to be recognized, members of minority cultures need recognition for the social forms which underpin their feelings of self-confidence, self-respect and self-esteem. Thus, in terms of 'national' cultures – defined by an intergenerational community and occupying a given territory or homeland – such a politics of recognition could lead to an infinite regress into parochialism. Ever smaller groups could claim self-government on an increasingly local level, as has happened for example in Nigeria. The same is true with regard to immigrants – which usually do not claim territory and whose cultures are not sustained by complete political institutions – who could claim 'group rights' on an ever decreasing scale (e.g. the Turks, the Kurds, the Alevis) in order to safeguard their cultural identity from a larger majority culture. But this kind of image of society as a mosaic of multiple *demoi* cannot supply the imaginative resources for the task of social and political integration – especially when 'demotic tribalism' is on the rise. The mere appeal to the mutual recognition of these *demoi* is hardly sufficient to contain the tension between the centrifugal pull of socio-cultural diversity in public life on the one hand, and the universalistic or 'centripetal' pull of constitutionalism in a multicultural state on the other.[24]

Taylor's undermining of his own dialogical theory of recognition is a result of his keeping with the 'substantialistic' communitarian idea that communication, and thus political deliberation, presupposes a shared language and historical tradition of an integrated, homogeneous cultural community. Accordingly, his *politics of recognition* requires cultural or ethnic boundaries – which are, of course, arbitrary – for the functioning of a community's self-government, as well as for the respect of other communities. Although he conceptualizes the larger political community as made up of a multiplicity of cultures or nations, in the end he reverts to what might be called a 'multi-*demoi*' thesis. Taylor's static view of self and culture does not allow him to see that pluralism and dialogue go 'all the way through' from the formation of self, to ethical-cultural practices and up to the practices of political deliberation. He does not envision multiculturalism as a politics of the mutual exploration of difference in public life.

Michael Sandel's theory of the self is similar to Taylor's. His well-known communitarian critique of the liberal conception of the self is that it is 'essentially unencumbered' and needs to be challenged by an 'enlarged self-understanding'.[25] While Sandel is certainly correct in underlining that the self is multiply constituted, subject to a variety of different – even conflicting – allegiances and identifications, its inner multiplicity is not bound by the practice of self-interpretation of its cultural community in an essentialist manner, as he seems to believe. As I argued above, situatedness or 'encumbrance' is a source of meaning and self-understanding, not a burdensome cultural imposition. Rather, intrasubjective multiplicity develops itself through intersubjective exchanges in a variety of communicative contexts, and is, therefore, the precondition for reflexivity and learning (see Part III).[26] Individuation arises intersubjectively by participating in communication in a variety of situations and positing oneself as one who is situated in the world with a particular, contingent life history.[27] In contrast to this dialogical self, the communitarian self – and, for that matter, the self of the *demos*-theorists – is 'constituted by friends and not by enemies'.[28] It is cocooned by a 'we-identity', invulnerable to experiential transformation or learning and closed to interactions in which the other (or the 'enemy') forces it to experience the

contingency of its own world view. Instead, this self challenges the enemy to justify his world view in an intercultural/ethical dialogue[29] (see Chapters 5 and 6).

Jürgen Habermas: the idea of an overarching political culture

In his essay 'Struggles for Recognition in the Democratic Constitutional State'
(1993/1994),[30] Habermas spells out an intersubjective approach to multiculturalism
which attempts to remove the false contradiction between individual rights and
the protection of collective identities by stressing that everyone is both an individual and a bearer of collective identity. On the one hand, he criticizes
communitarians (like Taylor) for overemphasizing 'collective rights' while undermining individual rights and thus the universalistic core of democratic principles.
On the other hand, Habermas also criticizes liberals preoccupied with rights because they concentrate on the needs of private individuals while failing to recognize that private and public autonomy are co-original (*gleichursprünglich*): there
is an internal, conceptually necessary, connection between them, because private
legal persons cannot attain the enjoyment of equal individual liberties unless they
themselves, by participating in public discourse and so jointly exercising their
autonomy as citizens, arrive at a clear understanding about what interests and
criteria (for what should be treated as equal or unequal) are justified.[31] In this
sense, the addressees of the law acquire autonomy (in the Kantian sense) only to
the extent that they can understand themselves to be the authors of the laws to
which they are subject as private legal persons. Therefore, a 'liberal' version of the
system of rights that fails to take this connection into account misunderstands the
universalism of basic rights as an abstract levelling of social and cultural differences.

Habermas argues that there is an inherent connection between democracy
and the constitutional state, in the sense that citizens can only be autonomous by
collectively exercising their political rights within the law-making process. The
system of rights is actualized simultaneously on two tracks: first, the handling of
problems by decision-making bodies or legal institutions on the basis of enforce-
able individual rights; and second, political and public discourse. In the case of
the latter, those who encounter one another do so as collective actors arguing
about collective goals and the distribution of collective goods, and struggling over
the interpretation of existing laws in view of new needs and interests. Once we
assume that the identity we ascribe to the bearers of individual rights is conceived
intersubjectively, the system of rights cannot be blind to unequal social conditions or cultural differences. Citizens, even when viewed as legal subjects, are not
abstract individuals cut off from their origins. Rather, persons become individu-
alized only through a process of socialization within varying social and cultural
contexts. Thus, Habermas's theory of rights

> requires a politics of recognition that protects the integrity of the individual in the
> life contexts in which his or her identity is formed[32]

– provided, that is, that the individual faiths and practices do not contradict reigning constitutional principles (as they are interpreted by the political culture of a citizenry), as can be seen, for example, in the tenets of 'fundamentalist' cultural traditions.

In contrast to Taylor, he argues that shared ethical conceptions of the good can never overrule individual rights (e.g. those of a citizen of Québéc who does not sympathize with the aspirations of 'the' French-Québécois culture). Democracy in a multicultural society therefore means guaranteeing social and cultural rights to every individual legal person, rather than just to members of specific groups. As Habermas points out, this does not happen by itself, but is rather the result of social movements and political struggle (e.g. the history of feminism). In the democratic process, the dialectics of legal and actual equality can give rise to extensive guarantees of status, rights to self-administration, infrastructural benefits, subsidies, etc. But these arise from legal claims and not – as Taylor seems to assume – from a judgement about the value of a certain group culture. A constitutional state can make the reproduction of cultural worlds possible (e.g. through a policy of 'reverse discrimination'), but it cannot guarantee the 'preservation of species by administrative means'.[33]

In Habermas's view, the law has to safeguard both private autonomy (i.e. the equal rights of citizens) and public autonomy (i.e. citizens' participation in the political struggle over collective goals). It is 'procedurally enacted', or, legitimized by a democratic process, and open to the influence of the society's collective goals. Since the process of actualizing rights is embedded in socio-cultural contexts, every legal system is also 'the expression of a particular form of life and not merely a reflection of the universal content of basic rights'.[34] And since a constitutional state can assert a certain conception of the good in its legal order, it can cause cultural battles in which disrespected minorities struggle against a 'majority' culture. But the coexistence of equal rights for different ethnic communities, cultural groups, and ethical forms of life should not be purchased at the cost of the fragmentation of society into a multiplicity of subcultures which are closed off from one another. Rather, Habermas argues, it is the binding force of a shared political culture that must prevent a citizenry from falling apart. Members of all cultural groups have to acquire a common political language and conventions of conduct to be able to participate effectively in the struggle for resources and the protection of group as well as individual interests in a shared political arena.[35] And it is 'constitutional patriotism'[36] – based on a distinctive interpretation of constitutional principles – that motivationally warrants the possibility of integration in a societal context of deep cleavages.

Let us briefly take a closer look at the relations between heterogeneous social/ethical practices, a shared 'homogeneous' political culture and the universalistic core of constitutional principles (for a more detailed discussion see Chapters 5 and 6).

(a) Habermas fears that an 'ethical grounding' for politics, as put forward by Taylor, undermines the universalistic core of democratic theory. But he exaggerates his 'transcendental' turn, arguing that the ethical substance of constitutional patriotism has to be distinguished from the legal system's neutrality towards the different cultural groups that are 'integrated at a subpolitical level'.[37] Although legal systems and political cultures are 'ethically permeated', they remain 'neutral' with respect to the differences among the cultural communities within a nation. The binding force of the common political culture becomes progressively more 'abstract' as subcultures reduce it to a common denominator, but without losing its binding force of integrating a multicultural society.[38]

In Habermas's approach, the coexistence of different forms of life with equal rights requires the mutual recognition of different ethical/cultural memberships. But for this to be so, his theory of multiculturalism has to distinguish between two levels of integration, that of the self and that of culture: ethical 'acculturation' and political socialization;[39] private (ethical-cultural) and public (political) self; (many different) ethical subcultures and (one common) political culture. As he puts it, 'the level of the shared political culture must be uncoupled from the level of subcultures and their pre-political identities'.[40] This distinction corresponds to the more fundamental distinction he draws between a substantive consensus on the (ethical) values of a certain cultural community or 'subculture' and a procedural consensus on the legitimate enactment of law and exercise of power within a political community.[41]

At the same time, however, Habermas claims not to take the national self-understanding of citizens in a political community as a historical-cultural a priori that makes the democratic process possible, but rather as the 'fluid content of a circulatory process' that is generated through the legal institutionalization of public discourse. In this sense, the people's shared political identity (e.g. identity as Europeans) need not precede the establishment of democratic institutions, but can be expected to arise from those institutions. Because of this 'constructivist' concept of the identity of a political community, he can conceive of transnational institutions (e.g. a European constitution) that would foster the integration of national and cultural identities. Nevertheless, his holistic notion of a postnational constitutional identity on the one hand, and his two-track model of law-making on the other, does not allow him to conceive of politics as plural and dialogical 'all the way up'. Habermas ends up with the idea of a European nation-state which cannot accommodate either the contemporary reality of dispersed sovereignty in a multilevel polity or the radical pluralism of ethical social practices in public life.

(b) Habermas's quasi-substantialist element of a holistically structured and shared life world or background understanding has an equivalent in his formal-pragmatic idealizations concerning identity of meaning (see Chapter 5). His constitutionalist justification of politics presupposes the universalistic epistemological tenets of an inclusive discourse or 'ideal speech situation' that are already implicit in the very idea of rational-critical or argumentative communication. When participants in the democratic process disagree, they nonetheless must share the assumption that there exists a point of convergence in respect to the reference of their debate. The adversaries are intersubjectively involved in their respective ethical/culturally situated justifications insofar as they understand themselves to be jointly committed to the principle of learning to understand each other. It is the aim of getting to the truth of this object that keeps disagreeing participants committed to the attempt to achieve mutual understanding. In dialogical encounters difference and heterogeneity cannot be transcended, only translated. As we will see in Chapter 5, they are ever functioning word-disclosing forces of linguistic hybridization (Bakhtin) – and, as such, are the presuppositions of meaningful understanding and learning. Moreover, many disagreements in ethical/cultural conflicts can be resolved in forms of social cooperation and discursive practices other than rational or 'inclusive-discursive' aiming at consensus, as, for example, through the use of narratives as a means of achieving mutual understanding or of persuasion.

Jeremy Waldron: the mongrel self in a global world

Jeremy Waldron proposes a cosmopolitan account of multiculturalism. Although he does not deny that culture plays a constitutive role in human life,[42] he questions two of the underlying assumptions of communitarian approaches such as Taylor's. The first concerns the notion that 'the social world divides up neatly into particular distinct cultures, one to every community', and the second that 'what everyone needs is just one of these entities – a single coherent culture – to give shape and meaning to his life'.[43] He discredits the idea of cultural integrity mainly by showing that this is not an adequate reaction to the contemporary world. Waldron sees the contemporary world as a global society characterized by considerable economic, moral and political interdependencies among different ethnic groups, national cultures, nation-states and civilizations. He presents his opponents with an argument that is frequently put forward by communitarians: since the free individual can only maintain his identity within a society/culture of a certain kind, he has to be concerned with the wellbeing of this society/culture.[44] In the modern world, Waldron says, we have to recognize the dependence of particular cultures and national communities on wider social, political, and civilizational structures and we should therefore participate in the wider, global context in which our immediate, local surroundings are embedded. In other words, Waldron argues, it is precisely because of (liberal and cosmopolitan) beliefs, rules and institutions, which acknowledge the existence of cultural pluralism and hybridism instead of cultural integrity that small-scale national or ethnic communities can remain true to their local allegiances.

Identity constituted under the auspices of 'cosmopolitanism' is a mélange or hotchpotch of many cultures. Against the communitarian model of 'one person, one culture', Waldron argues that his model of 'one person, many fragments' is both more realistic and more attractive as an account of individual identity in contemporary societies.[45] It is the hybrid or 'mongrel' self (the term is borrowed from Salman Rushdie) that Waldron celebrates in suggesting that it is possible for each of us to respond to a multifaceted world in new and creative ways; that is, chaotic, confused, incoherent. It thus requires 'management' of the (more or less comfortable) coexistence of ethical/cultural fragments. In this view, individual autonomy differs substantially from the liberal idea of the pursuit of a chosen conception of the good (Dworkin) or a plan according to which we live a human life (Rawls). For Waldron, autonomy is nothing but

> choice running rampant, and pluralism internalized from the relations between individuals to the chaotic coexistence of projects, pursuits, ideas, images, and snatches of cultures within an individual.[46]

(a) Such a seemingly postmodern theory of the self ('seemingly' because it may not be Waldron's intention to adopt such a label) is inspiring for its anti-essentialist zeal, but it does not help to create the conditions for cultural reflexivity and political dialogue. The 'mongrel self' risks being constructed in the image of a multilingual gourmet who tastes one global culture after another.[47] But, unlike many academics nowadays (and indeed Waldron himself), not everyone has a 'frequent flyer identity'.[48] Nor can everyone play with cultural fragments like Rushdie. In his work on the 'dialogic imagination', Bakhtin makes the important distinction between two different forms of hybridization, which he understands as a mixture of two different languages (or linguistic world views): conscious, intentional and unconscious, 'organic' hybridity.[49] The first category means the artistic invention of intended, challenging and often shocking or revitalizing fusions of dissimilar social languages and images (e.g. the rap songs of the Frankfurter 'Turkish Power Boys' or Salman Rushdie's novels). They build on the historical foundations of the everyday 'organic' hybridity of languages and cultures, which – despite the illusion of boundedness and homogeneity – evolve through unreflective borrowings, mimetic appropriations, exchanges and inventions. Organic hybridization does not disrupt the sense of order and continuity: new images, words and vocabularies are unconsciously integrated into language and culture.[50] Bakhtin's distinction seems a useful correction to Waldron's theory of hybridity, since it accounts for the simultaneous coexistence of both cultural change and resistance to change, for instance of ethnic and migrant groups or national minorities. For many 'transnational' migrants, intended, artistic hybridity is potentially threatening to their sense of moral integrity; it may be experienced as a deliberate, provocative challenge to an implicit social order. Cosmopolitanism seems a valuable rhetorical device by which to challenge any conception of the nation or ethnos as a cultural whole, but it is unsuitable as a theory of the self under conditions of denationalization (see Part III for further discussion).

b) Waldron's implied suggestion that we all have good reasons to live up to our global interdependencies and celebrate the liberating hybridization of culture is naïve and elitist. If 'culture', however, is merely a false intellectual construction, where does the destructive (e.g. xenophobia or fetishized ethnic culture) or revitalizing (e.g. black movements) power of cultural identities come from? Why should 'partisans of particular communities' feel a sense of allegiance to the cosmopolitan understanding of culture? Indeed, the globalization of economic, moral and political interdependencies cannot be said to have been instigated by, for instance, indigenous people or ethnic minorities in Western Europe. On the contrary, their loyalties are anchored in translocal social networks and cultural diasporas rather than in the 'global ecumene' (of some elites). It is also wholly understandable that people who do not receive full social recognition retreat to their 'imagined communities' in order to find a stable and secure cultural environment. [51] Waldron's cosmopolitanism plays down the socio-cultural and economic inequalities of those who cannot keep pace with the globalization of our interdependencies, and thus glosses over the actual differences of their ethical/socio-cultural positions within public life. But the resolution of these socio-economic and cultural conflicts starts with the acknowledgement of their existence, that is, with the recognition of the differential interests social groups have in maintaining boundaries. A theory of 'multiculturalism as *mélange*' turns out to be a political cul-de-sac which could trivialize social movements and the cultural politics of disadvantaged socio-cultural and national groups. In the end, Waldron implicitly suggests that we should all react to our global interdependencies in similar ways; that cosmopolitanism is a viable alternative for everyone. A cosmopolitan culture will be pluralistic, but it will be unitary in its cosmopolitan values. In this sense, he presupposes that liberal and cosmopolitan societies are, or should be, somehow culturally homogeneous or at least in the process of converging at the global level. He thus undermines his own argument for an immense plurality of normative outlooks in global society.

(c) A further fundamental problem with 'multicultural theory' like Waldron's is that it relegates difference and pluralism to the individual level[52] and cannot account for the 'intersubjectivity' of identity-formation in particular contexts and practices, nor for differences in access to cultural and political power. In the real world, political agency is constituted in given historical locations or committed socio-political or ideological positionings. And it is enacted liminally, on the boundaries of self and other, of identity and difference. Anthropologists have shown how liminality is itself structured processually[53] and how people 'play' with their identity while still giving it value. Their cultural positioning in public life (e.g. as a diasporic community at the margins) can have emancipatory motifs, not only as a response to the experience of racism but also as a gesture of reaching out to morally valued others.[54] This is similar to the Gramscian idea that hegemony or counter-hegemony must necessarily be constituted through allegiances which cut across differences. It is precisely the acknowledgement that culture and self are always situated and negotiated that enables us to argue for the possibility of transcending fragmentation through intercultural dialogue and sometimes for new, positive (anti-racist) identity fusions (e.g. those of third-generation migrants). Nonetheless, not all minority voices are progressive. Whether cultural politics are 'good or evil' depends on the ability of members of cultural or national collectivities to engage in critical self-distancing from their own cultural/ethical point of view.

(d) Recently, Waldron has developed the notion of 'intercultural deliberation',[55] arguing against the Wittgensteinian idea that effective communication presupposes some sort of agreement in judgements ('to play a language game'); a framework of common concepts and understanding. Whereas the communitarian political philosophy, which is influenced by Wittgenstein's idea of language, has a tendency to insist that a well-ordered society should be thought of as something constructed among those who share certain fundamental under- standings and beliefs,[56] Waldron begins with exactly the opposite assumption. In the tradition of Hobbes and Kant, he assumes that we are always likely to find ourselves, in the first instance, alongside others who disagree; and that

> if there is no community or a common framework for living, it has to be created in the form of positive law, constructed out of individual views or by views sponsored by particular cultures that are given initially as disparate and opposed.[57]

From this, Waldron deduces the duty of 'civic participation', which is the duty of the inhabitants of any country to deliberate responsibly among themselves about law and public policy. However, because we hold different world views and come from different cultures, the business of coming to terms with one another is a fragile enterprise.

Although his argument comes close to fulfilling the Rawlsian requirement of a 'reasonable pluralism', Waldron argues against the distinction between public reason and (many) non-public reasons.[58] The duty of civic participation requires inter-ethical/cultural deliberation which in Waldron's view means

> to make whatever effort we can to converse with others on their own terms, as they attempt to converse with us on ours, to see what we can understand of their reasons, and to present our reasons as well as we can to them.[59]

If politics means the difficult business of coming to terms with those with whom we have to come to terms (as opposed to those with whom we would like to), then public deliberation includes the will to reason about one's own norms and prac- tices in the light of other norms and alternative standards. Because Waldron's notion of pluralism is simultaneously too radical (lacking any idea of the constant co-production of shared meaning in normative political dialogue) and insuffi- ciently situated or contextualized, it cannot account for the problems of cultural translation and reflexivity, intercultural communication and transnational mobi- lization. He lacks a conception of deliberation which comprises ethical pluralism and disagreement without losing the centripetal or unifying force of dialogue that – as we will see from Chapter 5 on – derives from the practice of mutual transla- tion or exploration of difference and that itself generates an (always fragile and negotiable) common ground of shared constitutional identity.

Will Kymlicka's idea of a multicultural citizenship

Most liberal theorists have recognized that citizenship is not just a legal status, defined by a set of rights and responsibilities, but also an identity, an expression of one's membership in a political community. And it is precisely in the name of a strengthened civic-political identity that many liberals have clung to the principle of common citizenship. Will Kymlicka, however, proposes a theory of multicultural citizenship on the basis of what he calls 'group-differentiated rights'.[60] In a society which recognizes group-differentiated rights, the members of certain groups are incorporated into the political community not only as individuals, but also through the group, and their rights depend in part on their group membership.[61] He argues that many (but not all) of the demands for a politics of difference of ethnic and national groups are consistent with liberal principles of individual freedom and social justice.

Kymlicka argues that culture is a 'primary good' because people cannot choose a conception of the good in isolation, instead choosing among options in the context of 'societal cultures'. These societal cultures are closely tied up with the existence of nation-states, and membership of either a nation or a more or less 'distinct society' in the sense of an ethnic or regional/cultural nation (such as for example the French-speaking Québécois) is a prerequisite for leading a good life in modern societies. Only a societal culture can provide the rich cultural environment that is presupposed by the liberal idea of freedom – namely, the idea that choosing one's own direction in life (within a societal culture) is the greatest good.[62] Liberal states should therefore protect societal cultures through group-differentiated rights – Kymlicka chooses to use this term instead of the more common 'collective rights' – since such rights, he claims, are not 'about the primacy of communities over individuals'.[63] They are allocated to and exercised by individual members of a group (e.g. language rights for French-speaking Québécois), groups themselves (e.g. hunting rights for indigenous peoples like the Canadian Indians) or regions or provinces (e.g. the right of the Québécois to promote their national culture).

Kymlicka distinguishes two consequences of the existence of group-differentiated rights: first, 'internal restrictions', which are restrictions on individual freedom; and second, 'external protections', which can limit the impact of decisions made by the larger society on a particular group in question. Internal restrictions, which is to say the claims of a group against its own members made with the intention of protecting itself from the destabilizing impact of internal dissent, are what critics of 'group-differentiated rights' are most afraid of. They rightly fear that special rights for national or ethnic minorities may be misused to restrict the individual freedom of their members. For instance, they may be used to discriminate against members of such communities who want to loosen their ties with the community or simply do not follow traditional customs. External protections – that is, the claims of a group against the decisions of a larger society – are less controversial. Canadian Indians may, for example, protect their hunting grounds by such measures without implying that all members of the larger community will be forced to stick to traditional hunting practices or hunting grounds. Kymlicka argues against internal restriction on the basis that liberal societies cannot tolerate cultures which restrict the freedom of individuals to question substantive aspects of that culture. However, he argues in favour of external protections which support secure cultural membership by claiming that liberal societies have an obligation to provide individuals with a stable societal culture.[64] Weighing the advantages and disadvantages of group-differentiated rights, Kymlicka comes to the conclusion that liberal societies should accept them on the basis that, in principle, they should not be used to justify internal restrictions.[65] At the same time, the majority of citizens should be willing to change their ideas of what is just, right and good in light of the needs and interests of new citizens.

Kymlicka's notion of 'societal culture' – that is a culture which 'provides its members with meaningful ways of life across the full range of human activities, including social, educational, religious, recreational, and economic life, encompassing both public and private spheres'[66] – is much more substantive than either Rawls's model of 'overlapping consensus' among deeply opposed (though reasonable) comprehensive doctrines, or Habermas's idea of a 'constitutional patriotism' shared by different ethical subcultures. Compared to his liberal colleagues, Kymlicka takes socio-cultural diversity more seriously 'all the way up', accepting that real world pluralism doesn't simply dissolve once people participate in political debates. He claims that all political debate is in fact intrinsically imbued with an ethical/cultural and national dimension, whether it is in the drawing of boundaries and distribution of power, or in decisions about the language to be used in schools, courts and bureaucracies, or in the choice of public holidays. Moreover, these inescapable choices in political life give a profound advantage to the members of majority cultures or nations. Liberal societies should therefore be willing to endure social conflicts in which there is no 'neutral ground' to stand on, but should not give up hope that these conflicts may one day be overcome or at least mitigated.

Kymlicka is more in favour of interference than the political liberals, who, he argues, can recognize the personal autonomy of citizens only to the very limited extent of guaranteeing minority groups the minimal conditions needed to have both a voice in public affairs and the opportunity to live according to their own conception of the good life. He himself, by contrast, claims that without group-differentiated policies, liberal talk of 'treating people as individuals' is cheap, or is itself just a cover for ethnic or national injustice. Furthermore, he suggests, there may be good reasons to respect individual self-understandings and doctrines, even when they are illiberal: it is only by allowing the public defence of such doctrines – through the subsidization of cultural forms – that they can be controlled. For, once the private or the cultural becomes politically and publicly relevant, the grounds exist for engaging in debates that, although they will usually start from a modus vivendi only, might lead to stronger common understandings. In such inter-ethical/cultural debates liberals are obliged to promote the value of personal autonomy if they want to encourage change. But liberalism, argues Kymlicka, is only one doctrine among others, a powerful ideology that hopes to transcend pluralism and social conflict by the assumption that human reason must, in principle, be able to provide a rational and neutral solution to normative conflicts. It is exactly because of this belief that in social contention the liberal bottom line of personal autonomy is no less controversial to some than their own bottom line may be to liberals, that the kind of interference with cultures Kymlicka professes should be considered more 'humane' than the abstinence from interference which characterizes political liberalism.

(a) Kymlicka's pragmatic argument for regarding cultural membership as a primary good is probably a sound liberal strategy in practice. In a deeply pluralist world, the argument that we need to actively seek to establish the needs of those whose wellbeing is under threat is well taken. We should, in my view, understand his vocabulary as a new and as yet not properly tested proposal for a way of looking at the problem of access to cultural-political power. Nonetheless, he has no convincing solution to the problem of how to distinguish not only internal restrictions, but also external protections that frustrate individual autonomy. Kymlicka's 'politics of external protection', like Taylor's politics of recognition, provides no way of distinguishing group claims which arise from the value placed on a cultural structure or frame of meanings within a group from claims voiced in terms of 'essentialized' characteristics of this structure that may well be controversial within the group. His argument shows that people need cultural materials, but, contrary to what he claims, it does not show the importance of something called 'cultural membership'. It is, in other words, not clear why a person has to make ethical choices in relation to cultural frameworks via his or her membership to a particular group.[67] Although this may caricature his argument slightly, it seems as if Kymlicka means to say that the coherence that makes a particular community a single cultural entity will confer a corresponding degree of integrity or coherence on the individual self that is constituted under its auspices.

(b) A further problem is that Kymlicka has no normative concept of dialogue within which social and ethical/cultural conflicts can be – more or less – democratically negotiated. When he talks about social integration or the unity of a polity, he points out that shared political values or a common conception of justice (Rawls) are not sufficient for multicultural societies. But he has no theoretical means by which to conceive of the – in his words – necessary 'common identity' in a country which contains two or more ethnic or national communities. He can only empirically state that people from different cultural and national groups

> will only share an allegiance to the larger polity if they see it as a context within which their national identity is nurtured, rather than subordinated.[68]

Kymlicka adds that since people not only belong to separate ethnic and national communities, but also belong to the same political communities in different ways, a deeply pluralistic society will only stay together if people value profound diversity in itself, and want to live in a country with diverse forms of cultural and political membership. But a strong sense of solidarity and mutual identification (as Kymlicka claims is true in Switzerland and Canada) will hardly be generated by a vague commitment to the value of cultural diversity. Rather, as he admits, it is the product of this sort of allegiance.[69] In the end, he cannot find a way of conceiving how solidarity and trust among strangers of different cultures or nations can not only lead to deliberation about common issues, but also how the practices of deliberation can generate the basis for the social integration he is looking for.

As we will see later, only the idea of a dialogue understood as an exploration of difference – and, at the same time, the co-production of shared meanings – values diversity and pluralism as a precondition of communication and a source of social learning.

However, as alluded to in Chapter 2, there is a 'deliberative' line of political theory that suggests that the possibility of constitutional democracy under conditions of cultural pluralism does not depend on the recognition of diverse ethical/cultural communities without, at the same time, limiting democracy to a mere aggregation of competing individual interests and (ethical/cultural) preferences. Jürgen Habermas's idea of democratic constitutionalism tries to vindicate the universalistic core of this idea[70] which is challenged by the pluralistic character of today's polity. As we will see in Chapter 6, from a discourse-theoretical point of view, it is institutionally-enacted law and a shared constitutional-political identity or 'constitutional patriotism' that is tasked with integrating the ethical-cultural heterogeneity of the participants in the democratic process.

Multiculturalism: a way out?

To conclude our discussion of multiculturalism, we might say that, paradoxically, in contemporary multicultural societies, pluralism has often become the basis for an exaggeration of difference and, with it, the assertion of the incommensurability of cultures.[71] Much multicultural talk presupposes conceptions of collective identity that are empirically uninformed and thus remarkably unsuitable in their understandings of the processes by which identities develop. Such talk often assumes that culture is a given set of norms which is ultimately rooted in a sense of belonging to a community. Although multiculturalism allows for pluralism, it often comes close to assuming an essentializing conception of group cultures, which neglects the fact that cultural boundaries are fluid and negotiated in public discourse. On the basis of this latter assumption, the ethnology of the 1990s has analyzed processes of migration not in terms of 'loss' (of the homeland, an original identity, etc.), as might once have been the case, but has stressed the possibility of multiple belongings, of innovative cultural mixing and social change – without, of course, failing to recognize the power-relations involved in this process.[72] This transnational approach conceptually turns Robert Park's 'marginal man'[73] upside down, because migrants are no longer viewed as peripheral or uprooted, but as rooted in two or more cultures. For young second and third generation migrants in London, Paris, Frankfurt or other global cities, the position of 'in-between' has become a typical phenomenon. They happily withdraw from 'either-or' classifications of collective identity (see also Part III).

Taylor, on the other hand, was right to underline the significance of ethical/cultural practices for self and politics. Culture is not only what we live by, but also, in great measure, what we live *for*, and thus is an important motivation for public life with strangers. Everyday social interaction and relationships, which are embedded in concrete cultural/ethical practices, give us a sense of place, of memory and community, emotional fulfilment, intellectual enjoyment, a sense of ultimate meaning. But these affiliations need not be conceived 'retrospectively' as ethnic or ancestral (i.e. stemming from sameness), but instead as constantly produced in an intercultural dialogue which is sensitive to and curious about the other's difference. Such an inclusive-dialogical politics could expand its community without the danger of its shared political identity becoming increasingly abstract (bridging difference by an overarching identification with a political culture). At the same time, such intercultural citizenship practices would have themselves to produce more generous and more contextualized affiliations than cultural/ethical or national identities. Accordingly, a constitutional patriotism would be situated without being based on a *demos* (see Chapter 6).

Against a 'multiculturalism based on difference' which runs the risk of compartmentalizing cultural or ethnic groups by emphasizing their mutual distinctness, I have argued above (against Taylor) that we should underscore the *processes* that go towards the creation of culture and (collective as well as personal) identity.[74] As a consequence of the described overlapping, interacting and negotiating of cultures, the experience of cultural difference is *internal* to any culture. Against a 'cosmopolitanism' that risks the danger of glossing over the heterogeneity of existing social practices, I have argued (against Waldron) that democratic politics should not abstract from the existence of people's different socio-economic and ethical-cultural positions, nor the conflicts that may arise from them.

It follows that a 'critical' multiculturalism does not require the politics of authenticity or of affirmative action (which emphasizes 'fundamentalist' cultural self-definitions among national or cultural minorities), nor should it ignore the existing pluralism of cultural/ethical identities; but rather, should start from the idea that identity is dialogical 'all the way up': proceeding from the assumption that culture is always sited and negotiated,[75] *a 'critical' politics of multiculturalism argues for the constant possibility of new, positive identity-fusions in public life, transcending fragmentation, but at the same time recognizing the differential interests that (disadvantaged) social groups have in maintaining boundaries.* Its task should be to envisage policies – and the institutionalization of public deliberation – *where ethical-cultural or national collectivities engage in reflexive, self-critical distancing from their own discourses, and hence come to recognize the potential validity of other discourses.*

The process of mutual exploration of different ethical perspectives does not only have a pacifying function (i.e. to improve political cohabitation among ethical/cultural communities), but is also crucial for solving moral or legal conflicts. Although I insist on the separation of values and norms for heuristic-pragmatic reasons,[76] ethical and moral questions are interacting dimensions in the same political practice: opponents must first understand how the impact of the same situation is perceived from the perspective of a self- and world-understanding different from their own before they can, in a next step, mutually expand their value-orientations such that an overlap would then allow for the discovery of a norm deserving intersubjective recognition. A dialogical concept of justification needs to specify exactly this mechanism of 'generalization of values' as mutual perspective-taking (see Chapter 5). In this sense, a dialogical approach can be used not only as a heuristic device to explain given transformations of cultural self-understandings pointing beyond the multiculturalism debate, but also as new institutionalized forms of deliberative problem-solving, such as can be seen in the EU's Open Method of Coordination, which depends on neither uniform consensus nor uniform results, but rather produces cooperation (among representatives of EU member states) by continuously exploring different understanding of the 'best' policies or the most 'just' solutions to common problems like unemployment, health care, pensions etc. The interdependency of norms and values, of politics and identities is more evident that ever under contemporary conditions of pluralism and denationalization. Identities are themselves hybrids between assertions and world views – always normatively embedded in the constitutional project and thus acting as resources for law and politics. As we will see in Chapter 5, the structural relationship between the justificatory-cognitive and existential-word-disclosing dimension of politics can be spelled out as the linguistic relation between pragmatics and semantics. This would make it possible to envisage intercultural translation or 'multicultural literacy' in an ongoing constitutional dialogue (see chapter 6) as a possible alternative to a multiculturalism based on 'difference'.

Notes

1 Original transcript: 'Wenn ein Lehrer fragt: Wo kommst Du her? Ich hab nicht geantwortet. Ich hab gesagt: Hauptsache bin Mensch. Sie hat gelacht, ich weiß, daß Du Mensch bist, aber wo kommst Du her? Ich hatte gesagt, ich komme aus der Türkei, aber ich fühle mich nicht Türke, ich fühle mich auch nicht deutsch. Habe ich weitergeredet, hat sie gesagt, das darfst du nicht sagen. Ich hab gesagt: ich bin ein internationaler. Sie hat gesagt, das darfst Du niemals sagen! Entweder bist Du Türke oder Deutscher oder Italiener oder was weiß ich. Also wenn jemand sagt, ich bin internationaler, ist das schlimm? So gemischt.' (Cited from S. Sauter, *Wir sind 'Frankfurter Türken': Adoleszente Ablösungsprozesse in der deutschen Einwanderungsgesellschaft*, Brandes & Apsel, Frankfurt am Main 2000, p. 242. Translation by Lorraine Frisina.)

2 These remarks suggest that the term 'multicultural' is misleading if it implies that some cultures within a political system (e.g. German, Italian) are homogeneous. The term as used here instead conceives of cultures as always historically situated and negotiated. Cultures, in this sense, are not understood in terms of easily identifiable closed contexts which are internally characterized by well-defined and unquestioned standards of expectations and evaluation. If this were so, we would think of the social world as a patchwork of many relatively closed and therefore often incommensurable contexts of value and action. Rather, cultures organize and thereby distribute the conditions of individual and collective self-understandings according to the (interaction of) the always produced and changeable organizational standards of many cultures, which together make up a social order that is called 'a culture' (in the sense that inspires a reifying perspective).

3 B. Parekh, 'Dilemmas of a Multicultural Theory of Citizenship', in: *Constellations* 4:1, 1997, p. 54.

4 The ideological impact and political legacy of the nation-state building of the late nineteenth and early twentieth centuries has in fact ignored or actively discouraged differences

of language, religion and ethnic identity within particular political states (see D. Baggioni, *Langues et nations en Europe*, Payot, Paris 1997).

5 The minorities are often defined (by the majority, host population) as temporary inhabitants, such as asylum-seekers and economically driven 'guest-workers' in Germany.

6 I take this distinction from W. Kymlicka, although he calls the second a 'polyethnic state' (W. Kymlicka, *Multicultural Citizenship*, Oxford University Press, Oxford 1995, p. 18).

7 By contrast, Rawls refers to this as 'reasonable pluralism': the comprehensive doctrines will never be affirmed by all citizens, but they are the result of the exercise of human reason within the framework of free political institutions and do not reject the essentials of a constitutional democratic regime (see: J. Rawls, *Political Liberalism*, Columbia University Press, New York 1993, p. xvi).

8 M. Dunne, 'Postscript: Multiculturalism on Europe and America', in: M. Dunne and T. Bonazzi (eds.), *Citizenship and Rights in Multicultural Societies*, Keele University Press, Keele 1995, p. 265.

9 The Habermasian idea of 'constitutional patriotism' refers to a kind of post-nationalism whose normative reference point is the democratic constitution rather than the nation-state, territory or a dominant cultural tradition (see Chapter 6).

10 Many classical liberals believed that liberal democracies could be made secure, even in the absence of a particularly virtuous citizenry, by creating checks and balances. Accordingly, institutional and procedural devices such as the separation of powers, a bicameral legislature and federalism could all serve to block would-be oppressors. Even if each person pursued his or her own self-interest without regard for the common good, one set of private interests would check another set of private interests. However, it has become clear that institutional mechanisms to balance self-interest are not enough and that some level of civic virtue or democratic political culture (public-spiritedness) is required. Leaving questions of legitimacy aside for a moment, we can say – even in pragmatic terms – that in the absence of this motivational support, democracies have become difficult to govern and even unstable.

11 Raz points to the connection between private autonomy and a pluralism of comprehensive doctrines: 'A pluralistic society, we may say, not only recognizes the existence of a multiplicity of values, but also makes their pursuit a real option available to its members' (J. Raz, 'Liberalism, Skepticism and Democracy', in: *Iowa Law Review* 74:4, 1989, p. 771).

12 Majoritarian democracies can, for instance, systematically ignore the voices of minorities.

13 C. Taylor, 'The Politics of Recognition', in: C. Taylor and A. Gutman (eds), *Multiculturalism and the Politics of Recognition*, Princeton University Press, Princeton 1992, pp. 25–73.

14 *Ibid.*, p. 25

15 C. Taylor, *The Ethics of Authenticity*, Harvard University Press, Cambridge, MA, 1992, p. 33.

16 The politics of difference can be fought out only in societies in which the idea of equal dignity has become part of the moral self-understandings of citizens; only if citizens feel that they should be recognized as equals per se does it make sense to claim recognition of their more concrete traits in terms of equal respect.

17 C. Taylor, 'The Politics of Recognition', in: C. Taylor and A. Gutman (eds.), *Multiculturalism and the Politics of Recognition*, Princeton University Press, Princeton 1992, p. 59.

18 See also: C. Taylor, *Sources of the Self: The Making of Modern Identity*, Harvard University Press, Cambridge, MA, 1989.

19 Fraser therefore proposes an alternative approach: to treat recognition as a question of social status, and therefore to treat *mis*recognition as an institutionalized relation of social subordination, i.e. the lack of equal access in social and public life. Such a politics of recognition would have to examine institutionalized patterns of cultural value for their effects on the relative standing of the social actor. It concentrates on the status of the individual group member as full partner in social interaction rather than on group-specific, collective identities. Redressing misrecognition would aim to change the modes of interaction that

impede parity of participation at all relevant institutional sites (see: N. Fraser, 'Rethinking Recognition', in: *New Left Review* 3, 2000, pp. 107–120).

20 K. A. Appiah, 'Identity, Authenticity and Survival: Multicultural Societies and Social Reproduction', in: C. Taylor and A.Gutman (eds.), *Multiculturalism and the Politics of Recognition*, p. 157.

21 When Jozeph Raz defends a 'right of exit' from the group, he argues precisely against prescribed affiliations on the basis of descent (J. Raz, 'Multiculturalism: A liberal Perspective', in: *Dissent* 1, 1994, p. 73).

22 Taylor, 'The Politics of Recognition', in: Taylor and Gutman (eds.), *Multiculturalism and the Politics of Recognition*, p. 67; H.-G. Gadamer, *Wahrheit und Methode*, Mohr, Tübingen 1965.

23 *Ibid.*, p. 63.

24 Although J. Tully stresses intercultural dialogue within the process of the constitutionalization of a multicultural or national polity, his position is similar to Taylor's: 'Universality is a misleading representation of the aims of constitutional dialogue because ... the world of constitutionalism is not a universe, but a multiverse: it cannot be represented in universal principles or its citizens in universal institutions' (J. Tully, *Strange Multiplicity: Constitutionalism in an Age of Diversity*, Cambridge University Press, Cambridge 1995, p. 131). Tully loses the integrative force of dialogue because he does not conceive of universality as 'idealized shared meanings' in the process of intercultural translation (see Chapter 5).

25 M. Sandel, *Liberalism and the Limits of Justice*, Cambridge University Press, Cambridge 1982, pp. 87 and 143.

26 'This ego always retains an intersubjective core because the process of individuation from which it emerges runs through the network of linguistically mediate interactions.' (J. Habermas, *Postmetaphysical Thinking: Philosophical Essays*, MIT Press, Cambridge, MA, 1992, p. 170.)

27 Habermas argues that the great change in the affirmation of a projection of self-realization and self-determination comes about in autobiographical texts, whose essence is a public dialogue: 'Rousseau's confession can be most properly understood as an encompassing ethical self-understanding with justificatory intent, put before the public in order for the public to take a position on it.' (Habermas, *Postmetaphysical Thinking*, p. 167.)

28 B. Honig, *Political Theory and the Displacement of Politics*, Cornell University, Ithaca 1993, p. 172.

29 Historical epochs and societal cultures give rise to different conceptions of self. Some stress self-enclosure or sharp individuation, some encourage openness to others. And of course, these different conceptions interact and modify each other in multicultural societies.

30 J. Habermas, 'Anerkennungskämpfe im demokratischen Rechtsstaat', in: C. Taylor and A. Gutman (eds.), *Multikulturalismus und die Politik der Anerkennung*, S. Fischer Verlag, Frankfurt am Main 1993, pp. 147–196; this essay has been inserted in the second English edition: C. Taylor and A. Gutman (eds.), *Multiculturalism and Politics of Recognition*, Princeton University Press, Princeton 1994.

31 See for example the women's movement: 'Rechte können die Frauen nur in dem Maße zu einer privatautonomen Lebensgestaltung ermächtigen, wie sie zugleich eine gleichberechtigte Teilnahme an der Praxis staatsbürgerlicher Selbstbestimmung ermöglichen, weil nur die Betroffenen selbst die jeweils "relevanten Hinsichten" von Gleichheit und Ungleichheit klären können.' (J. Habermas, *Faktizität und Geltung*, Suhrkamp Verlag, Frankfurt am Main 1992, p. 506, not included in English version: *Between Facts and Norms*, MIT Press, Cambridge, MA, 1996, roughly p. 419.) See also J. Habermas, 'On the Internal Relation between the Rule of Law and Democracy', in: *European Journal of Philosophy* 3:1, 1995, pp. 12–20.

32 J. Habermas, 'Struggles for Recognition in the Democratic Constitutional State', in: Taylor and Gutman (eds.), *Multiculturalism and Politics of Recognition*, 1994, p. 113.

33 *Ibid.*, p. 130.

34 *Ibid.*, p. 124.

35 See J. Habermas, 'The Nation, the Rule of Law, and Democracy', in: J. Habermas, *The Inclusion of the Other*, MIT Press, Cambridge, MA, 1996, p. 146.

36 His notion of 'constitutional patriotism' has two aspects: (a) citizens' acknowledgement of what a constitution has to be in order to fulfill its role in the moral justification of legal coercion (epistemic aspect) and (b) citizens' sentiments of identification with an actual, historical community with its specific ethical character (empirical aspect). In this sense, loyalty to a country's constitution means loyalty to the common life of its people and its actual public institutions (see: M. Michelman, 'Morality, Identity, and "Constitutional Patriotism"', in: *Denver University Law Review* 76:4, 2000, p. 1011).

37 J. Habermas, 'Struggles for Recognition in the Democratic Constitutional State', in: Taylor and Gutman (eds.), *Multiculturalism and Politics of Recognition*, p. 134.

38 J. Habermas, 'The Nation, the Rule of Law, and Democracy', in: J. Habermas, *The Inclusion of the Other*, MIT Press, Cambridge, MA, 1996, p. 146.

39 Accordingly, immigrants can be expected to enter into the political culture of their new country without having to give up the cultural form of life of their origins.

40 J. Habermas, 'The European Nation-State', in: J. Habermas, *The Inclusion of the Other*, MIT Press, Cambridge, MA, 1996, p. 146

41 'Citizens who are politically integrated in this way share the rationally-based conviction that unrestrained freedom of communication in the political public sphere, a democratic process for settling conflicts, and a constitutional channeling of political power together will provide a basis for checking illegitimate power and ensuring that administrative power is used in the equal interest of all.' (Habermas, 'Struggles for Recognition in the Democratic Constitutional State', in: Taylor and Gutman (eds.), *Multiculturalism and Politics of Recognition*, 1994, p. 135.)

42 'To put it crudely, we need culture, but we do not need cultural integrity. Since none of us needs a homogeneous cultural framework or integrity of a particular set of meanings, none of us needs to be immersed in … small-scale communities which … are alone capable of securing this integrity and homogeneity. Some, of course, still may prefer such immersion, and welcome the social subsidization of their preference. But it is not … a necessary presupposition of rational and meaningful choice.' (J. Waldron, 'Minority Cultures and the Cosmopolitan Alternative', in: T. van Willigenburg, F. Heeger and W. van der Burg (eds.), *Nation, State and Coexistence of Different Communities*, Kok Pharos, Kampen 1995, p. 135.)

43 *Ibid.*, p. 131.

44 C. Taylor, 'Atomism', in: C. Taylor, *Philosophy and the Human Sciences. Philosophical Papers*, vol. 2, Cambridge University Press, Cambridge 1985, p. 207

45 J. Waldron, 'Multiculturalism and Mélange', in: R. Fullinwider (ed.), *Public Education in a Multicultural Society: Policy, Theory, Critique*, Cambridge University Press, Cambridge 1996, p. 90.

46 *Ibid.*

47 I borrow this metaphor from Bert van den Brink (see: B. van den Brink, *The Tragedy of Liberalism: An Alternative Defense if a Political Tradition*, SUNY Press, Albany, NY, 2000, p. 204.)

48 I owe this metaphor to Bert van den Brink.

49 M. Bakhtin, *The Dialogic Imagination: Four Essays*, University of Texas Press, Austin 1981, p. 358.

50 In this sense, they are unintentionally 'pregnant with potentials for new world views' (*Ibid.*, p. 360).

51 'They actively construct "community" to shield themselves from racist rejections, but also to compete for honour, to have fun, to worship, and to celebrate – together – collective rites of passage or ceremonies of nostalgic remembrance for a lost home' (P. Werbner, 'Introduction: The Dialectics of Cultural Hybridity', in: P. Werbner and T. Modood (eds.), *Debating Cultural Hybridity: Multicultural Identities and the Politics of Anti-Racism*, Zed Books, London

1997, p. 12).

52 Waldron, 'Multiculturalism and Mélange', in: Fullinwider (ed.), *Public Education in a Multicultural society: Policy, Theory, Critique*, p. 113.

53 In this process, categories (e.g. 'black') are exaggerated and caricatured in order to be worked upon and reconfigured so as to reconstitute the condition of participants. Ritual hybrids (e.g. hyphenated third-generation migrants) not only raise consciousness; they are performatively powerful, transgressive and fertile (see P. Werbner, *The Migration Process: Capital, Gifts and Offerings among British Pakistanis*, Berg Publishing, Oxford 1990).

54 The materiality of racial suffering can potentially lead to the invention of allegories that travel, and thus to an imagining of moral and aesthetic communities of suffering across social and cultural divisions (see: P. Gilroy, *The Black Atlantic: Modernity and Double Consciousness*, Verso, London 1993).

55 J. Waldron, *Law and Disagreement*, Oxford University Press, Oxford 1999.

56 See for instance: M. Walzer, *Spheres of Justice*, Basic Books, New York 1983.

57 J. Waldron, 'Cultural Identity and Civic Responsibility', in: W. Kymlicka and W. Norman (eds.), *Citizenship in Diverse Societies*, Oxford University Press, Oxford 2000, p. 15.

58 J. Rawls, *Political Liberalism*, Columbia University Press, New York 1993, p. xix.

59 Waldron, 'Cultural Identity and Civic Responsibility', in: Kymlicka and Norman (eds.), *Citizenship in Diverse Societies*, p. 8.

60 Kymlicka, *Multicultural Citizenship*.

61 He agrees with B. Parekh that citizenship today 'is a much more differentiated and far less homogeneous concept than has been presupposed by political theorists' (see: W. Kymlicka, *Contemporary Political Philosophy: An Introduction*, Oxford University Press, Oxford 1990).

62 His starting point is not so much the communitarian commitment to the intrinsic value of culture or community, but a Rawlsian conviction about the importance to persons of the freedom to form, reform, and revise their individual beliefs about what makes life worth living.

63 Kymlicka, *Multicultural Citizenship*, p. 47.

64 Kymlicka rightly points out that, in practice, the situation is more complex than this analytical distinction suggests. In a very pragmatic vein, he analyzes some concrete problems of multiculturalism and differentiates between the practical social and political consequences of three kinds of group-differentiated rights which foster internal and external limitations to a rather different extent. The first category he identifies is that of 'special group representation rights', i.e. quotas that are intended to correct the under-representation of disadvantaged groups within the political institutions of a larger society. These rights, which may be understood as instituting a form of 'affirmative action', are attractive in particular to regionally scattered minorities. The second category is that of 'self-government rights' which decentralize political power to smaller political units. They aim to ensure that a geographically-concentrated national minority cannot be outvoted on important cultural issues such as education, family law, etc. If democracy is rule by the people, national minorities can claim that there is more than one people, each with the right to rule itself. The third category Kymlicka calls 'polyethnic rights'. These protect specific religious and cultural practices which might not be adequately supported by the market (e.g. the funding of minority language programmes), or which are disadvantaged by existing legislation (e.g. dress codes that conflict with religious beliefs) (Kymlicka, *Multicultural Citizenship*, p. 95). Kymlicka argues that we should not discard these rights for the simple reason that they can be used to enforce internal restrictions on group members. The polyethnic right of Sikh men not to wear a helmet when riding a motorcycle, for example, does not oblige all Sikh motorcyclists to wear a turban instead of a helmet. He points out that, generally speaking, most demands for representation rights by disadvantaged groups or polyethnic demands are a demand for 'inclusion', i.e. they are evidence that members of minority groups want to participate in the public life of a society (*Ibid.*, p. 176).

65 Kymlicka places two limits on group rights: (1) they must respect the equality of groups,

i.e. minority rights should not allow one group to dominate other groups; and (2) they must respect equality within groups, i.e. minority rights should not enable a group to oppress its own members.

66 Kymlicka, *Multicultural Citizenship*, p. 176.

67 W. Kymlicka, *Liberalism, Community, and Culture*, Clarendon Press, Oxford 1991, p. 165.

68 Kymlicka, *Multicultural Citizenship*, p. 189.

69 *Ibid.*, p. 191.

70 'Universal' constitutional justification means that the exercise of legal force and political power can be justified if everyone affected has reason to accept them in the light of his or her interest as well as in the light of everyone else's.

71 See Werbner and Modood (eds.), *Debating Cultural Hybridity*, Zed Books, London 1997 and P. Werbner and T. Modood (eds.), *The Politics of Multiculturalism in the New Europe*, Zed Books, London 1997.

72 A. Ackermann, 'Ethnologische Migrationsforschung: ein Überblick', in: *Kea. Zeitschrift für Kulturwissenschaften* 10, 1997, pp. 1–28; T. Faist, 'International Migration and Transnational Spaces. Their Evolution, Significance and Future Prospects', in: *IIS-Arbeitspapier (Universität Bremen)* 9, 1998; L. Pries (ed.), *Transnationale Migration, Soziale Welt*, Sonderband 12, Nomos Verlag, Baden-Baden 1997.

73 Robert Park describes the 'marginal man' as 'a man living and sharing intimately in the cultural life and traditions of two distinct peoples; never quite willing to break, even if he was permitted to do so, with his past and his traditions, and not quite accepted, because of racial prejudice, in the new society in which he now sought to find a place. He was a man on the margins of two cultures and two societies, which never completely interpenetrated and fused.' (R. Park (ed.), *The University Studies in Urban Sociology*, Chicago University Press, Chicago 1925).

74 See for instance: T. Turner, 'Anthropology and Multiculturalism: What is Anthropology that Multiculturalists Should be Mindful of It?', in: *Cultural Anthropology* 8:4, 1993, pp. 411–429.

75 That is, culture can be understood properly only as the historically negotiated creation of more or less coherent symbolic and social worlds.

76 This is in order to maintain a concept of justification that is not naturalizing.

5

'Multicultural literacy': questions of translatability

Jede Sprache zieht um die Nation, welcher sie angehört, einen Kreis, aus dem es nur insofern hinauszugehen möglich ist, als man zugleich in den Kreis einer andren Sprache hinübertritt. Die Erlernung einer fremden Sprache sollte daher die Gewinnung eines neuen Standpunkts in der bisherigen Weltansicht seyn, da jede das Gewebe der Begriffe und Vorstellungsweise eines Theils der Menschheit enthält. Da man aber in eine fremde Sprache immer mehr oder weniger
seine eigne Welt – ja seine eigne Sprachansicht hinüberträgt,
so wird dieser Erfolg nie rein und vollständig empfunden.

Wilhelm von Humboldt[1]

The idea of political deliberation which is implicit in the *demos*-thesis (Chapter 2) is of a dialogue between people who – being transparent to one another – form a 'common mind' (Taylor). A 'we-feeling', so the argument goes, ensures relationships of trust and solidarity among citizens, and thus is the necessary basis for legitimate majority rule, especially with respect to redistributive policies, where the market economy's 'winners' must be willing to compensate its 'losers'. The attachment to a *demos* is seen as the pre-political presupposition of democratic politics (Offe, Scharpf, Grimm). There is a communitarian aspect to this kind of political theory and to the presuppositions which underpin it. The possibility of political integration is seen as dependent upon the existence of shared cultural values and a prevailing sense of unity.

At this point, it is necessary to introduce the argument that concepts of politics (implicitly or explicitly) correspond to concepts of language. In the *demos* view of politics, language is valued because the speech community is erected and maintained through it: language carries cultural traditions and thereby ensures a common belonging or 'we-identity'. Since plurality and difference are surmounted in advance by shared background understandings, there are no radically diverging interpretations or misunderstandings within a community. For the *demos*-

theory of politics, the problem of translation or multicultural literacy either does not exist (because the people of a *demos* have a common mind) or is insurmountable (because the worldviews of different *demoi* are incommensurable).

As we have seen, however, regardless if one takes up a historical or sociological view, suggesting that the cultural background of speakers in any given community is totally shared is simply wrong. If societies were homogenous in this way, there would be no need for their members to have to agree on a common framework for concerted action. In other words, there would be no 'circumstances of politics'.[2] As Hannah Arendt once put it, 'The human condition of plurality ... is the condition *sine qua non* for ... the public realm.'[3] This is all the more obvious in contemporary pluralistic societies where there is no common mind about the cultural norms and world views which can be taken for granted. Under conditions of denationalization and socio-cultural pluralism the problem of translatability is exacerbated. Once the shelter of the *demos* drops, the contingency of agency comes to the fore.

In pluralistic societies, politics always involves conflicting perspectives of the world, society and self. Accordingly, the achievement of a common political culture has to be conceived as an ongoing project, something always to be achieved anew through deliberation among peoples of different ethical or socio-cultural perspectives. As we will see in Part III, we seem to be living at a historical moment in which a constructivist approach to democracy seems plausible; where the legitimacy of political decisions no longer depends on the pre-political national feelings of a *demos*, but rather on deliberation among citizens. From this perspective, language is valued because the basis for agreement in democratic politics is understood to be discussion and deliberation, not because it carries the cultural commonalities of a *demos*. Putting public reasoning at the centre of political justification, the deliberative conception of democracy is based on a normative notion of communication which aims at rationally-motivated agreement. In contrast to the ethical constriction of political discourse characteristic of the *demos* view, the idea of deliberative politics takes into account a multiplicity of communicative forms (including fairly regulated bargaining among different interests, pragmatic reasoning about efficiency in material reproduction, justice-related arguing and dialogue between different ethical/cultural perspectives).[4]

It seems clear that political deliberation in complex contemporary societies can no longer be insulated from the consequences of pluralism. Nonetheless, rather than being a burden, the existence of a diverse range of perspectives or interests may in fact be a resource for cooperative learning. A situation in which political decision-making processes are characterized by a high degree of decentralization and of indeterminacy of knowledge (for example within the EU) suggests the need for a theory of 'translation' or of an 'exploration of difference', in which the plurality of perspectives is valued as a 'search engine' for political problem-solving. In order to spell out such a dialogical theory of politics understood as the exploration of difference, or as an epistemic struggle between different ethical/cultural identities or 'vocabularies', I propose to draw on arguments derived from the philosophy of language. In particular, I will consider the possibilities for 'translating' linguistically encoded world views, self-understandings and ways of knowing. Whereas in Chapter 4 I looked at some political theories as implicit (Kymlicka, Waldron) or explicit (Habermas, Taylor) extensions of theories of language, I will now analyze this cross-fertilization the other way round, which is to say, I will consider some theories of language and the concepts of identity they imply as models of political will-formation. I take the theories of Davidson, Putnam and Bakhtin to be particularly promising as accounts of how the plurality of languages 'divide up' reality in significantly different ways. The accounts I give of these theories of language will obviously be limited by my larger purpose of drawing out their implications for political theory.

The aim of this chapter, then, is to explore how political theory might benefit from some of the important insights of the philosophy of language, in particular those involving the notion of translation. I will argue that the generation of shared interpretations of constitutional principles is akin to the dialogical generation of shared meanings in a given speech community at a certain time.[5] It will be suggested that conceptual norms, and for that matter the meaning of constitutional norms, rather than being given along with the linguistic world view of a particular language community/*demos*, are constantly intersubjectively (re)produced or ratified through dialogue. Shared meanings, as well as shared interpretations of legal or constitutional principles, are thereby understood as idealizations, something always to be achieved anew. If this is the case, then political theorists need to take into consideration not only the *pragmatic* dimension of language – which ensures the orientation of a 'community of justification' towards the common goal of discursively achieved agreement, as well as the reciprocal recognition of participants, but also its *semantic* (or world-disclosing) dimension: the reservoir of potential meanings and interpretations of the world which can be made explicit[6] in public deliberation and which are, as it were, the socio-historical 'fleshing-out' of our interpretations. It is precisely this 'fleshing-out' which opens the possibility of finding innovative solutions to political problems.

Shared meanings or shared principles as used in everyday communicative practices are always exposed to revision when new interpretations turn out to be more adequate to the dynamics of success-oriented action within a speech/political community. In this sense, shared meanings are 'coagulated' from their ongoing use in different communicative contexts just as shared principles of law are coagulated from democratic politics understood as ongoing public deliberation or epistemic struggle between different interpretations of these principles. The semantic reservoir of potential meanings may trigger new understandings of conceptual or legal norms, but these linguistic/interpretative innovations have to be intersubjectively 'proven' in discursive practice. Innovative interpretations which are successful are comparable to the claims of precedent in case law.[7] The constitution is therefore not a closed meaning-space of (already) shared principles, but can be conceived as a procedural design for the exploration of ambiguity in the continuing clarification of the meaning of these principles. This exploration takes place in a multiple network of decentralized arenas of public deliberation (we can call this 'bottom-up' constitutionalism).

In what follows, I will first briefly outline some of the problems that the notion of translation poses for the philosophy of language, moving on to discuss the relevance of translation for political theory. I will then outline Davidson's idea of a 'conceptual scheme' or the shared 'metalanguage' which bridges the idiolects of two speakers, subsequently criticizing the residual substantialism of his ideas, which ultimately presuppose a prior consensus about truth. The next step is to show how Putnam's 'internal realism' gets rid of the problem of a substantial metalanguage by idealizing the truth conditions understood as 'warranted acceptability' among speakers. Finally, I shall reconstruct Bakhtin's theory of meaning in which plurality and difference 'go all the way down' in concrete dialogical encounters and thus can be regarded as a crucial empirical counterweight to idealizing presuppositions.

Two conceptions of translation

In both the analytical and the hermeneutic traditions, translation is often analyzed as the limiting case which helps to elucidate what is going on in the 'normal' case of interpretation. Quine's analytic philosophy postulates the epistemic conditions of a radical translator as crucial for the understanding of semantic interpretation. His famous thesis of the indeterminacy of translation suggests that there will always be two or more equally acceptable theories which differ in assigning clearly non-synonymous sentences of mine as translation of someone else's utterance.[8] Quine thereby assumes that translating is an activity in which one gives a descriptive theory of the features of 'meaning in use'. His empiricist account of correct translation, however, focuses on verificationism, that is, the thesis according to which the meaning of a sentence is given by the observational consequences that it logically entails. By contrast, the hermeneutic/formal-pragmatic tradition of Humboldt/Habermas focuses on the establishment of understanding via linguistic communication (*Verständigung*).[9] Accordingly, the telos of translation is reaching understanding with someone from another speech community about something:

> In der Erscheinung, entwickelt sich jedoch die Sprache nur gesellschaftlich, und der Mensch versteht sich selbst nur, indem er die Verstehbarkeit seiner Worte an Andren überprüft.[10]

Understanding/translation, however, is embedded in the social game of giving and asking for reasons.

From within the hermeneutic/formal-pragmatic tradition, we can conceive of translation as a normative project or, more precisely, as a procedure of 'accounting for norms' in terms of discursive practices. To accept translational norms or other claims about meaning is in an important way analogous to the mutual ratification of an agreement or the writing of a constitution (i.e. the act which makes such codes binding upon oneself and one's fellows).[11] The ends of translation are not secured by describing the utterances of another speaker from an objective stance (whether by antecedent regularity of usage or correspondence to the world), but by mutually 'legislating' one another's meaning talk (and its inbuilt truth claims) from the stance of a participant.[12] From this hermeneutic/pragmatic perspective, ethical/cultural world views and inherited traditions carry with them a socially-instituted – albeit revisable – justificatory burden. The semantic exploration of difference is oriented towards intersubjective recognition: cross-cultural translation and any eventual new interpretations of the world have to be accepted or validated by both linguistic communities.[13] The validated (shared) meanings – which are always (re)produced anew in each speech situation – are akin to a constitutional principle on the interpretation of which the citizens of political community agree; or more precisely, the interpretation of which is constantly (re)generated by citizens in public communication.

In this sense, the normative goal of translation or cross-cultural dialogue is the formation of one large community where previously there had been two. A single set of linguistic norms – which are nothing but the 'anticipation' of shared meanings or idealizations and which always have to be interpreted anew – comes to govern the linguistic practice of the translator and the translated. The choice of those norms has to be recognized by both participants (and their respective linguistic/cultural communities).[14] To fail to translate a term of another language is to fail to make it possible either to agree or to disagree with utterances made involving that term. The most basic point of translating is to enable cross-cultural agreement or disagreement on interpretations of the world. The cognitive dimension of both intra- and inter-linguistic translation is the clarification of what is really at stake in disagreements between speakers. Translating in this sense is also a procedure for becoming informed. No single individual or social group possesses all the information which may be relevant to the solution of a particular problem.

From the *semantic* point of view, the telos of translation is that of seeing the world from the other's perspective. From the formal-pragmatic point of view, the telos of translation is reaching mutual understanding about something, notwithstanding the different perspectives of the participants. In what follows, I wish to argue that the semantic emphasis on 'difference' – which is maintained but can be coordinated in communicative practices – is the precondition for understanding the (formal-pragmatics) impulse of communication, that is, 'the imperative of social integration'.[15] While the purpose of cognitive activity is merely to acknowledge how things already are, the chief purpose of our practical reasoning is to agree about norms for the regulation of our joint activities. Whereas epistemic reasoning aims at the convergence of assertive sentences of facts (consensus), practical reasoning – relevant for undertaking joint projects and thus for political decision-making – may only aim at agreement to norms on the part of wilful agents (cooperation).[16]

Politics as translation

'*Gebrochene Intersubjektivität*' is the constant (and constitutive) dialogical interaction between two subjectivities where each is recognized as (formally) equal
and (substantively) different and unique. This is because efforts to increase mutual understanding between subjects can never completely remove the element of
the unshared,[17] and total transparency between them is impossible:

> Keiner denkt bei dem Wort gerade und genau das, was der andre, und die noch so
> kleine Verschiedenheit zittert, wie ein Kreis im Wasser, durch die ganze Sprache fort.
> Alles Verstehen ist immer zugleich ein Nicht-verstehen, alle Übereinstimmung in
> Gedanken und Gefühlen zugleich ein Auseinandergehen.[18]

The 'inter-space' of intersubjectivity is a precondition for the social integration at
which communication – understood as an ongoing process of mutual (intra- and
interlinguistic) translation of perspectives – aims. What is 'shared' (the meanings
of utterances or constitutional principles) in the ongoing pursuit of the cooperative undertaking of deliberation are 'idealizations' which are specifiable only by
reference to the various perspectives from which they are viewed. In the process
of cross-cultural translation, agreement can be reached without a converging of
views or consensus, but participants may nonetheless learn from each others' stand-
points, thereby eventually revising their respective world views and sometimes
developing surprising new perspectives. If deliberative cooperation (the game of
giving and asking for reasons) continues, the participants may still be able to reach
mutual agreement (which is certainly weaker than a consensus but stronger than
a mere compromise 'tit for tat') on what the common will should consist of, on
which norms should coordinate their action plans and on which constitutional
principles they want in order to regulate their co-existence legitimately. Thus, even
under conditions of '*gebrochener Intersubjektivität*' and of ethical/cultural pluralism, the (semantic) exploration of difference can be a resource for moral or justice-related reasoning. When embedded in a praxis of justification, the clash of
differing interpretations of the meaning of 'fair distribution' and 'equality' can
lead to the decentring and eventual revision of the perspectives of participants.

A dialogical account conceives of deliberation as a dialogical exchange of public
reasons for the purpose of resolving common problems that makes participants
answerable and accountable to one another. Dialogue does so in such a way that
their interpretative horizons must not necessarily converge into an agreement.
Rather, it triggers a process of mutual perspective-taking – an 'exploration of difference' – which results in reflective social learning. As will be shown in this chapter, even agreements elicit clarification or amplification; for example, in discourses
of contextual application of norms, they lead to further disagreements or (critical) comments aiming at a 'better' or 'deeper' agreement etc. According to this
definition, deliberation is not so much a form of discourse or argumentation aiming at reaching a consensual understanding, but a joint, cooperative activity of
mutual translation and justification of viewpoints aimed at finding the 'best' or
most 'just' solution in an ongoing process of pragmatic experimentation. Politics

can thus be conceived as the public deliberation of all citizens (coming from their various ethical/cultural perspectives) on the meaning of constitutional rights, the entitlements they entail, their objective and enforcement.[19] By translating, we are trying to make communication, deliberation and argumentation possible. And by doing so, we generate the sort of cognitive openness and conditions for mutual trust – for being taken seriously, for being included in deliberation, for being held accountable and so on – which are taken for granted in any speech community. As a consequence, the process of translation forces one to adopt an 'enlarged mentality' (Arendt).

Instead of containing pluralism through 'reasonable disagreement' (Rawls), the deliberative/dialogical approach sees the diversity of perspectives as a resource for democratic politics. In what follows, I will suggest a theory of translation which connects semantics to formal pragmatics and which can help to elaborate such deliberative, dialogical approach to democratic politics. *The procedures of democratic politics can be understood as methods for translating and eventually revising world views and articulating, examining, and cooperatively weighing conflicting interests.* The very process of mutually translating each other's views in public – making them explicit and thus entering the game of giving and asking for reasons – entails a certain reflexivity with respect to one's own preferences or ethical/cultural perspectives. Procedural models of democracy allow the articulation of the plurality of world views and interests under conditions of social cooperation and exploration of difference which are acceptable to all. We can conceptualize translation or 'multicultural literacy' as a constant exploration of different vocabularies or ethical/cultural perspectives with the anticipation of establishing shared conceptual norms, or for that matter, constitutional principles. The discursive practice of translation can thus be regarded as a model for deliberative procedures in democracies where conflicts of ethical/cultural perspectives and interests prevail.

Donald Davidson's principle of charity

The American analytical philosopher Donald Davidson points out that the idea of incompatible, or reciprocally unintelligible, language-games is a pointless fiction, and that in real cases of communicative interaction, representatives of different cultural traditions can always find a way to talk over their differences. Any (national or socio-cultural) language can be learned by one who is able to use any other language. He argues against the conceptual relativism of Kuhn and Feyerabend (i.e. the idea of a total failure of translatability) and, at the same time, against the empiricism of philosophers such as Quine (i.e. the dualism of conceptual scheme and empirical content). He does this by showing that the presupposed dualism of conceptual scheme and empirical content is inconceivable. The metaphor of a single space within which each scheme has a position or point of view with respect to a 'theory-neutral' reality, he argues, makes no sense.[20] There is no intelligible basis on which to say either that conceptual schemes are totally different or incommensurable, or that we share a wholly common scheme or 'ontology'.

By way of an alternative to the two positions he challenges, Davidson develops an empirical theory of translation that makes no assumptions about (pre-given) shared meanings or concepts, but instead describes their usage.[21] While Wittgenstein analyzes the concepts of meaning and understanding primarily from the performative perspective (i.e. the actor's capacity to follow rules and to participate in a common practice), Davidson thematizes these concepts from the interpretative perspective of a translator. His analysis thus focuses on the capacity of the actor to understand the communicative intentions of a speaker in a situation in which a common understanding of words is not possible. Since Davidson's theory of meaning does not start from shared language games or common practices, it is more useful than Wittgenstein's for the analysis of deliberation and translation in pluralistic societies. In fact, Davidson's analysis concentrates on situations of 'radical interpretation' where the main problem is learning the meaning of words from a foreign language.

Davidson argues that understanding *within* a language is itself always a continuing translation of the idiolects of speakers, and thus that translation between languages is, in fact, only an extension of what native speakers do all the time when trying to make sense of one another's meaning. The argument is that it is precisely the plurality of perspectives (within and between languages) – the 'non-identity' of the speakers and their idiolects – that makes meaningful (intra- and inter-linguistic) translation possible. In this sense, understanding requires the exploration of ambiguity in the continuing clarification of meaning between the speakers.[22] It involves a process of constructing a viable 'passing theory' of beliefs and meanings from sentences held true by another speaker. We implicitly assume a great deal about a speaker's beliefs: in the case of a malapropism, for example, we decide to understand a different word from that actually spoken in order to preserve a 'reasonable theory of belief'. For Davidson, communicative practice therefore presupposes that we assume general agreement on beliefs, that is, a widespread sharing of sentences held true by speakers of the same language. Davidson's theory accounts for partial failure in translatability, which at the same time is the precondition for the possibility of making changes in conceptual schemes intelligible by reference to what remains common: meanings can be innovative (e.g. malapropisms, metaphors) if they become accepted by the larger speech community, or, in other words, if they become shared meanings.

Interestingly, Davidson starts from an a priori 'verificationist' position: an interpretation is true, he claims, if it accords with the interpretation we would be disposed to give were evidential conditions favourable.[23] He holds that the conceptual resources of different languages cannot differ dramatically, since the conditions of access to any such reputed conceptual scheme require shared knowledge. As a consequence – and in the face of general scepticism – Davidson claims that the very possibility of communication presupposes that we have mostly true beliefs: 'Successful communication proves the existence of a shared, and largely true,

view of the world'.[24] We can only start translation by assuming a general agreement of beliefs, that is, a widespread sharing of sentences held true by speakers.
His verificationist approach does not allow him to properly distinguish between
the questions, 'What counts as evidence for an interpretation?' and 'What constitutes the truth of an interpretation?' (This will be elaborated in the discussion of
Putnam in the following pages).

On the basis of this position, Davidson proposes the 'principle of charity' as a
non-negotiable guiding principle of ordinary interpretation. According to this
principle, what counts in favour of a translation is if it represents the translated
speaker as saying, believing or otherwise implying things that are true. This principle is (a) an epistemic guide, which helps to explicate what we think makes an
interpretation of someone's words reasonable; and (b) a constitutive principle,
that is, part of an account of what constitutes the truth of some statement. The
'charitable' interpretation of anomalous details of another's idiolect against the
background of common beliefs is a precondition for understanding (here understood as a method of translation). For Davidson, 'charity' is the presupposition
for the possibility of making sense of what other speakers say. Interpretative charity thus limits the arbitrariness of interpretation: 'Charity is forced on us; whether
we like it or not, if we want to understand others, we must count them right in
most matters.'[25] The principle of charity leads us to prefer theories of interpretation that minimize disagreement. We can make sense of the utterances of others
only when we interpret in a way that maximizes agreement. We improve the clarity of a conceptual scheme or an opinion by 'enlarging the basis of shared (trans-
latable) language or of shared opinion'.[26] Since Davidson has an 'internal holistic'
approach, the translator operates from a descriptive point of view and therefore
has to interpret speakers as speaking truths. This is in contrast to a normative
point of view where truth has to be negotiated intersubjectively and charity is
only necessary as an epistemic guide that grants a degree of reasonability to the
statements made by strangers.

I wish to argue that although Davidson claims to present a 'theory of translation and interpretation that makes no assumptions about shared meanings, concepts, or beliefs',[27] he ultimately falls back into a residual substantialism that he
assumes a fundamental pre-agreement – 'a vast common ground'[28] – as a precondition of access to meaning. Davidson's approach is 'empirical', that is, it accounts
for the workings of natural language, and relies on an 'internally holistic' correspondence theory of truth which abandons the concept of reference. He argues
that truth precedes reference: A speaker's understanding of the reference of words
consists in his grasping the truth conditions for a sentence which contain those
words. If for any given language, our theory of meaning is no more than the truth
definition of that language – the argument goes – then the understanding that a
native speaker has amounts to the knowledge of its truth definition: 'We make
maximum sense of words and thoughts of others when we interpret in a way that
optimizes agreement.'[29] Davidson's theory of truth is 'substantial', because he sees
truth as a property which sentences have or lack depending on what they mean
and how the world is.[30]

The reason why Davidson's theory of translation requires a prior, given consensus lies both in the verificationism of interpretation mentioned above and in his residual 'subject-philosophical assumption'. Both of these positions limit the relevance of pluralism in communication; the former because it assumes that we always already share true beliefs, and the latter because the sentence of another person is interpreted on the basis of a kind of methodological individualism (i.e. by the observation of another speaker without taking into consideration his or her recognition of the validity of the observer's translation/interpretation). Davidson assimilates understanding a participant in communicative interaction to the 'theoretical' interpretation of the observer. Instead of analyzing communication intersubjectively (as a process of mutual translation between alter and ego), his starting point is always a speaker (with a subject language) who translates another speaker's object language into his own. Thus, Davidson's theory of translation involves three languages:

> [T]he object language, the subject language, and the metalanguage (the language from and into which translation proceeds, and the language of the theory, which says what expressions of the subject language translate which expression of the object language).[31]

In his path-breaking essay on linguistic innovation, 'A Nice Derangement of Epitaphs' (1986), Davidson dilutes the concept of the metalanguage into that of the 'passing theory' which generates shared meaning in each speech situation. In every communicative situation speakers negotiate anew a passing theory which they need in order to know how to interpret a particular utterance on a particular occasion.[32] However, the passing theory is conceived from the perspective of the subject (third person) and not as something intersubjectively negotiated by participants in communicative interaction. Looking at the actual intersubjective conditions of communicative interaction, however, it seems evident that a metalanguage can be no more than a set of idealizations of the shared meanings which are constantly produced between alter and ego. If this is the case, then truth is conceivable as an idealization of justification,[33] and linguistic charity in the process of mutual translation goes in two directions, at the same time from alter to ego and from ego to alter. In an intersubjective theory of language, charity is not paternalistic but reciprocal.

Furthermore, Davidson's theory of interpretation does not allow for an account of how linguistic knowledge refers to world knowledge, that is, of how we can learn from confrontation with the world and with each other. Lacking the notion of 'reference', it excludes the extralinguistic dimensions of communication: the objective world and the socio-historical dimensions of communication, as well as the contexts in which it takes place. In short, Davidson makes no claims about the relation of utterances and extralinguistic contexts. Since he excludes the social world (and social languages) from analytical philosophy, he overlooks the fact that speech is differentiated according to the plurality of life worlds and contexts, and that these 'speech genres' are more or less open to interpretation. Just as social practices constrain the interpretation of meaning, speech genres help to control the shift of meaning which necessarily occurs in the constant chain of decontextualization and recontextualization in a new context of speech. Moreover, Davidson's theory overlooks the fact that the negotiation of a passing theory between two or more speakers is always imbued with cultural-political power, that is, that the speech situation can be more or less symmetrical or democratic. It can account for linguistic innovation (for example enlarging the basis of shared language to include malapropisms), but hardly for innovative interpretations of the world which might lead to social change.

Despite these problems, a *political* theory of translation should retain Davidson's idea of charity because it is necessary for mutual understanding that is understood as the exploration of ambiguity in the ongoing clarification of meaning between alter and ego. However, instead of ultimately tying semantics to metaphysics (for Davidson, semantic interpretation is guided by the constitutive rule of charity whereby we are required to interpret people as speaking the truth), it seems more plausible to postulate a principle of 'reasonable charity', according to which, one should take people to be saying things that would be reasonable given their circumstances and abilities. *In its reciprocal version, this principle requires participants in communication to converge in their intersubjective recognition of validity claims (which is not to say to substantially converge in their views).*[34] If we 'translate' this idea into a theory of democratic politics it would correspond to the idea of a dialogue between ethical/cultural groups that generates cross-cultural universality (shared meanings), which is then inevitably challenged again by new ambiguities. Interpretive charity – the precondition for 'multicultural literacy' – ensures the possibility of expanding not only one's own horizon, but also that of one's (political) community with respect to new data, new ideas or concepts, and new solutions to problems. By exploring difference (within a normative context) it takes the monological edge off universalism. This kind of theory of politics could accommodate phenomena such as socio-cultural denationalization and innovative forms of life or situations of cross-cultural communication where the background of shared generic expectation (i.e. of how to interpret an utterance in a speech situation) is minimal. It would also make it easier to investigate whether – in instances where linguistic charity is lacking – differences in asymmetrical speech situations lead to domination or the silencing of another's perspective. With the notion of charity, we can empirically distinguish good talk from bad talk, dialogical consensus from monological compromise, and situations of mutual learning from situations of hegemony.

Hilary Putnam and the idea of situated idealizations

Hilary Putnam combines a theoretical pluralism with an 'internal realist' theory of knowledge. His approach to communication allows for an already stronger notion of pluralism since the different perspectives of speakers (or the mutual translation of their idiolects) are epistemically oriented toward the 'idealization' of shared understandings. Putnam criticizes Davidson's (postempirical) correspondence theory of truth with the pragmatic argument that 'what is true' has to be analyzed on the basis of true statements that are accepted as valid by everyone everywhere. Language represents something in the objective world that is not itself part of the social world of utterances (realist perspective).[35] However, Putnam emphasizes that truth is relative to the sort of language we are using and the sort of context we are in (i.e., he adopts an internalist perspective). Truth is deeply dependent on the criteria of rational acceptability that we use, and thus on our ethical/cultural values.[36] Nonetheless, to abandon the notion of truth as (unique) correspondence is not to favour a position of cultural relativism, but to adopt the balanced position of a pluralism which, rather than being transcended by a metalanguage or a prior consensus, is constrained by reason. What is 'right' or 'wrong' is interpreted from a certain cultural perspective, but this cultural perspective can be criticized with reasons. Using a word presupposes knowledge of the history of its 'use', but also the ability to interpret that tradition, to 'appropriate' it in new contexts and to criticize it. Certainly we cannot speak meaningfully if we place ourselves outside of cultural traditions, something which, in turn, affects our understanding of what interpretations of a word or a principle are 'rationally acceptable'.[37] However, cultures and social practices cannot define what reason is, since they presuppose reason for their interpretation:

> Reason is, in this sense, both immanent (not to be found outside of concrete language games or institutions) and transcendent (a regulative idea that we use to criticize the conduct of *all* activities and institutions).[38]

Putnam therefore conceives truth as an epistemological and not a merely cultural or sociological notion. Truth is an idealization of the intersubjectivity of rational acceptability[39] or, more precisely, of the 'warranted assertibility' of sentences. He claims that we cannot eliminate the normative – that is, we cannot separate the notion of truth from what is rationally acceptable at a particular time or within a certain culture.[40] From this internal realist point of view, 'shared meanings' are not seen as constructions but rather as idealizations without which we could not communicate and socially interact. We have no choice but to engage in the exploration of new (and perhaps better) conceptual schemes and interpretations of constitutional principles from the perspective which arises from our historical and socio-cultural context or 'situatedness'. The 'true' concept of interpretation is the idealization of what speakers rationally accept in the ongoing process of dialogical translation.

As in the hermeneutic/formal-pragmatic tradition of Humboldt and Habermas, Putnam's theory of translation presumes (a) that the objective world is one and the same for all, and (b) that the social worlds of our different reference systems are commensurable, i.e. that the same objects can be described from various linguistic/ethical perspectives.[41] Putnam has a pragmatic approach to rationality, since for him it is not defined by a set of principles but by the regulative ideal of the 'evolving conception of the cognitive virtues to guide us'.[42] The differences between the perspectives of alter and ego (and between their idiolects) cannot be transcended by a metalanguage (Davidson) but are the precondition for constant mutual translation.

But, it may be asked, how do we ever know that a translation scheme 'works' if conceptions always turn out to be different? The answer to this question, as given by various thinkers from Vico down to the present day, is that interpretive success does not require that the translated beliefs come out the *same* as our own, but it does require that they come out *intelligible* to us. This is the basis of all the various maxims of interpretative charity or 'benefit of the doubt', such as ... Vico's own directive to maximize the *humanity* of the person being interpreted. It is a constitutive fact about human experience in our world of different cultures interacting in history while individually undergoing slower or more rapid change that we are, as a matter of universal human experience, able to *do* this; able to interpret one another's beliefs, desires, and utterances so that it all makes some kind of *sense*.[43]

At bottom, the notion of rationality is, as Putnam argues, just one part of our idea of the good. Since we cannot speak from nowhere, we can only search for truth or the correct interpretation of principles from the perspective of our specific perspective/'situatedness'.

In his recent writings, Putnam has emphasized the entanglement of facts and values, as well as of science and ethics. He argues that we cannot have a view of the world that does not reflect our interests and values and that we are 'committed to regarding some views of the world – and, for that matter, some interests and values – as better than others'.[44] From a 'realist' perspective, he claims that values have objectivity in the sense that they are 'ought-implying facts' and thus can be true or false.[45] Giving up the idea of objectivity as an absolute answer to perspective-independent questions, he favours the idea of objective resolutions to problems that are situated, or what Dewey called 'objective resolutions of problematical situations'.

Putnam's idea of translation is of a dialogue where a purely procedural rationality prevails and with the help of which we arrive at a common vocabulary. However, if we understand 'common vocabulary' as an idealization of the telos of mutual translation (of two vocabularies becoming one), then translation has not only an epistemological but also a moral aspect: the transcendental claim of a symmetrical speech situation which allows a *reciprocal* adoption of different perspectives. Claims about the validity of beliefs and values have to be intersubjectively accepted and thus in terms of the 'structure' of dialogue they imply the mutual recognition of the speakers. In other words, the dialogical generation of shared meanings unavoidably involves the symmetrical mutual recognition of the *concrete* other.

Furthermore, we have to distinguish between theoretical and practical reason. Justified epistemic claims aim at a consensus of facts; justified practical projects aim at cooperation when reaching agreements on norms. Contrary to what Putnam's theory of 'value-realism' implies, justified epistemic claims about facts do not constitute the essential basis for the justification of practical projects or cultural practices (moral and ethical reasoning). Rather, it is willingness to learn from one another's ethical/cultural perspective – not in terms of convergence or the elimination of differences, but in terms of seeing the world from the other's point of view – which allows both ethical/cultural communities to form a common will. Putnam's theory of meaning puts more emphasis on difference than

Davidson's, but his (epistemological) understanding of values does not allow him to translate his (formal-pragmatic) idealizations of shared meanings into the idealization of shared interpretations of constitutional principles. Therefore his (semantic) pluralism of values is unable to valorise difference as a resource for intercultural/ethical deliberation on justice-related issues. Instead, the exploration of difference is a normative project since it aims to give rise to a broadly shared vocabulary – or body of constitutional principles – no doubt ambiguous and indeterminate (and therefore unstable), but for that very reason capable of providing a common framework of public discourse. Only the telos of creating one horizontal speech/political community (e.g. the EU) out of many can accommodate plurality in the process of translation or intercultural deliberation.

A semantically relevant learning process has formal-pragmatic conditions. It assumes that participants reciprocally acknowledge one another as responsible subjects who are both members of *one* community of justification, that is, that they recognize one another as partners in the normative constitutional project which takes place via the dialogical translation of different ethical/cultural world views. Different cultural values do not simply coalesce into legal norms; rather, the mutual translation of perspectives in formal and informal public debate is expected to create enough common ground and willingness to facilitate an agreement about what norms the different participants want in order to legitimately regulate their co-existence:

> Die im Diskurs erwartete Dezentrierung lebensweltlicher Perspektiven fördert in moralisch relevanten Handlungskonflikten diejenige gegenseitige Erweiterung des je eigenen Horizonts von Wertorientierungen, die nötig ist, um auf dem Wege der Wertegeneralisierung zu gemeinsam anerkannten Normen zu gelangen.[46]

The 'shared meaning' of these norms are 'idealizations' which secure the co-reference of all perspectives, something, without which we could not communicate or translate (and indeed without which we would have no grounds for disagreement). What is shared in such a process can only be specified as a pragmatic vantage point (a 'third-party perspective') to which the various perspectives refer.

> Die lichtvolle Erkennung der Verschiedenheit fordert [vom Interpreten] etwas Drittes, nämlich ungeschwächt gleichzeitiges Bewußtsein der eigenen und der fremden Sprachform.[47]

This third-party perspective can be understood as the 'shared meanings' or 'principles' which amount to the (idealized) norms of translation or political deliberation. From the participants' stance, however – and in the context of pluralistic societies this is more evident than ever – intra- and inter-linguistic translation can only mean a constant reflexive decentring (and eventually revising) of one's own perspective or world view in light of the other's perspectives or world views (see also the interviews in Chapter 8). To engage in the normative project of translation (or constitutional patriotism) when mutually accounting for world views and social practices (or the interpretation of principles) is not equivalent to transcending differences:

Da man aber in eine fremde Sprache immer mehr oder weniger seine eigne Welt- ja seine eigne Sprachansicht hinüberträgt, so wird dieser Erfolg nie rein und vollständig empfunden.[48]

According to the dialogical approach, political deliberation takes place within a particular society with a particular civic culture, history and traditions. Its participants are not abstract moral beings but are socio-culturally situated in a certain way. Where disagreement arises, for example, it is not about whether a disputed cultural practice (acutely, female circumcision, polygamy, Muslim girls wearing headscarves at school, etc.) is desirable 'in general' or 'in principle', but whether it is justifiable in their society according to their constitutional principles (which, of course, are (re)interpreted in the course of a public debate by the disagreeing parties).[49] In justice-related reasoning it is the translational imperative of social integration, not a mere commitment to (justified) epistemic claims which enables mutual agreement and learning processes. It is the shared citizenship or constitutional identity of the participants in deliberation that allows them to overcome the phases of incomprehension and irreconcilable disagreement which intercultural/ethical debates often involve and instead to generate (dialogical) solidarity over time. I will spell out this idea of an inclusive (but not assimilationist) 'constitutional patriotism' which reconciles the legitimate but occasionally conflicting demands of achieving political unity and avoiding the imposition of cultural uniformity in Chapter 6.

Mikhail Bakhtin: the centrifugal and centripetal forces of language

The Russian philosopher and cultural theorist Mikhail Bakhtin[50] makes a striking, but yet under-explored contribution to the definition of the democratic project. His originality as a social critic is often overlooked since he did not write about politics or society but about the theory of language, the epistemology of the human sciences and, in particular, about the history of the European novel. Bakhtin is convinced that through a socio-historical analysis of various forms of communication (both those of contemporary society and of the past) he can discover fundamental patterns of social relationships, for instance the modern types of intersubjectivity embodied in the language of the European novel.[51] He analyzes the ways in which, in novels, communicative structures take the historical shape of a particular kind of modern social life. For him there exists no culturally unmediated or 'pure' intersubjectivity and no language 'purified' of history. Dialogue, Bakhtin tells us, was there all along, but certain historical conditions (e.g. the shift to European modernity) disclose its intersubjectivity or 'multivoicedness' more than others. It was, for instance, the creation of national cultures with new standard languages[52] which gave rise to the (intra-)linguistic stratification typical of modernity. Bakhtin sees his idea of 'heteroglossia'[53] (i.e. the national vernaculars internally differentiated by various socio-cultural contexts), represented in the novel. For example, he analyzes Dostoevksy's novels as 'artistically organized social heteroglossia'.[54] As we will see, the notion of heteroglossia (which literally means 'different speech-ness') provides a valuable framework within which to outline the mechanism of the constant 'disequilibrium' within language that is due to the ambiguity or indeterminacy of meaning. Compared to Putnam, Bakhtin radicalizes the relevance of the socio-cultural plurality and situatedness of language. At the same time, however, his sociological account of various 'speech genres' can counterbalance the formal-pragmatic idealization of the symmetrical recognition of alter and ego with an empirical analysis of 'addressivity' (the sociological equivalent of Davidson's 'charity') – that is, the quality of turning symmetrically to the listener and the willingness to see the world from their perspective within a certain dialogical speech situation.

Without being aware of the Western tradition of pragmatic linguistics, Bakhtin sets out a theory of 'dialogue' which focuses on human speech understood as the social event of communicative interaction.[55] He thereby claims dialogical structures to be the ideal-typical form of all linguistic interaction. Dialogue becomes an emphatic category of symmetrical or undistorted communication. It can be more or less 'dialogical', depending on whether ego addresses alter with charity rather than silencing his or her voice or standpoint:

> In rhetoric … there is complete victory and destruction of the opponent. In dialogue the destruction of the opponent also destroys that very dialogic sphere where the word lives. … This sphere is very fragile and easily destroyed (the slightest violence is sufficient, references to authority, and so forth).[56]

Bakhtin's theory of language focuses less on the cognitive dimension of speech (its function of representing something in the world) than on the communicative and the expressive dimension of dialogue as an encounter between world views. Unlike most Western pragmatic linguists, he stresses not only the intersubjective quality of all linguistic meaning, but also its sociological and historical aspect, its situatedness in a plurality of contingent contexts which constitutes its (semantic) meaning: 'verbal interaction' can never be understood in isolation from its connection with a concrete 'extraverbal situation' and 'its audience'.[57] Therefore, utterances are impregnated with the power and social conflicts that constitute their context. Since Bakhtin's theory of language lacks a categorical frame, the following rather 'constructive' reconstruction interprets his ideas about linguistic interaction – which are implicit in his analysis of the history of literature, his cultural semiotics and his late notebooks – against the backdrop of Western philosophy of language and its terminology.[58]

Bakhtin's starting point is that what we experience as meaningful, we experience dialogically, as an event of communication which is not so much reproduction as response. Language is radically dialogical in the sense that all utterances are part of an open-ended dialogue where meanings are negotiated in the interaction between the discourses of the speakers' different socio-cultural and ideological positions. Bakhtin's concept of dialogism is not to be misunderstood as a description of actual verbal interaction between two people, but rather points to the fundamental philosophical idea that meaning is always produced intersubjectively in the (semiotic) space between expression and understanding. According to this view, the 'in-between' separating subjects (and the resulting indeterminacy and ambiguity of meaning) is not a limitation but the very condition of meaningful speech:

> Any understanding is imbued with response and necessarily elicits it in one form or another: the listener becomes the speaker. A passive understanding of meaning of perceived speech is only an abstract aspect of the actual whole of actively responsive understanding, which is then actualized in a subsequent response that is actually articulated.[59]

Thus, Bakhtin's argument is that the internal structure of language and the internal structure of utterances reflect the fact that they are always responding to and anticipating other utterances.

Bakhtin's notion of dialogism goes far beyond the more conventional conception of dialogue, so dear to liberal democracy, as a mere negotiative give-and-take aimed at compromise over exogenous preferences.[60] A dialogical theory of meaning questions the notion that individual interests and preferences precede verbal interaction (liberal individualism) but also the idea that a shared cultural tradition is a precondition for understanding and, consequently, that traditions are ultimately incommensurable (communitarian culturalism). However, to interpret Bakhtin's concept of dialogue in a proceduralist way (i.e. as the mere agreement to observe certain procedures when resolving conflicts), misses the socio-historical import of his analysis. Rather, it points to the constant semiotic co-production of shared meanings – the exploration of difference – which takes place in a particular discursive form according to a concrete socio-cultural context. All arguments are articulated and conducted in a particular social language or 'speech genre' which cannot be purged of its deep socio-cultural and evocative associations. Dialogue refers both to (a) the formal/structural dimension of communicative interaction, that is, the radically inter-subjective nature of meaningful utterances which presupposes (rather than contains) the plurality of perspectives and cannot be determined outside a particular speech situation; as well as to (b) the substantial/socio-historical dimension, that is, the fact that the dialogical conventions governing ordinary linguistic practices have historically concrete shapes (speech genres).

During the process of mutual translation or of reaching understanding between two or more speakers there is also a process of dialogical semiosis which takes place at the level of words. Dialogue, Bakhtin argues, can therefore be interpreted as an epiphenomenon of the internal dialogism of all discourses. The (semiotic) dialogism which takes place within a word reflects, so to speak, the dialogical process of mutual understanding. It is due to the implicit interaction between two utterances or texts, and between their diverging contexts or perspectives, which constitute the 'shared interpretation' of that utterance/text. Dialogism refers to all those relations, immanent within an utterance, which generate its meaning – that is, its reference to an object, its relation to the speaker, the addressee, the system of language, to other utterances, to the socio-cultural context and the specific speech situation. Dialogical relations are neither merely logical nor linguistic-syntactical, but are rather *semantic* relations, which penetrate the micro-level of language, the word. In the semiotic process, they mediate between the univocal meaning of a word and the plurality of its contexts. For Bakhtin a word is not an isolated linguistic element – always identical to itself – but rather a flexible sign, which has as many meanings as contexts in which it can be used. Each application in a new context undermines its semantic unity or identity:

> I live in a world of other's words. … All of each individual's words are divided into the categories of his own and other's, but the boundaries between them can change, and a tense dialogic struggle takes place on the boundaries.[61]

The resulting ambivalence does not, however, have a purely 'internal' semantic-linguistic nature as Julia Kristeva's post-structuralist Bakhtin interpretation and her notion of 'polysemy' suggests,[62] but a semiotic one that does not abstract from the speakers as agents. Ambivalence arises from the intersubjective interpretation of a word in the multiple contexts of its use.

Bakhtin's concept of dialogism thus stresses both the pragmatic/communicative dimension of language and its semantic/world-disclosing dimension. Bakhtin discovers this latter dimension of language in the history of its use, of the many socio-cultural contexts and speech situations which have existed. The actual meaning of a word is determined by its heterogeneous relations and changes in each communicative interaction. Accordingly, understanding a word within an utterance cannot be reduced to the recognition of its 'identical' meaning. Rather, we must capture the difference or newness of meaning in a concrete (linguistic and extra-linguistic) context. Meaning lies neither within the word as significant (de Saussure), nor within the intention of the speaker (Grice, Schiffer, Bennett), but is the result of the semiotic interaction between speaker and addressee in each actual speech situation.

The continuous splitting up of the consolidated (identical) meaning of a word through the innumerable contexts of utterance in which it is used can be thought of as the 'centrifugal forces' of language. However, while Bakhtin stresses the plurality of contextual meaning, it is always in relation to the rules of the system of language, the norms of discursive practice which are the 'centripetal forces' of language. Similarly to Putnam, he claims that without the idealization of shared meaning we could not communicate at all. The intersubjective interpretation of a word presupposes an identical meaning. But the word is given only within actual utterances and discursive practices. Bakhtin's most innovative idea is that the production of meaning in any utterance is a dialectical process involving 'centralization' by the centripetal forces of shared meanings, and 'decentralization' by the centrifugal forces of the unique meaning-in-context; of unification by the normative system of language and disunification by language as action (i.e. speech in all its aesthetic-stylistic density and ethical/cultural situatedness).[63] The centripetal forces guarantee a shared reference and thus

> a certain maximum of mutual understanding and crystallizing into a real, although still relative, unity – the unity of the reigning 'correct language'.[64]

This centrifuge constitutes the condition for semantic innovation, the reflexivity of world views and, eventually, social change. This does not, of course, imply total linguistic freedom.

Bakhtin's theory avoids any movement towards analytical abstraction, since language as an enabling code or system is seen, not as a mere summation of separate and distinct social languages, nor as the dialectical overcoming (*Aufhebung*) of antagonisms. Rather, Bakhtin stresses the constant empirical disequilibrium of language due to the dynamics of (semiotic) contestation over the fit between the language of the code (i.e. of learned conventions and regularities) and the language of practice in specific contexts. The centripetal forces ensure relatively stable shared meanings (e.g. interpretations of constitutional principles), whereas the centrifugal forces ensure that these meanings are open to new contexts, new social practices, and new interpretations (e.g. by strangers or migrants) and thus that the 'dialogical community' is inclusive, or, available to new participants (see also the idea of 'mixing' in Chapter 8).

These dialogic relations[65] of heteroglossia institutionalize indeterminacy and ambiguity as a precondition of meaningful experience between alter and ego: they ensure that meaning remains in the process of being (re)produced and modified in each speech situation.[66] They take place in the social interaction between a speaker and a *concrete* other.

> His orientation toward the listener is an orientation toward a specific conceptual horizon, toward the specific world of the listener; it introduces totally new elements into his discourse; it is in this way, after all, that various different points of view, conceptual horizons … come into contact with one another. The speaker strives to get a reading of his own word, and on his own conceptual system that determines this word, within the alien conceptual system of the understanding receiver; he enters into dialogical relationships with certain aspects of this system. The speaker breaks through the alien conceptual system of the listener, constructs his own utterance on alien territory, against his, the listener's, aperceptive background.[67]

Consequently, understanding the utterances of others involves constant (implicit) reflection on the kind of language one is hearing and its appropriateness within the speech situation, as well as the socio-cultural position of the other. Understanding language is not a simple and unreflective process, but often a highly self-conscious interpretative one – an active and engaged understanding means response. If all meaning is intersubjective (dialogism), the 'inter' separating two people (Humboldt's idea of '*gebrochene Intersubjektivität*'), difference and pluralism is not a limitation but a precondition for meaningful dialogue.[68] 'Multicultural literacy' is not new but has been there all along.

We can say that Bakhtin's idea of heteroglossia 'applies' Humboldt's principle of linguistic relativity (i.e. that world views are relative to national languages) within a given language.[69] In the sense of reflecting an internally-differentiated life world, a language discloses not only our common world, but also the many social worlds within society. It is by using this notion of speech genres – stressing the rhetorical and expressive aspects of language use that are characteristic of specific socio-historical contexts[70] – that we can theorize the plurality of ethical/ cultural or ideological perspectives on the world. Speech genres are historically and socio-culturally specific forms of utterance[71] which 'organize our speech in almost the same way as grammatical (syntactical) forms do'.[72] Like grammar, speech genres both constrain and enable communication. As well as representing the idealizations of 'identical meanings', Bakhtin thinks of these typologies of speech acts as part of the (normative) preconditions for reaching understanding: they 'maximize' mutual interpretation or the translation of 'idiolects'. Similarly to Wittgenstein's idea of language games, Bakhtin conceptualizes speech genres as 'relatively stable types', which impose restrictions on individual speakers as to thematic content, style and compositional structure.[73] They do so with a different degree of flexibility (from brief standard military commands to oral anecdotes).[74] They reflect the actual settings in and through which social practices are reproduced (e.g. unofficial political discussions, the exchange of opinions at the theatre, speech performances at court, etc.); in this sense, the production of deliberative communities (e.g. neighbourhoods, associations) is always socio-historically grounded and contextual.[75] Speech genres are, thus, historically evolved, context-specific or 'conventionalized' passing theories (Davidson) or interpretative framings, on which speakers in a given social situation more or less tacitly agree.[76] In this sense, genres both unify and stratify language.[77]

Bakhtin conceptualizes speech genres with an essential openness: the understanding of situations is always negotiated between alter and ego. In actual language, he observes, speech genres are more or less open to interpretation and change or innovation. He distinguishes between two ideal types of genre: 'authoritative discourse', which is absolute or 'undialogized' and permits no play with its framing context (e.g. fundamentalist discourses); and 'internally persuasive discourse', which is more akin to retelling a story in one's own words, with one's own emphases and modifications. Whereas the first type of discourse 'demands our unconditional allegiance',[78] the second type (or comprehensive doctrine) undergoes 'dialogization' because it is relativized, de-privileged, and aware of competing discourses on the same issue. Thus, speech genres are characterized not only by a particular 'referentially semantic content', and by a characteristic composition and style, but also by a characteristic conception of the addressee, that is, they are more or less 'dialogical' (or monological) and open to new appropriations in each speech situation. They have, normatively speaking, more or less 'addressivity'.[79] Only internally persuasive discourse creates 'fertile soil for experimentally objectifying'[80] one another's discourse since it exposes itself to critique. It is this second (ideal) type of speech genre, then – that which is intersubjectively negotiated in argument – that represents a promising contribution to the analysis of democratic deliberation under conditions of ethical/cultural pluralism.

Bakhtin's concept of speech genres is therefore useful for two reasons: (a) it can counterbalance analytical theories of (intra- and inter-linguistic) translation with a sociological approach in which linguistic knowledge is held to be intertwined with world knowledge. From a sociological perspective, the idealizations of shared meanings become situated and always unstable passing theories which relate different idiolects and which are facilitated through speech genres; and (b) the notion of speech genres 'historizes' the ideal speech situation of a symmetrical dialogue into actually existing, more or less dialogical speech situations or genres.

(a) Adapting the notion of speech genres to the purposes of a theory of inter-cultural deliberation, we could say that in moving between highly differentiated life worlds we are compelled to make constant choices about social languages, as well as to constantly learn new ones. The fact that through socialization every person learns not a single system of language but many speech genres makes it possible to conceive the possibility of cultural reflexivity and the capacity to re-spond to an age of heightened flexibility (and autonomy), in which we are en-meshed in multiple bonds of belonging within a proliferating number of symbolic worlds (see Part III). In this sense, inter-linguistic translation is only a radical case of intra-linguistic translation, that is, what we do all the time when we mutually negotiate a speech genre with another person (cooperatively 'appropriating' it to the situation). Communicative capacity requires the flexibility to move from one speech genre to another according to the social context. For Bakhtin as well as Habermas, the fragmenting effect of modern socio-cultural pluralism, or for that matter denationalization, produces the conditions for an

> ever more finely woven net of linguistically generated intersubjectivity. Rationaliza-tion of the life world means differentiation and condensation at once – a thickening of the floating web of intersubjective threads that simultaneously holds together the ever more sharply differentiated components of culture, society and person.[81]

(b) At the same time, the concept of speech genres can help to empirically contextualize Habermas's notion of intersubjective recognition (an in-built ori-entation of all communication) by situating it in concrete social practices. In this way, existing genres of public deliberation can be analyzed according to the extent to which the 'universalizing' force of dialogue (i.e. its capacity for symmetrical mutual translation or understanding, is realized in practice). We are directed to consider their degree of inclusiveness or openness to the interpretations of all participants (e.g. in situations of social or cultural conflict over the meaning of constitutional principles). There are clearly more or less symmetrical or 'demo-cratic' speech situations in public debates, and with a concept of contextualized dialogical practices, scholars of politics could expose the limits of existing demo-cratic or participatory structures and explore – within a particular political com-munity – which dialogic practices (or which speech genres) are most suitable to a fair or symmetrical exploration of difference and to problem-solving in situa-tions of divergent interpretations of public justice.

'Multicultural literacy' – communication/translation across lines of socio-cultural and national differences – is possible precisely because in public discourse cultural identities and selfhood are enacted liminally, on the boundaries of self and other, of identity and difference.[82] In other words, Bakhtin says, we always communicate by crossing barriers, leaving behind the limits of our own idiolect, point of view, or conceptual scheme, or making another's view our own. It is a process of mutual learning: by 'appropriating' one another's perspectives of the world, we may revise parts of our own world view. In this sense, we can, for instance, conceive of the cultural and national margins of today's Europe as battlegrounds for contested world views, or we can think of European politics in terms of a conflictual process between different interpretations within a constitutional dialogue (e.g. different interpretations of 'subsidarity').

Starting from a constructive interpretation of Bakhtin's theory of self and dialogue we can develop an epistemic concept of democracy that allows us to think of politics (under conditions of pluralism) as the constant polarizing and pooling of different ethical or socio-cultural perspectives which generates shared interpretations of constitutional principles: *radically 'pragmatizing' and 'contextualizing' communication may help to analyze the mechanism through which the weft of principles are interwoven with the warp of social practice.* The appropriation of principles of justice in a specific social situation is, so to speak, negotiated among different ethical perspectives or comprehensive doctrines.[83] Accordingly, trust and solidarity, as well as the motivation to engage in public dialogue, are not based on the sameness of people within the boundaries of a *demos*. Rather, the moral resources of democracy are produced by sharing such practices of dialogue and enforced by the emotional fulfilment and the intellectual enjoyment of curiosity and learning which arise from the process of reaching mutual understanding. Given that this is the case, difference has to be perceived as both unavoidable *and* desirable, because the precondition for dialogue is the mutual attraction of the participants or, to put it less emphatically, the hope of discovering new solutions to social problems together.

> Languages of heteroglossia, like mirrors that face each other, each reflecting in its own way a piece, a tiny corner of the world, force us to guess and grasp for a world behind their mutually reflecting aspects that is broader, more multi-levelled, containing more and varied horizons than would be available to a single language or a single mirror.[84]

Dialogism, then, refers to the constant process of differentiation or polarization and pooling between the 'universalizing centre' of norms and 'contextualizing periphery' of ethical values and social practices, and between different peripheries, perspectives or ethical subcultures. The opposition between centre and periphery in terms of codification and indeterminacy can be translated for our purposes into a constant tension in the definition of norms and in the interpretation of constitutional principles. Social transformation is then seen in a processual way: as ideas or world views (the Rawlsian 'comprehensive doctrines', Habermas's ethical life forms or subcultures, Rorty's 'vocabularies') interact with one another, they undergo an internal process of reworking until the transformed world views displace those from which they evolved. This approach goes beyond both the idea of an overarching political culture which contains difference and pluralism of perspectives as the many voices of an uni-vocal public reason, and 'demotic' contextualism that celebrates pluralism and ends up with the incommensurability

of different cultures. For Bakhtin, political culture – since it grows out of dialogical interaction between different cultures – is internally plural and also unifies
and respects diversity. Political culture is not a presupposition of deliberation but
its product, and it is constantly reconstituted and pluralized by it. And political
deliberation is always contextualized and culturally embedded. Therefore the public
sphere should welcome new languages/speech genres, modes of deliberation, forms
of speech and political sensibilities, and create conditions in which their innovative interplay could over time lead to a broad-based political culture. Bakhtin's
idea of dialogism can serve as a metaphor for the process of non-holistic, but also
non-decontextualized collective identity-formation that is produced in these con-
junctions and which is the basis for a constitutional patriotism situated in practices of social exchange. Such a notion of 'constitutional identity' recognizes that
we all speak from a particular place, a particular history, a particular culture, without losing a core of universalism. Our interpretative reference to constitutional
principles becomes both inclusive and situated.

For Bakhtin, communication is a *concrete* aesthetic and ethical act.[85] This move
to the concrete means a shift to an ethical point of view, that is, the perspective of
the participant in dialogue, where understanding what is said cannot be dissoci-
ated from entering into the sphere of 'openings' and 'recognitions' and from en-
suing ethical commitments.[86] In this sense, Bakhtin (normatively) defines the
concrete utterance as the trigger for a kind of reciprocal activity. He theorizes the
linguistic utterance as the act of a 'responsible' subject, with the weight and density of his or her specific position in an ethical world. Such an ethical conception
of language (i.e., a language which is suffused with the historically-framed intentions of responsible subjects) enforces the demand that we respond to the utterances and the behaviour of others, not with a knee-jerk application of moral norms,
but with a sound interpretation of our social and historical situation. Just as norms
are sites of competing conceptions or interpretations, language, rather than reflecting society, is itself an object of struggle within it.

Accordingly, the 'uniqueness' of an utterance in Bakhtin's theory is not a matter of a distinct location or a distinctness of person, but of whether one feels
uniquely obliged by a norm rather than compelled on principle. By extension,
utterances are unique only in relation to values and social practices because it is in
this context that they become a real assertion or negation, representing an irreducible moment of commitment or position-taking with intersubjective consequences.[87] Grounding the validity of meanings (linguistic, cultural, scientific,
ethical, etc.) in a dialogue where the participants disclose themselves and are committed to symmetrical relations implies an ideal of intersubjectivity against which
actual dialogues can be measured.[88] The dialogical community instanced in every
attempt to grasp truth should link the act of assuming a position or making a
claim to the validity of the claim itself, thus ensuring a relationship of responsibility between subjects and their objective culture. Objectivity of understanding is
linked to the engagement of mutual exploration of difference or, as Bakhtin says,
'with dialogic vigour and a deeper penetration into discourse itself'.[89] In this sense,

universalism, understood as the translatability of world views, is situated in the plurality of ethical practices, action and context. Compared to his emphatic underlining of the recognition of the concrete other (his or her distinctness), Bakhtin, however, de-emphasizes the structural recognition of each other (as equal). The (semantic) exploration of difference can only be adapted to the democratic project if it is intertwined with the (formal-pragmatic) acknowledgement of the symmetry/equality of the speakers with regard to the idealization of shared meanings.

In the co-production of meaning through public deliberation, the centripetal or universalizing forces of dialogue produce a shared constitutional identity, not necessarily through consensual understanding, but through the exploration of the many cultural/ethical interpretations of constitutional principles. The constant semiotic contention between universalizing or centripetal, and destabilizing, decentralizing or centrifugal forces within language as praxis can explain the mechanism by which in Habermas's pragmatic-linguistic theory, deliberation among representatives of different subcultures can, in the long run, change their common constitutional identity (i.e. the interpretation of a polity's constitution which is shared in otherwise conflictual debates). We can then understand the political deliberation of citizens as a form of decentred or dialogical constitutionalism 'from below', since constitutional identity or political culture is not in itself a warrant of democracy but something to be constantly co-produced in public life. The production of shared meanings in a given language or the generation of a common interpretation of constitutional principles in a given socio-historical context is always fragile, challenged by new disagreements and by its own ambiguity. The centrifugal or decentralizing forces of difference challenge conventionalized meanings and interpretations of norms, but by means of an 'epistemic struggle' the process of semiotic dialectics arrives at new shared understandings. It is precisely the pluralism of contexts which causes linguistic indeterminacy or ambiguity, something which at the same time, however, is the precondition for the application of norms in social practices. For Bakhtin, language is continually stratifying under the pressure of the centrifugal force which challenges fixed definitions or given interpretations of norms and principles. These centrifugal, dispersing forces of dialogue cause the constant proliferation of new contexts and appropriations. They may thus help to explain the empirical mechanism of dialogical 'inclusiveness' behind the Habermasian notion of discourse, and at the same time its situatedness – that is, the ability to expand the political community beyond ethical/cultural or national boundaries.

An alternative to the *demos*-thesis: the mutual exploration of difference

Whereas theorists of the *demos* believe that meanings are always *already* shared by all members of an (integrated) cultural or national community (i.e. pre-given by the sort of tradition in which the speakers stand), I have argued along with Davidson, Putnam and Bakhtin that meanings are always dialogically negotiated between alter and ego within certain socio-cultural contexts. And it is precisely because of the 'inter-space' between alter and ego that social practices and traditions can be criticized. There is no such thing as a clearly defined, transparent language and, accordingly, speakers are not transparent to one another simply because they share the same language:[90] there are only speakers with certain socio-cultural positions who co-produce shared meanings with other speakers by translating one another's idiolects. This semiotic interaction – the dialogical generation of meaning – is, however, facilitated and constrained by forms of language – namely, the speech genres which are specific to certain socio-cultural contexts and upon which speakers (mostly implicitly) agree in their interpretation of the speech situation. Thus, meanings are produced dialogically in a semiotic process which 'institutionalizes indeterminacy or ambiguity' within certain socio-cultural contexts and practices. These (relatively) stable generated meanings are in turn decentralized and challenged in every new context or speech situation. In this way (dominant or official) discourses are in principle always exposed to critique. It is the very fact of heterogeneity and pluralism that is the precondition for any process of reflexive learning and social change.

The internal (linguistic) relation between meaning, validity and mutual recognition in dialogue points to an 'existential' approach to politics – an approach where the disclosing of difference or otherness opens up a space for the exploration of new contexts and the expression of pathologies at the margins of our social world. It is the idea that different existential-ethical narratives are more than the many voices of a single political reason. Rather, they pluralize and dialogize meaning and the interpretation of norms 'all the way up'. At the same time, however, in the political realm the world-disclosing capacity of language has a cognitive core. All our practices come to us with norms already contained within, which is to say, we are perpetually in the game of giving and asking for reasons. It is from within those implicitly normative practices of justification that we frame our questions, interpret each other, and assess the properties of the application of norms. In other words, innovative (disclosing) interpretations of principles are always embedded within a constitutional project. If in politics, the existential world-disclosing dimension of language is intertwined with the justificatory-cognitive one, then social actors/citizens (and their ethical self-understandings) can become the suppliers of constitutional interpretations. In this way, the heterogeneity of the citizenry is transformed into a resource for an ongoing process of constitutional learning (we might call this the 'horizontalization' of politics). Democratic deliberation is not seen as sociologically naturalized (by the boundaries of a common culture/language or *demos*), but as situated in dialogical interaction, creating an always more densely differentiated network of contexts within which the constitutional project is critically interpreted and becomes potentially inclusive, extendable to new members of a political community. Constitutional patriotism becomes the deliberative process of normative translation within which citizens explore their different ethical/cultural perspectives and preferences and (re)produce (always fragile) shared interpretations of two ethical self-understandings – namely, the kind of society they wish to have, and the specific constitutional principles they wish to guide it.

Notes

1 W. von Humboldt, *Werke, vol. III: Schriften zur Sprachphilosophie*, Wissenschaftliche Buchgesellschaft, Darmstadt 1963, p. 224/225. English translation follows: 'Every language draws about the people that possesses it a circle whence it is possible to exit only by stepping over at once into the circle of another one. To learn a *foreign language* should therefore be to acquire a new standpoint in the world-view hitherto possessed, and in fact to a certain extent is so, since every language contains the whole conceptual fabric and mode of presentation of a portion of mankind. But because we always carry over, more or less, our own world-view, and even our own language-view, this outcome is not purely and completely experienced.' (W. von Humboldt, *On Language: On the Diversity of Human Language Construction and its Influence on the Mental Development of the Human Species*, M. Losonsky (ed.), trans. P. Heath, Cambridge University Press, Cambridge 1999, p. 60.)

2 J. Waldron, *Law and Disagreement*, Oxford University Press, Oxford 1999, p. 102.

3 H. Arendt, *The Human Condition*, Chicago University Press, Chicago 1958, p. 220

4 J. Habermas, 'Three Normative Models of Democracy', in: S. Benhabib (ed.), *Democracy and Difference: Contesting the Boundaries of the Political*, Princeton University Press, Princeton 1996, p. 25.

5 This is not to conflate norms of rationality (e.g. conceptual norms) with norms of action. Whereas the latter bind the will of agents, the former direct their minds. However, in both cases, whenever we apply a concept or comply with a constitutional principle or a moral norm, we move in the 'space of reasons'. In drawing this parallel I would like to stress that the world-disclosing or semantic dimension of language can be brought into a theory of politics when hooked up to the pragmatic dimension, i.e. when the exploration of different world views is intersubjectively generated. If language and reality are inextricably intertwined from a semantic point of view, but if we presuppose that the world is one and the same for all (from the pragmatic point of view), no matter from which linguistic perspective we describe it, then we can learn from each other's interpretations of the world, either by confronting them with the empirical world (justification as descriptive sentences of facts) or by giving and asking for reasons for coordinated action (justification of norms). Agents commit themselves to epistemic claims in a similar way as they commit themselves to practical projects.

6 For a convincing theory which connects formal pragmatic with inferential semantics, see R. Brandom, *Making Explicit: Reason, Representing, and Discursive Commitment*, Harvard University Press, Cambridge, MA, 1994 and R. Brandom, *Articulation Reasons: An Introduction to Inferentialism*, Harvard University Press, Cambridge, MA, 2000. Brandom claims that there is a tendency towards a reflexive upgrading built into language. Norms of speaking that guide behaviour by way of implicit knowledge can be made explicit. In this sense, discursive practices generate shared meanings (out of the semantic reservoir of potential meanings) which are mutually recognized as 'suitable and appropriate' by members of a linguistic community.

7 I owe this analogy to Oliver Gerstenberg.

8 Quine argues that the totality of actual and potential speech behaviour of a linguistic community – which he takes to be the only ontological ground that exists for claims of meaning – does not suffice to determine a single correct translation manual from one language to another. All that indeterminacy shows is that if there is one way of getting it right there are other ways that differ substantially in non-synonymous sentences used after 'said that' (W. V. Quine, *World and Object*, Harvard University Press, Cambridge, MA, 1960).

9 In the formal-pragmatic theory of language, to understand a speech act means to know the conditions and consequences of the rationally motivated agreement that a speaker could achieve with that speech act. (J. Habermas, 'Toward a Critique of the Theory of Meaning', in: J. Habermas, *On the Pragmatics of Communication*, MIT Press, Cambridge, MA, 1998, pp. 277–306).

10 W. von Humboldt, *Werke, vol. III, Schriften zur Sprachphilosophie*, Wissenschaftliche Buchgesellschaft, Darmstadt 1963, p. 196. English translation follows: 'In appearance, however, language develops only *socially*, and man understands himself only once he has tested the intelligibility of his words by trial upon others.' (W. von Humboldt, *On Language*, M. Losonsky (ed.), p. 56).

11 'Adopting a translation manual is … like adopting a constitution or set of laws in the following specific way: (1) It is not a process of describing a prior set of standards, either implicit or explicit. Rather, it is a matter of agreeing to a normatively binding document, a set of constraints on future behavior. (2) This is not to say that the process is independent of prior standards, both implicit and explicit. There will be a wide range of previously adopted social conventions which constrain new adoptions and provide for the mechanisms for rational emendation of them into the new document. (3) Neither is the new set of rules accepted once and for all. Sets of laws and translation manuals both carry with them mechanisms for emending themselves. (4) If we come to a situation in which previously accepted standards, previously dominant methodological principles, and facts about the environment do not determine which of a pair of rules to adopt, it is up to us simply to decide' (M. Norris Lance and J. O'Leary Hawthorne, *The Grammar of Meaning: Normative and Semantic Discourse*, Cambridge University Press, Cambridge 1997, p. 63). However, this semantic theory of translation does not differentiate between practical and epistemic reasoning (justification of norms and justification of assertions).

12 When we withdraw from the participant stance, we somehow restrain ourselves from treating the other as an accountable agent. This objective stance toward people is, however, atypical in ordinary communicative action or is a sign of an asymmetrical power-relation.

13 There is an in-built conservatism that consists in the fact that linguistic innovation, i.e. the attempt to go against accepted usage, carries with it an onus of proof.

14 In order for a people to discuss what they are going to mean by a term, they must use it. In cases of mutual translation or cross-cultural dialogue, both communities have a say in the matter of which of them is correctly using words. Unlike the case of interpreting the language of living people, historical translation – which was the focus of the hermeneutic of H. G. Gadamer – is essentially asymmetrical (or 'undemocratic').

15 J. Habermas, 'From Kant to Hegel: On Robert Brandom's Pragmatic Philosophy of Language', in: *European Journal of Philosophy* 8:3, 2000, p. 346.

16 I think that Brandom is right in pointing this out (R. Brandom, 'Facts, Norms, and Normative Facts: A Reply to Habermas', in: *European Journal of Philosophy* 8:3, 2000, p. 363). However, I agree with Habermas that 'communication is not a self-sufficient game with which the interlocutors reciprocally *inform* each other about their beliefs and intentions. It is only the imperative of social integration – the need to coordinate the action-plans of independently deciding participants in action – that explains the point of linguistic understanding (*Verständigung*).' (Habermas, 'From Kant to Hegel', p. 346).

17 J. Habermas, 'Motive nachmetaphysischen Denkens', in: J. Habermas, *Nachmetaphysisches Denken*, Suhrkamp Verlag, Frankfurt am Main 1988, p. 56.

18 W. von Humboldt, *Werke, vol. III, Schriften zur Sprachphilosophie*, Wissenschaftliche Buchgesellschaft, Darmstadt 1963, p. 439. English translation follows: 'Nobody means by a word precisely and exactly what his neighbour does, and the difference, be it ever so small, vibrates, like a ripple in water, throughout the entire language. Thus all understanding is always at the same time a not-understanding, all concurrence in thought and feeling at the same time a divergence.' (W. von Humboldt, *On Language*, M. Losonsky (ed.), p. 63.)

19 'Democratic debate is like a ball game where there is no umpire to interpret the rules of the

game and their application definitively. Rather, in the game of democracy the rules of the game no less than their interpretation and even the position of the umpire are essentially contestable.' (S. Benhabib, 'Toward a Deliberative Model of Democratic Legitimacy', in: Benhabib (ed.), *Democracy and Difference*, pp. 79–80.

20 D. Davidson, 'The Very Idea of a Conceptual Scheme', in: D. Davidson, *Inquiries into Truth and Interpretation*, Oxford University Press, Oxford 1984, p. 195.

21 Davidson calls his theory of meaning 'empirical' because its ambition is to account for the working of a natural language. His notion of translation is purely syntactic and thus does not deal with questions of reference (D. Davidson, 'Reality Without Reference', in: Davidson, *Inquiries into Truth and Interpretation*, p. 221).

22 D. Davidson, 'A Nice Derangement of Epitaphs', in: E. LePore (ed.), *Truth and Interpretation: Perspectives on the Philosophy of Donald Davidson*, Blackwell, Oxford 1986, pp. 433–446. This conception of language comes close to Wilhelm von Humboldt's dictum 'Alles Verstehen ist … immer zugleich ein Nicht-verstehen' (W. von Humboldt, *Werke*, vol. III, p. 439). English translation: '… all understanding is always at the same time a not-under-standing' (W. von Humboldt, *On Language*, M. Losonsky (ed.), p. 63).

23 'A general requirement on a theory of interpretation is that it can be supported or verified by evidence plausibly available to an interpreter.' (D. Davidson, 'Radical Interpretation', in: Davidson, *Inquiries into Truth and Interpretation*, p. 128).

24 D. Davidson, 'The Method of Truth in Metaphysics', in: Davidson, *Inquiries into Truth and Interpretation*, p. 201.

25 Davidson, 'The Very Idea of a Conceptual Scheme', in: Davidson, *Inquiries into Truth and Interpretation*, p. 197.

26 *Ibid.*

27 *Ibid.*, p. 195.

28 *Ibid.*, p. 200.

29 *Ibid.*, p. 197.

30 H. Putnam has criticized him in these terms, see: H. Putnam, 'Vagueness and Alternative Logic', in: H. Putnam: *Realism and Reason: Philosophical Papers III*, Cambridge University Press, Cambridge 1983, p. 278.

31 Davidson, 'Radical Interpretation', in: Davidson, *Inquiries into Truth and Interpretation*, p. 129.

32 Davidson, 'A Nice Derangement of Epitaphs', in: E. LePore (ed.), *Truth and Interpretation*, p. 443.

33 Putnam, *Realism and Reason: Philosophical Papers*, p. 84.

34 See also R. Bernstein's description of a dialogue based on charity (although he does not call it 'charity'): 'Here one begins with the assumption that the other has something to say to us and to contribute to our understanding. The initial task is to grasp the other's position in the "strongest" possible light. One must always attempt to be responsive to what the other is saying and showing. This requires imagination, sensitivity and perfecting hermeneutical skills. There is a play, a to-and-fro movement in dialogical encounters, a seeking for a common ground in which we can understand our differences. The other is not an adversary or an opponent, but a conversational partner. Conflict is just as important in dialogical encounters, because understanding does not entail agreement.' (R. Bernstein, *The New Constellation: The Ethical-Political Horizons of Modernity/Postmodernity*, Polity Press, Cambridge 1991, pp. 336–337).

35 H. Putnam, 'The Question of Realism', in: H. Putnam, *Words and Life*, Cambridge University Press, Cambridge, 1994.

36 H. Putnam, 'Analyticity and Apriority: Beyond Wittgenstein and Quine', in: H. Putnam, *Reason, Truth and History*, Cambridge University Press, Cambridge 1981, p. 136.

37 *Ibid.*, p. 203.

38 H. Putnam, 'Why Reason Can't be Naturalized', in: H. Putnam, *Realism and Reason. Philosophical Papers, III*, Cambridge University Press, Cambridge 1983, p. 234.

39 H. Putnam, 'Analyticity and Apriority: Beyond Wittgenstein and Quine', in: H. Putnam, *Reason, Truth and History*, Cambridge University Press, Cambridge 1981, p.55.

40 'Theory of truth presupposes theory of rationality which in turn presupposes our theory of the good.' (Putnam, *Reason, Truth and History*, p. 215)

41 Similarly see Walter Benjamin: 'Die Sprache der Dinge kann in die Sprache der Erkenntnis und des Namens nur in der Übersetzung eingehen – so viele Übersetzungen, so viele Sprachen, sobald nämlich der Mensch einmal aus dem paradiesischen Zustand, der nur eine Sprache kannte, gefallen ist.' (W. Benjamin, *Über die Sprache überhaupt und über die Sprache des Menschen, Schriften II*, Suhrkamp Verlag, Frankfurt am Main 1955, p. 85.)

42 H. Putnam, *Reason, Truth and History*, p. 163

43 H. Putnam, 'Philosophers and Human Understanding', in: Putnam, *Realism and Reason*, p. 195.

44 H. Putnam, 'The Science-Ethics Distinction', in: M. Nussbaum and A. Sen (eds,), *The Quality of Life*, Oxford University Press, Oxford 1993, p. 156.

45 He thereby conflates theoretical with practical reason, assertive sentences with moral judgments and ends up with an epistemological understanding of democracy which does not allow him to account for justice-related reasoning (see: J. Habermas, 'Werte und Normen. Ein Kommentar zu Hilary Putnams kantischem Pragmatismus', in: *Deutsche Zeitschrift für Philosophie* 48:4, 2000, pp. 547–564).

46 J. Habermas, 'Hermeneutische und analytische Philosophie. Zwei komplementäre Spielarten der linguistischen Wende', in: J. Habermas, *Wahrheit und Rechtfertigung: Philosophische Aufsätze*, Suhrkamp Verlag, Frankfurt am Main 1999, p. 98. English translation follows: 'It is expected that discourse leads to a decentering of lifeworld perspectives. In cases of conflicts of interaction that have to do with morality, this decentering fosters the mutual expansion of each participant's horizon of value orientations.' ('Hermeneutic and Analytic Philosophy: Two Complementary Versions of the Linguistic Turn', in J. Habermas, *Truth and* Justification, MIT Press, Cambridge, MA, 2003, pp. 78–79.)

47 W. von Humboldt, *Werke*, vol. III, *Schriften zur Sprachphilosophie*, Wissenschaftliche Buchgesellschaft, Darmstadt 1963, p. 156.

48 W. von Humboldt, *Werke*, vol. III, *Schriften zur Sprachphilosophie*, Wissenschaftliche Buchgesellschaft, Darmstadt 1963, p. 225. English translation follows: 'But because we always carry over, more or less, our own world view, and even our own language-view, this outcome is not purely and completely experienced.' (W. von Humboldt, *On Language*, M. Losonsky (ed.), p. 60.)

49 B. Parekh has shown how debates about a minority practice have a profoundly transformative effect on all involved. It triggers off (self-reflexive) debates within the minority community, within the wider society, and between the two (see: B. Parekh, *Rethinking Multiculturalism: Cultural Diversity and Political Theory*, Macmillan, London 2000).

50 For a long time we knew very little about Bakhtin's intellectual life (1895–1975). One of the reasons is that his biography depends upon a network of (often contradictory) sources. Another reason is that so few of his texts were published at or near the time they were written. A third reason is the extensive reference to obscure literary figures (from classic and medieval sources of several languages) which accompany his works and the lack of secondary sources. On Bakhtin's myths and history see K. Hirschkop, *Mikhail Bakhtin: An Aesthetics for Democracy*, Oxford University Press, Oxford 1999, pp. 111–193.

51 *Ibid.*, pp. 225–248.

52 For the importance of a print culture in this development see: B. Anderson, *Imagined Community: Reflections on the Origin of Nationalism*, Verso, London 1983.

53 That is, the 'internal stratification of a unified national language' (M. Bakhtin, 'Discourse in the Novel', in: M. Bakhtin, *The Dialogic Imagination: Four Essays*, University of Texas Press, Austin 1981, p. 262). His emphasis on social language rather than individual voices is indicated by the shift in terminology from 'polyphony' to 'heteroglossia'.

54 *Ibid.*, p. 262.

55 This is exactly what de Saussure called 'language', but considered to be an inadequate start-ing point of linguistics because of his heterogeneity (F. de Saussure, *Cours de linguistique générale*, Payot, Paris 1922). He therefore elaborates a structuralist theory of language as a system of norms ('langue') which abstracts from an extralinguistic reality (the reference to something in the world, the relation between speaker and addressee, the socio-cultural context of an utterance, etc.).

56 M. Bakhtin, 'Notes Made in 1970–1971', in: M. Bakhtin, *Speech Genres and Other Late Essays*, Texas University Press, Austin 1986, p. 150.

57 See: V. Vološinov, *Marxism and the Philosophy of Language*, Harvard University Press, Cambridge, MA, 1986. The authorship of the books signed by Valentin Vološinov and Pavel Medvedev is unclear. I follow Todorov's thesis that these texts were outlined by Bakhtin but elaborated and formulated also by these two members of the 'Bakhtin circle'. For the reconstruction of Bakhtin's theory of language I therefore used the whole corpus of texts of the 'Bakhtin circle' (see: T. Todorov, *Mikhail Bakhtine, le principe dialogique*, Le Seuil, Paris 1981, p. 20).

58 Bakhtin's semiotic turn is, for example, strikingly similar to the early Charles S. Peirce (unknown, of course, in the Soviet Union at that time): 'Das Erlebnis – das Auszudrückende und seine äußere Objektivation – bestehen … aus ein und demselben Material. Denn es gibt kein Erlebnis ohne Zeicheninkarnation.' (V. Vološinov, *Marxismus und Sprachphilosophie*, Ullstein Verlag, Frankfurt am Main/Berlin 1975, p. 145.)

59 Bakhtin, 'The Problem of Speech Genres', in: Bakhtin, *Speech Genres and Other Late Essays*, p. 68.

60 For this kind of liberal interpretation which overlooks Bakhtin's emphasis on conflictual plurality and power see: C. Emerson and G. Morson, *Mikhail Bakhtin: Creation of Prosaics*, Stanford University Press, Stanford, CA, 1990; M. Holquist, *Dialogism: Bakhtin and his World*, Routledge, London/New York 1990.

61 M. Bakhtin, 'Notes made in 1970–71', in: Bakhtin, *Speech Genres and Other Late Essays*, p. 143.

62 J. Kristeva, *Essays in Semiotics*, Mouton, Paris 1971.

63 Accordingly, Bakhtin distinguishes between the 'theme' or 'actual meaning' of an utterance, which designates all that is contextually unique in the utterance, and its 'neutral significa-tion' which refers to those elements of the utterance – semantic, syntactic, etc. – which are not context-specific (cf. G. Frege's distinction between 'Bedeutung' and 'Sinn').

64 Bakhtin, 'Discourse in the Novel', in: Bakhtin, *The Dialogic Imagination*, p. 270.

65 Bakhtin conceives of dialogic relations not only among speakers but also (a) among whole utterances and words (the double-voiced micro-dialogue), (b) between language styles (perceived as semantic positions or world views) and (c) toward one's own utterance as a whole, its parts and even a word (if we distance ourselves from them, speak with inner reservation, etc.).

66 'Stratification and heteroglossia widen and deepen as long as language is alive and devel-oping.' (Bakhtin, 'Discourse in the Novel', in: Bakhtin, *The Dialogic Imagination*, p. 272.)

67 *Ibid.*, p. 282.

68 Hirschkop, *Mikhail Bakhtin*, p. 5.

69 For a lengthier discussion of this argument, see: P. Nanz, 'Vielstimmige Lebenswelt. Zum Begriff der "Redegenres" in der Sprachtheorie Mikhail Bakhtins', in: *Deutsche Zeitschrift für Philosophie* 2, 2003, pp. 199–212.

70 The structure of context has only lately become the focus of systematic attention (see for instance: A. Duranti and C. Goodwin, *Language as an Interactive Phenomenon*, Cambridge University Press, Cambridge 1992). Beyond sociolinguistics, the ethnography of speech and anthropological linguistics, contexts remain a poorly defined idea, an inert concept referring to an inert environment, a social frame within which specific actions or represen-tations can best be understood. Contexts are produced in the complex imbrication of dis-cursive and nondiscursive practices. From a sociocultural point of view, a theory of

globalization would require a theory of intercontextual relations (which cannot be conceived as intertextual relations). See: D. Hymes, *Foundations in Sociolinguistics: An Ethnographical Approach,* Tavistock, London 1977.

71 'Utterance' means speech act. It is Bakhtin's extension of what de Saussure called the 'parole' aspect of language, but where utterance is made specifically social, historical, concrete and dialogized (see: Vološinov, *Marxism and the Philosophy of Language,* p. 40).

72 M. Bakhtin, *Speech Genres and Other Late Essays.*

73 Speech genres seem more open to innovation than Wittgenstein's language games (see: Bakhtin, 'The Problem of Speech Genres', in: Bakhtin, *Speech Genres and Other Late Essays,* pp. 60–102). Bakhtin argues that understanding a language game or speech genre is only a necessary and not a sufficient condition of such a 'situational' understanding, since situations may be perceived and understood differently from different (and controversial) perspectives on situations.

74 Bakhtin distinguishes between primary (simple) and secondary (complex) speech genres. The latter arise in relatively highly developed and organized communication (socio-political, scientific, artistic and so on). During the process of their formation they absorb various primary speech genres that have taken form in unmediated everyday speech situations (talking to the neighbour about the weather, ordering a round of drinks etc.).

75 Existing social spaces, e.g. within a historically-produced neighbourhood and with a series of localized social practices, experts and informed audiences, are required in order for new members (strangers, guests, adolescents, etc.) to be made temporary or permanent local subjects. But these taken-for-granted localities contribute to the creation of contexts which might exceed their own existing material and conceptual boundaries: as social subjects engage in the social activities of production, representation, and reproduction, their aspirations extend marriage networks to new villages, fishing expeditions yield refinements of what are understood to be navigable and fish-rich waters, trading activities look for new commodity-worlds and thus new partnerships with as-yet-unencountered regional groupings, social conflicts force new strategies of exit and solutions, etc. All these cross-cultural encounters contribute to subtle shifts in language, world views, social practices, and collective self-understandings. In this sense, locality-producing activities are not only context-driven, but also generate their own larger context through interaction with social subjects beyond their community-boundaries. The extent to which such an interaction takes place, e.g. the Yanomami with the Brazilian and Venezuelan nation-state, is a matter of social power and the different scales of organization within which social spaces are embedded. Yet, today, the task of producing locality is increasingly a struggle, especially because of the growing disjuncture between territory, the formation of personal identity, and collective social movements and democratic politics, e.g. the disjuncture between neighbourhoods as social formations, and the mass-mediated discourses and transnational practices such as multiculturalism, human rights, and refugee claims (see: A. Appadurai, 'The Production of Locality', in: A. Appadurai, *Modernity at Large,* Minnesota University Press, Minneapolis, 1996).

76 It is only in the context of speech genres that modernity creates the secular, historical and differentiated world which gives actual intersubjectivity its shape (K. Hirschkop, 'It's Too Good to Talk: Myths and Dialogue in Bakhtin and Habermas', in: *New Formations* 41, 2000, p. 90).

77 A speech genre is also (re)produced in every utterance: 'A genre is always the same and yet not the same, always old and new simultaneously. … A genre lives in the present, but always remembers its past, its beginning.' (M. Bakhtin, 'The Characteristics of Genres and Plot', in: M. Bakhtin, *Problems of Dostoevsky,* Minnesota University Press, Minneapolis 1984, p. 106.)

78 Bakhtin, 'Discourse in the Novel', in: Bakhtin, *The Dialogic Imagination,* p. 343.

79 Bakhtin, 'The Problem of Speech Genres', in: M. Bakhtin, *Speech Genres and Other Late Essays,* p. 99.

80 Bakhtin, 'Discourse in the Novel', in: Bakhtin, *The Dialogic Imagination*, p. 348.

81 J. Habermas, 'The Normative Content of Modernity', in: J. Habermas, *The Philosophical Discourse of Modernity*, MIT Press, Cambridge, MA, 1987, p. 346.

82 Bakhtin conceives of the self as always directed towards an actual, concrete other. Such a self is radically multiple and unique when compared to the self portrayed by symbolic interactionists (e.g. G. H. Mead and C. Morris (eds.), *Mind, Self and Society*, University of Chicago Press, Chicago 1934) whose conception of the self seems more ossified in roles and in communities with a shared set of knowledge.

83 Regarding the concept of 'appropriation' see R. Chartier, *Cultural History: Between Practices and Representations*, Polity Press, Cambridge 1988.

84 Bakhtin, 'Discourse in the Novel', in: Bakhtin, *The Dialogic Imagination*, pp. 414–415.

85 Bakhtin points out that one can recover the 'concreteness' of language from two points of view: (a) from the point of view of a participant, meanings are concrete in so far as they are the sediment of an intersubjective encounter; their validity is inseparable from the ethical act of confronting another in discourse; (b) from the point of view of the observer/author, meanings are concrete when endowed with an aesthetic thickness and worldly weight which reflect their origins in a particular social situation.

86 Bakhtin conceptualizes a kind of representation of language, which, by sketching in the details of occasion, social context, speaker, and addressee, reveals the unique connection of that language with a certain social or public sphere and certain forms of practices and actions.

87 Cf. Habermas's 'yes or no position', J. Habermas, *Theorie des kommunikativen Handelns*, vol.1, Suhrkamp Verlag, Frankfurt am Main 1981, Chapter III.

88 Truth, in Bakhtin's view, is inseparable from the dialogical community maintained in its pursuit. This community points permanently to the possibility of a 'redeemed life' – it is a value in itself in a way that Habermas's discursive community is not.

89 Bakhtin, 'Discourse in the Novel', in: Bakhtin, *The Dialogic Imagination*, p. 352.

90 Even the self-transparancy of speakers is relative. In many cases – e.g. in philosophical discussions and especially in situations of indeterminacy of knowledge – we learn from the interpretations and responses of our interlocutors that we do not really know what we meant to say (A. Wellmer, 'Conditions of a Democratic Culture', in: A. Wellmer, *Endgames*, MIT Press, Cambridge, MA, 1998).

6

A situated constitutional patriotism beyond the nation-state

Im Diskurs soll sich eine Weltansicht am Widerspruch der anderen in der Weise abarbeiten, daß sich mit fortschreitender Dezentrierung der je eigenen Perspektive die Sinnhorizonte aller Beteiligten erweitern – und immer weitergehend überlappen.

Jürgen Habermas[1]

In this chapter I will address the question of how to conceive a European constitutional patriotism that has the necessary integrative force of mutual solidarity without thereby transcending cultural/ethical diversity through the idea of an overarching European political culture or *demos*. I will start by considering the problem of EU constitutionalization which is related to the problem of legitimacy. I will go on to reconstruct Habermas's proceduralist theory of constitutional deliberation and Michelman's critique of it. Finally, on the basis of the theory of mutual translation (as discussed in Chapter 5), I will propose a conceptualization of the constitutionalization of the EU as an ongoing exploration of different cultural/ethical perspectives which takes place both within formal institutions and the informal, wider public sphere. I will argue that with this conceptualization in hand, constitutional patriotism can be understood as a dialogical process of interpretative disagreement of principles which (re)produces shared (but always unstable) understandings. This does not mean that democratic politics is always and at all times involved in (re)interpreting constitutional principles, but that 'ordinary' politics cannot but be informed by such principles.[2]

The problem of legitimacy in the European Union

In general terms, the fundamental idea of democratic legitimacy is that

> the authorization to exercise state power must arise from the collective decisions of the members of a society who are governed by that power.[3]

A sovereign people impose the principles, rules and procedures of a political system on themselves, but are always able to call them into question and enter into (rule-governed) deliberations about them with those who govern. Put simply, legitimacy converts power into authority and, thereby, simultaneously establishes an obligation to obey and the right to rule. Its function is to ensure effective and democratic government in liberal polities: citizens are obliged to comply with government policies even if they violate their own interests or preferences. Government is obliged to serve the 'common good' of the respective constituency, which must be protected against both the self-interest of governors and the strategies of special societal interests or the potential tyranny of the majority. Legitimacy, therefore, depends on political institutions that protect public policy against both dangers (electoral accountability, independent judiciaries, complex interdependencies between political actors, etc.) and the trust of citizens in these institutions.[4] Finally, legitimacy makes up an important element of citizens' (political) identity. It is contextual or 'situated' because it is based on the shared norms of a particular community granting authority.

There are two closely inter-related dimensions of legitimacy:[5] on the one hand, there is the social dimension, which refers to the acceptance of political authority by citizens – that is, whether and to what extent authority is rooted in popular consent of a constituency. On the other hand, there is the normative dimension, which is concerned with the justifiability of political authority, or, whether or not its decision-making institutions are just and democratic. Social legitimacy is democratic only if it is grounded in a deeper normative legitimacy – that is, when the justificatory discourses of political authorities are 'checked' by citizens in the formation of the collective will and when they are 'tested' against the outcome of actual or hypothetical processes of public deliberation. Equally, normative legitimacy is only satisfactory when it is vindicated by social acceptance, or, when those affected by political authorities acknowledge that authorities in question as a component part of their political identity. That is why political theory that deals with the conditions under which government is legitimate, should be informed by sociological research on citizens' political loyalties and their sense of belonging to a political and legal community (see Part III).[6] Such a double disciplinary perspective allows us to reconstruct the meaning of collective identities and the understanding of citizenship in contemporary societies, as well as to recognize the value of these concepts for political theory.

In social scientific literature, legitimacy usually enters into the analytical picture either when it is missing or deficient. Only when a political order is being manifestly challenged by its citizens, do scholars tend to invoke a lack of legitimacy as a cause for crisis. When it is functioning well, legitimacy recedes into the background and citizens seem to take for granted that the actions of their political authorities are justified. If this is true for polities (i.e. national states) that have fixed boundaries, unique identities, established constitutions, well-established practices and sovereignty over other claimants to authority, it is much more difficult to imagine legitimacy in the case of a polity 'above the nation-state', as, for example, the EU. There is a widespread perception (in the academic world, as well as with the general public) of a deficiency in the EU's democratic credentials. From a normative point of view, European citizens are, under current conditions, only the addressees of binding and coercive Community law, and are not the ultimate authors of the basic laws and constitutional principles that constitute a polity.[7] While this system of political authority is based on international treaties and, therefore, has its ultimate source of legitimacy in the sovereignty of the member states, the authority of the single nation-state is nonetheless being undermined by the EU institutions' accretion of substantial authority. The member states do not control the constitutional-legal context within which the European-level decision-making process takes place; furthermore, EU law is gradually developing into an autonomous, distinct and independent supranational legal order, the provisions of which take precedence over national law and are directly applicable to the citizens of the member states. The resulting democratic deficit can therefore be formulated as 'the possibly unbridgeable discrepancy between the pervasive effects of the regulative power of the EU and the weak authorisation of this power through the citizens of the Member States who are specifically affected by those regulations'.[8]

From an empirical point of view, there is a widespread perception of a lack of a European (political) identity. In the literature on integration, we find profound disagreement among scholars as to the impact of EU institutions on identities. It is still questionable whether European citizens acknowledge that the EU provides a framework of norms which connects them to the authoritative institutions of the Union in a chain of reciprocal rights and obligations. In any case, there is a significant gap, wider in some countries than in others, between elite and mass attitudes towards the EU.[9] Empirical research on public attitudes toward the EU generally has characterized the public's outlook as 'permissive consensus' that supports elite initiatives favouring more integration without actively demanding such steps.[10] Their attachment to EU institutions – what could be called 'patriotism' – is still weak. It seems clear that a European (political) identity will not take on a national shape. But the question remains open as to whether Habermas's idea of a constitutional patriotism – linked to a thin (post-national) identity – is enough to foster mutual commitment among fellow Europeans and a spirit of transnational cooperation. Or, perhaps the conception of constitutional patriotism should be better 'situated', incorporating substantive features of self-imagining or a 'common desire to live together' (Ernest Renan) into its formulation of democracy. But this is a point that I will later return to.

Let us first re-examine the concept of 'constitutional patriotism'[11] with respect to the EU. How can European political institutions draw their legitimacy from citizens' commitment to constitutional principles?[12] How can we, given the enormous cultural and ethical diversity within the European polity, foresee the power of EU institutions (and in particular the primacy and direct effect of EU law over national law) as the political will of the public – that is, of free and equal citizens acting as a collective body?[13] According to the liberal principle of legitimacy,

> our exercise of political power ... is justifiable only when it is exercised in accordance with a constitution the essentials of which all citizens may be expected to endorse in the light of principles and ideals acceptable to them as reasonable and rational.[14]

The goal of constitutional theory is to show that democracy, rather than a mere aggregation of individual interests, involves the mutual justification of political choices by citizens in the light of a shared understanding of constitutional principles. This constitutionalist justification of politics takes place not only in strong institutionalized (democratic and constitutional) procedures, but also in a decentred public sphere where citizens deliberate about fundamental questions which affect the integration of society and ask for normatively legitimate treatment (see Chapter 3). The idea is that constitutional law is a 'higher' law that is sufficiently removed from the pluralism of citizens' world views and interests to allow it to be reasonably acceptable to all. It is in this sense that we refer to a constitution as expressing what citizens hold in common beyond their differences, which is to say, their shared constitutional identity.

As early as 1991, the European Court of Justice started referring to EU treaties as collectively forming a constitution for Europe. At the same time, it is evident that the EU, even if the Constitutional Treaty is enacted, is not comparable to a traditional state. Much would have to be said about the language of European constitutionalism and the questions it raises about the adequate institutional embodiment of constitutional ideals in transnational political and legal practices, but this is not the place here.[15] Rather, it is important to notice that constitutional patriotism does not necessarily mean a commitment to a particular constitution (e.g. the Constitutional Treaty), but to its underlying constitutional ideals or principles and European constitutional practices seen as a whole.[16] And, as we will see, these ideals, together with their more practical and institutional implications, remain open to contestation and interpretations from heterogeneous national perspectives.

Michelman's idea of the constitutionalist justification of politics

Michelman argues that in contemporary liberal-minded forms of political justification the idea of the democratic constitution is 'pivotal', 'because there can be no settled agreement among the governed on a description of the actual thing in all its concrete specificity'.[17] The diversity of citizens' comprehensive outlooks reaches 'all the way up' into the realm of constitutional interpretations. Constitutional principles cannot be applied to real social controversies without some further specification that will itself necessarily be open to different interpretations. If discussing multicultural issues, for example, we often (mostly implicitly) disagree about the application and meaning of constitutional principles. Parents who wish to withdraw their children from religious education, for example, might appeal to a constitutional principle of religious freedom. The 'higher law' of lawmaking is itself up for grabs in political disputes over the application of constitutional principles to major classes of cases. Thus, we need constitutional patriotism as an empirical warrant to morally motivate people to see themselves as co-participants in the constitutional justification of politics.

Michelman distinguishes three features of the constitutionalist justification of politics – namely, universalism, legal dualism and moral responsivism. According to the first of these, universalism,

> everyone, each judging from his or her own standpoint and with due regard for his or her own interests, should be able to see how everyone else, each judging similarly, could find prevailing reason to accept the political act in question.[18]

In other words, the legitimacy of intersubjective norms should ultimately be judged from the allegedly ethically neutral perspective of communicative rationality or 'inclusive discourse'.[19] In the case of legal dualism, the acceptance of a constitutional lawmaking system as right or as fair and worthy of respect, commits one to accept as legitimate whatever decisions issue from that system. Michelman's third feature, moral responsivism, is the presupposition that participants consider themselves to be among a company of free and equal co-inhabitants, all of whom are under the same moral motivational pressure to find agreement on fair terms of cooperation. Before moving on, we might briefly note that in order to have practical bite, the criterion of universalism must involve acceptability, not acceptance – that is, hypothetical consent rather than an agreement in actual democratic practice.[20]

Michelman's argument is that the universal appeal or acceptability of a given set of constitutional principles 'must presuppose the experience by all concerned of that particular, empirically contingent moral motivation' which arises from seeing oneself as a co-participant in a collective constitutional project. Moral justification of constitutional democracy cannot be explained without attributing to everyone a certain empirical attitude, that is, a socio-historically situated constitutional patriotism. According to Michelman, constitutional patriotism is the cultural substratum[21] or empirical warrant that is necessary to bridge the conceptual gap in proceduralist theory between hypothetical consent to constitutional principles and the actual constitutional justification of politics. The core of constitutional patriotism is

> the morally justified readiness of a country's people to accept disagreement over the application of constitutional principles, without loss of confidence in the univocality of the principles, because and as long as they can understand the disagreement as strictly tied to struggles over constitutional identity [which is] to a certain degree known and fixed.[22]

Only citizens' loyalty to the ethical bases of the democracy of their country can transform their disagreement over the interpretation of constitutional principles into differences that remain internal to a collectively shared discourse about a community's political identity or self-understanding. With regard to the EU, this could mean that constitutional patriotism signifies the willingness 'to reflect on the ethical components of the historical identities of Europe'.[23]

Against this cultural/ethical reading, Habermas insists on the universalistic core of constitutional patriotism. Proceduralist theories of democratic legal and political procedures are meant to protect the 'discursive level of public debate'[24] and the use of practical reason. Procedural rules serve to integrate citizens into a community of justification. They shape public deliberation, thereby prescribing the limits of cultural/ethical diversity, and structure the political debate about minority practices by ensuring that the settlement of claims to equality and justice does not depend on the vagaries of normal politics (i.e. are ruled out by majority votes). However, Habermas's post-nationalism tends to underestimate the indeterminacy of procedural rules or constitutional ideals. There can be disagreement even about discursive norms, and the nature of 'rational' procedures or 'just' genres of discourse. What we mean when we refer to the idea of public deliberation can itself become a crucial issue of political debate. It is, in fact, through deliberative practices that we eventually agree upon a common standard for what counts as reasonable. The interpretation of 'just' procedures cannot be safeguarded against pluralism. There are no uncontroversial principles for deciding the procedures by which to settle 'reasonable disagreement'. Thus, the aspiration of procedural constitutional theory to establish a set of relatively removed, framing principles for a lawmaking system leads to an infinite regress. In other words, democratic procedures are themselves always embedded in the particular social practices of an actual historical community. The debate about the substance of the institutional arrangements of deliberative democracy remains open-ended. Nonetheless, a shared political culture with a given set of social practices – able to unify citizens beyond their different ethical life forms or sub-cultures – itself includes a certain, socio-historically situated mode of public discourse and of self-understanding, and a particular set of political values (e.g. socio-cultural pluralism, human rights and so on). If so, then in a formal-pragmatic theory of discourse, procedures, 'identical meanings' of principles and 'a shared political culture' remain quasi-substantialist reminiscences.

Toward a situated constitutional patriotism

Whereas Michelman emphasizes that the idea of constitutional patriotism refers to a community's concrete ethical character,[25] Habermas insists on its universalistic core, beyond the particularism of any specific national (political) culture.[26] I want to defend a third position, however, in which a contextualized or situated constitutional patriotism can nonetheless have a universalistic core. This position relies on the 'dynamizing' of situatedness – that is, on conceiving cultural/ethical pluralism as an epistemic resource for an ongoing process of constitutional interpretation. In the resulting dialogical or interdiscursive approach, the residual substantialism of a shared political culture or the meta-values of a concrete ethical community are internalized by the participants of political justification as the idealized shared meanings of the constitutional principles to which interpretative disagreement refers. In this ongoing exploration of perspectives, the semantic or (substantive) world-disclosing dimension of language, which Humboldt once emphasized, is linked to its (universalizing) formal-pragmatic dimension.[27]

Following the argument made in Chapter 5, we can therefore conceive of democratic procedures as idealized patterns of intercultural or interethical deliberation; a translational constitution, so to speak. The meaning of 'just' procedures and the 'best' interpretation of principles is constantly (re)negotiated in public discourse, thereby always remaining exposed to different cultural/ethical perspectives. As we have seen, validity claims are necessary idealizations in communicative interaction (Putnam, Habermas). Validity claims, however, are always made from a certain cultural/ethical perspective, which is the 'facticity' of convictions and the state of affairs they call into question: constitutional patriotism is always 'situated' within particular social practices. Or, as Bakhtin would say, constitutional dialogues have specific socio-historical forms or genres, which are themselves negotiated between participants. In their concrete socio-historically contextualized shape, procedures (e.g. the modes of political deliberation in the European Parliament) can be more or less dialogical (or oppressive towards alternative modes of discourse),[28] or more or less conducive to the deliberative-democratic ideal of respecting the beliefs of others, even if they ultimately question the very reasonableness of these procedures.

Because of the indeterminacy of the meaning of principles and rights, the idea of a constitution is more like an endless series of negotiations and agreements (on shared understandings) reached by intercultural/ethical public deliberation, than an original contract reached in the distant past. In this sense, a constitution can be seen as citizenship practices involving the constant exploration of different (constitutional) interpretations which are institutionalized in democratic politics.[29] It corresponds to the idea of *constitutional horizontalization,* which understands citizens as constitutional interpreters in an ongoing process of social learning. In this sense, the deliberative force of social integration arises not only from participants' (formal) reciprocal recognition of one another, but also from the 'charity' of trying to understand the (substantial) difference or distinctness of the other's world view (cf. Humboldt's idea of mutual understanding as also recognizing the non-identical or non-shared, the *gebrochene Intersubjektivität*). It is this interpretative charity, the ability to change perspective (reflexive disequilibrium), which empirically counterbalances the ambiguity or indeterminacy of meaning. The everyday mastery of intra- and inter-linguistic translation or intercultural/interethical communication is not qualitatively different from the understanding demanded by constitutional dialogue. In both cases, the shared meaning of a term or principle is semiotically (re)negotiated between alter and ego (see Chapter 5).

Mutual translation can only come from engaging in practical discourse. We need public deliberation as a form of citizenship practice in order to become aware of all the different existing perspectives and interpretations of constitutional rights. The constitutionalist justification of politics cannot mean that we suppose ourselves to have understood things from the other's viewpoint simply 'by representing to ourselves imaginatively the many perspectives of those involved'.[30] Rather, mutual understanding arises only from engaging in (intra- and intercultural and intra- and interethical) translation and retranslation of a practical dialogue, in which each participant is gradually able to see a given issue or social conflict from the point of view of the other and to subsequently put together an acceptable inter-cultural/interethical 'translational constitution' capable of accommodating each world view. In this way, we understand the concept of constitutionalization of a polity as the weaving together, rather than the fusing, of many perspectives:

> In spinning a thread we twist fibre on fibre. And the strength of the thread does not reside in the fact that some fibre runs through its whole length, but in the overlapping of many fibres.[31]

In pluralist societies, cultures or world views encounter one another formally and informally in the public realm. Guided by curiosity, incomprehension or the desire to settle a conflict, they interrogate one another, challenge one another's assumptions, widen their horizons, eventually establish agreements, and undergo both major and minor revisions (intercultural learning) to their own views. Even when actors' interactions are limited, the very awareness of other perspectives and traditions alerts each to its own contingency, and subtly changes the manner in which people define and relate to it (reflexivity). Constitutional patriotism rests on a critical relationship to one's history: It demands that political communities (through an obligation of remembrance) come to terms with repugnant legacies.[32] The idea is that – through intercultural or transnational dialogue – Europeans learn to resist uncritical identification with a 'closed' national memory and recognise instead the crimes committed against others. Here, I would like to follow Etienne Balibars' depiction of European history as a series of successive encounters between cultures, which keeps taking place *within* its territory, enclosing cultural patterns from the whole world: the idea of 'Europe as Borderland', as 'Cross-Over' or 'overlapping folds'.[33]

The fact that cultures or world views are not excluded from the public sphere ensures that political culture itself is an object of democratic deliberation. Through the practices of this kind of intercultural/interethical dialogue, participants will tend to produce a new composite political culture which builds on their respective contributions and insights. Such an 'interdiscursive' or 'pastiche' political culture rests on neither the lowest common denominator, nor an abstract commitment to political institutions purified of socio-cultural traditions (as is suggested by some of Habermas's formulations);[34] but rather a more or less distinct mode of political deliberation (a speech genre) in which both substantive beliefs and traditions and the modes of deliberation themselves are constantly redefined and brought into a new relationship to other perspectives, composing a loosely-knit whole or 'thread'.[35]

Learning and solidarity across national and cultural boundaries

Active participation in dialogue helps one to develop a reflective attitude towards one's view and to gain conceptual clarity about another's points of view. This then becomes the basis for new interpretations, which can reconcile normative standards of justice with divergent conceptions regarding facts and norms. In this way, public deliberation leads to an intercultural/interethical learning process whereby one comes to acknowledge and appreciate other people's unique, different and multiple ways of being. With regard to political justification, this dialogical notion of learning is weaker than a search for consensus (the transcending of difference), but is certainly stronger then a mere compromise ('tit for tat') between the exogenous constitutional interpretations or preferences of actors. Accordingly, a dialogical notion of solidarity[36] is both universalistic and situated at the same time. It is more than mere tolerance or (formal) respect for the other – it engages in and is generated by actual intercultural/interethical dialogue with a concrete other, trying to understand his or her needs or interests – but less than a communal feeling or intimacy based on the parochial sameness of a culture or *demos* – it aims to have collective political concerns viewed reciprocally from the other's perspective, thereby exposing every viewpoint to criticism. Such reflective solidarity[37] is capable of dealing with plurality and avoids the problem of exclusion which affects conventional solidarities since it is based on the integrative force of dialogue. In the process of learning about different perspectives or interpretations of constitutional principles, the 'we' of a community of political justification is always (re)negotiated and inclusive – there is an in-built drive to expand its boundaries in order to explore the possibilities arising from the application of new viewpoints to social problems or to the interpretation of a constitution. Constitutional patriotism presupposes a 'postconventional' ego-identity[38] that has learned to do without the certitudes of tradition and social convention (see Chapter 7). Accordingly, a 'post-conventional' collective identity is the appropriate form of affect for a mature politics that has outgrown the need for 'a prior homogeneity of descent or form of life'.[39]

In pluralistic societies, rather than finding a few moral axioms that no reasonable person could reject, the aim is to construct an interpretation of procedural rules that all reasonable persons can be asked to share and, through which, we can aim for the widest possible comprehension (from all perspectives) when settling disagreements. Only in few cases do we find a plural public sphere and a political culture based on broad cross-cultural consensus. As political dialogue occurs within a particular society (with a unique moral structure and history), disagreements are not about whether a disputed social practice is desirable in general, but whether it is desirable in a *specific* society, in accordance with *its* constitutional principles. The meaning of 'gender equality', for example, is not the same over time or space. Meanings and principles are not static, but change in response to developments in societal circumstances and self-understandings.

Meanings and principles are idealizations which have to be intersubjectively recognized in order for communication to be possible at all. If we recognize the other's viewpoint not only formally, but try to see the world from her or his perspective, we recognize her or his (substantive) distinctiveness or otherness through capturing the (semantic) world-disclosing dimension of language, genre, argumentative style etc. 'Multicultural literacy' presupposes considerable interpretative charity. Unless an interpretation is patently irrelevant or wholly unintelligible to others, it cannot be ruled out. Inclusive political dialogue, understood as mutual translation, generates a broadly shared constitutional identity or common framework of discourse. While nurturing a wide plurality of views, it improves the quality of deliberation and fosters a common sense of belonging which is based on mutual commitment to a political community or shared citizenship. In this dialogical perspective, the aim of political deliberation is not exclusively to resolve contentious issues, but also to deepen mutual understanding between people of different world views – that is, to enlarge their mentality, to sensitize each to the concerns and needs of the other and to build up a 'dialogical' or 'reflective' solidarity among participants.

As previously argued, in the political realm, the semiotic dialectic of the centripetal and centrifugal forces of language can be interpreted as a dialectic of the unifying discourses of norms and the plurality of contextual discourses of values; of the shared interpretation of constitutional principles and heterogeneous ethical self-understandings and social practices. The universalistic idea of constitutional patriotism is understood here as a deliberative process involving the interpretative disagreement about principles. The idea is that shared meanings (i.e. language as a system of identical norms) and shared interpretations of constitutional principles are both the precondition (as idealizations) and the ultimate outcome of communication. The meaning of utterances and of constitutional principles is only available through an ongoing process of interpretation in particular contexts. There can be no non-interpretative grasp of the 'objective' meaning of a word or of a constitutional norm.[40] Since the constitution is not a closed or homogenous space of meaning, the fantasy that the 'right' laws or constitution might some day free us from political responsibility is to be rejected. Because of the ambiguity or indeterminacy of meaning, constitutional interpretations are never settled, always remaining exposed to critique and contestation. At the same time, however, constitutional interpretations, because they always take place in the public realm of reasons, are never an arbitrary imputation of meaning in an utterance or text. They have to be intersubjectively justified within democratic politics that are understood as an ongoing constitutional project for which pluralism is an enriching rather than inhibiting force.

In this radically proceduralized constitutional patriotism (in contrast to Michelman's version), disagreements and conflicts are not checked by a shared political culture, but are resources for an 'epistemic' struggle of perspectives in search of the interpretation of principles most suitable to a given case. Shared meanings and interpretations are always in process, they are never faits accomplis. Reasonably radical pluralism is counterbalanced by interpretative charity or the capacity for 'multicultural literacy' (i.e. the willingness to see the world from the viewpoints of other participants). This functions as an empirical warrant for the constitutional project of citizens who have internalized their orientation towards the idealized shared meanings of principles.

As discussed in Chapter 5, it is discursive practice that always determines anew what elements of the semantic reservoir of potential meanings will count as conceptual norms. With a theory of interpretation that is both pragmatic and semantic, the plurality of world-disclosing perspectives, instead of being contained by a shared ethics or political culture, can be conceived as a resource for the exploration of sometimes surprisingly innovative interpretations. In such a dialogical or 'interdiscursive' concept of politics, plurality is reasonably radicalized. Just as meaningful dialogue presupposes a plurality of speakers with their different understandings (their non-identical socio-cultural situatedness), controversies about the correct interpretation of constitutional principles are part of their very being. Plurality can therefore be seen as a precious asset. A democracy which values (individual, group-based and national) self-interpretation, world views and ways of knowing as worthy of consideration in the encounters of public life, gradually expands its horizon of enquiry so as to encompass new data, new hypotheses, and new solutions to problems. In a process of epistemic contention, which forces us to revise conceptual norms, our vocabularies are subject to (empirically-driven) alteration.[41] Without conceiving the plurality of world-projects across the board, there would be no moment of freedom or indeterminacy, and no chance for innovative interpretations. Interpretative innovation, however, is not a self-sufficient game (i.e. the purely poetic force of the extraordinary) if 'checked' through world-knowledge. Being embedded in the discursive practice of giving and asking for reasons, semantically relevant learning processes – which may, for example, lead to a changed interpretation of constitutional principles – have to be intersubjectively recognized.

In summary, it may be concluded that constitutional patriotism cannot but be situated; there is no view from nowhere, no non-interpretative grasp of constitutional principles. However, we do not need to be afraid of the disintegrating force of different viewpoints or non-shared meanings in communication as long as they are always already articulated within a project of mutual justification. Diversity also provides the polity with a positive critique of its institutions, which is vital if such institutions are to remain responsive and dynamic.[42] This does not mean that a constitutional project presupposes membership of a certain political culture or community, because its meaning or boundaries can themselves be a crucial object of contention (as for example in the case of Europe). Interpretations of constitutional principles are socio-historically situated but always exposed to new decentralizations of meanings. Constitutional patriotism can thus be conceived as an institutionalized 'exploration of difference' or intercultural/interethical translation which presupposes the constant willingness to see the world from another's perspective. In a manner that reasonably radicalizes cultural/ethical pluralism, the core of constitutional patriotism can then be seen as the readiness of a people to accept disagreement about the application of constitutional principles without loss of confidence in their idealized univocality – that is, provided that they understand this disagreement as strictly tied to the co-operative project of exploring different possible interpretations in order to (re)generate a shared understanding of the principles and find the best possible solution for the settlement of concrete socio-cultural disagreements. In this way, the (substantive) semantic divergence of meaning or the situated interpretations of constitutional principles are bound to the pragmatic function of dialogue (i.e. alter and ego's joint commitment to learn from each other's competing accounts and viewpoints). If we take multicultural literacy or mutual translation to be a heuristic device for the practice of constitutional justification, the acknowledgment of alter and ego's reciprocal claim to (formal) equality is accompanied by the motivational resources of charity and curiosity, which are necessary preconditions for learning about alter's (substantive) distinctness or difference. In Part III of the book, I will set out to explore the specific role that these two conditions play in shaping the experiences of migrants living in Germany. And in doing so, the book can now turn from theory to empirics.

Notes

1 J. Habermas, 'Hermeneutische und analytische Philosophie: Zwei komplementäre Spielarten der linguistischen Wende', in: J. Habermas, *Wahrheit und Rechtfertigung: Philosophische Aufsätze*, Suhrkamp Verlag, Frankfurt am Main 1999, p. 73. English translation follows: 'In discourse a worldview is supposed to prove itself against the opposition of others in such a way that, with the progressive decentering of individual perspectives, the meaning horizons of all participants expand – and increasingly come to overlap.' ('Hermeneutic and Analytic Philosophy: Two Complementary Versions of the Linguistic Turn', in: J. Habermas, *Truth and* Justification, MIT Press, Cambridge, MA, 2003, p. 58.)

2 Although we cannot transform and abrogate basic rights and liberties without extremely elaborate political and juridical procedures, we are always discussing their meaning, their extent and their jurisdiction. Principles guide politics by ruling out certain policies as unacceptable, requiring others, and often leaving a range of permitted policies (see: A. Føllesdal, 'Union Citizenship: Unpacking the Beast of the Burden', in: *Law and Philosophy* 20:3, 2001, p. 327).

3 J. Cohen, 'Procedure and Substance in Deliberative Democracy', in: S. Benhabib (ed.), *Democracy and Difference: Contesting the Boundaries of the Political*, Princeton University Press, Princeton 1996, p. 95.

  See also Rawls's famous formulation of the liberal principle of legitimacy: 'Our exercise of political power is fully proper only when it is exercised in accordance with a constitution the essentials of which all citizens as free and equal may reasonably be expected to endorse in the light of principles and ideals acceptable to their common human reason' (J. Rawls, *Political Liberalism*, Columbia University Press, New York 1993, p. 137).

4 To be sure, democratic legitimacy, i.e. legitimacy provided by democratic procedure, is not the only basis for legitimacy. Others are, for example, the rule of law, the protection of human rights and fundamental liberties, the problem-solving capacity etc.

5 For a more elaborate discussion see: P. Nanz, 'Democratic Legitimacy and Consitutionalisation of Transnational Trade Governance: A View from Political Theory', in C. Joerges and E.-U. Petersmann (eds.), *Constitutionalism, Multilevel Trade Governance and*

Social Regulation, Hart Publishing, Oxford 2006.

6 See also S. Benhabib, *Kulturelle Vielfalt und demokratische Gleichheit: Politische Partizipation im Zeitalter der Globalisierung*, Fischer Verlag, Frankfurt am Main 1999.

7 The democratic deficit in the emerging supranational system of political authority shared among the EU member states has been largely discussed in the literature. See: De Bùrca Gràinna, 'The Quest of Legitimacy in the European Union', in: *The Modern Law Review* 59:3, 1996, pp. 349–376; W. Norman, 'Justice and Stability in multinational societies', in: A. Gagnon and J. Tully (eds.), Multinational Democracies, Cambridge University Press, Cambridge, 2001, pp. 90–109; O. Gerstenberg, 'Law's Polyarchy: A Comment on Cohen and Sabel', in: O. Gerstenberg and C. Joerges (eds.), *Private Governance, Democratic Constitutionalism and Supranationalism*, European Communities, Brussels 1998, pp. 31–46; D. Grimm, 'Does Europe need a Constitution?', in: *European Law Journal* 1:3, 1995, pp. 282–302; J. Weiler, 'The Transformation of Europe', in: *The Yale Law Journal* 100, 1991, pp. 2403–2483; J. Weiler, *The Constitution of Europe: 'Do the New Clothes Have an Emperor' and Other Essays on European Integration*, Cambridge University Press, Cambridge 1999.

8 U. K. Preuss, 'Citizenship and Democracy in Europe: Foundations and Challenges', paper presented at the Conference on European Citizenship at Columbia University, 21 November 2003 [on file with the author], p. 5.

9 In 1996, Eurobarometer conducted what it called a *Top Decision-Takers Survey*, which asked the respondents whether their countries' membership in the EU was a 'good' or a 'bad' thing, and whether their country had benefited from membership (Eurobarometer, 'The European Union: "A view from the top"', 1996). Among these top decision makers, 94% concluded that their country's membership was a 'good' thing, and 90% felt that their country had benefited from membership. These figures were far higher than recorded among the wider population, and there was far less variation than found in the attitudes of the mass public.

10 See J. Citrin and J. Sides, 'More Than Just Nationals: How Identity Choice Matters in the New Europe', in: R. H. Herrmann, T. Risse and M. B. Brewer (eds.), *Transnational Identities: Becoming European in the EU*, Rowman & Littlefield, New York 2004, pp. 161–185. The data available to us via Eurobarometer unfortunately provide no information about the subjective conceptions of European identity.

11 The term 'constitutional patriotism' was first coined by Dolf Sternberger, see: J. Habermas, *The New Conservatism: Cultural Criticism and the Historians' Debate*, MIT Press, Cambridge, MA, 1989, p. 193.

12 For the conceptual link between legitimacy and constitutional patriotism see: C. Laborde, 'From Constitutional to Civic Patriotism', in: *British Journal of Political Science* 32, 2002, pp. 591–612.

13 As Joshua Cohen has argued, it is the fact of reasonable pluralism that constitutes the core conceptions of democracy, namely the conception of citizens as free and equal: 'To say that citizens are free is to say, inter alia, that no comprehensive moral or religious view provides a defining condition of membership or the foundation of the authorization to exercise political power. To say that they are equal is to say that each is recognized as having the capacities required for participating in discussion aimed at authorizing the exercise of power. (J. Cohen, 'Procedure and Substance in Deliberative Democracy', in: S. Benhabib (ed.), *Democracy and Difference: Contesting the Boundaries of the Political*, Princeton University Press, Princeton 1996, p. 96.)

14 J. Rawls, *Political Liberalism*, Columbia University Press, New York 1993, p. 217.

15 According to Mattias Kumm, there are four challenges to European constitutionalism: constitutional supremacy, democracy, subsidarity and human rights (see: M. Kumm, 'The Idea of a Thick Constitutional Patriotism and its Implications for the Role and the Structure of European Legal History', in: *German Law Journal* 6:2, 2005, p. 349).

16 *Ibid.*, p. 353.

17 F. Michelman, 'Morality, Identity and "Constitutional Patriotism"', in: *Denver University*

Law Review 76:4, 2000, p. 1010.

18 *Ibid.*, p. 1015.

19 'A law is valid ... when [it] could be accepted by everybody from the perspective of each individual.' (J. Habermas, *The Inclusion of the Other*, MIT Press, Cambridge, MA, 1996, p. 31).

20 F. Michelman, 'The Problem of Constitutional Interpretative Disagreement: Can "Discourses of Application" Help?', in: Aboulafia M., Bookman M. and Kemps C. (eds.), *Habermas and Pragmatism*, Routledge, New York 2002, p. 6.

21 To be fair, Michelman's notion of politics does not always have this ethical/cultural over-load as it may seem from his critique of Habermas, but is also envisioned as a 'field of epistemic contention – an encounter among world views, self-understandings, and ways of knowing' (F. Michelman, 'Private Personal But not Split: Radin versus Rorty', in: *Southern California Law Review* 63:6, 1990, p. 1786).

22 Michelman, 'Morality, Identity and "Constitutional Patriotism"', p. 1032 fo.

23 See Laborde, 'From Constitutional to Civic Patriotism', p. 601.

24 J. Habermas, *Between Facts and Norms*, MIT Press, Cambridge, MA, 1996, p. 304.

25 Such an interpretation is similar to the idea of a 'civic patriotism', see Laborde, 'From Con-stitutional to Civic Patriotism', p. 601.

26 For a 'neutralist' interpretation of J. Habermas conception, see: J. Lacroix, 'For a European Constitutional Patriotism', in: *Political Studies* 50, 2002, pp. 944–958.

27 Michelman misinterprets Humboldt's idea of world views as a plurality of mutually non-translatable, 'semantically closed universes'.

28 In intercultural dialogue there are for instance different kind of arguments which do or do not count in the political discourse of a certain community (e.g. analogical arguments: since cohabitation with multiple partners is allowed, polygamy should be as well). See: B. Parekh, *Rethinking Multiculturalism*, Macmillan, London 2000, p. 294.

29 This may lead to an institutional arrangement which shifts the burden of public decision-making from the formal institutions of representative democracy back to civil society. Through a theory of 'directly-deliberative polyarchy' O. Gerstenberg and C. Sabel have interpreted the 'exploration of difference' as a new principle of differential, democratic problem-solving, thereby broadening the debate about the possibilities of EU constitutionalization and democratization. O. Gerstenberg and C. Sabel, 'Directly-Delib-erative Polyarchy: An Institutional Ideal for Europe?', in: R. Dehousse and C. Joerges (eds.), *Good Governance and Administration in Europe's Integrated Market. (Collected Courses of the Academy of European Law, XI)*, Oxford University Press, Oxford 2002.

30 S. Benhabib, *Situating the Self*, Routledge, London/New York 1992, p. 52.

31 L. Wittgenstein, *Philosophical Investigations*, Blackwell, Oxford 1967, p. 67.

32 In contrast, David Miller argues for the necessity of a 'thick' national identity that 'depends on a pre-reflexive sense that one belongs to a certain historical group' (D. Miller, *On Na-tionality*, Oxford University Press, Oxford 1995, p. 143). According to him a national iden-tity 'involves an essentially historical understanding in which the present generation are seen as heirs to a tradition which they then pass on their successors' (*ibid.*, p. 175).

33 E. Balibar, 'Europe as Borderland, Lecture Presented in Human Geography', University of Nijmegen, 10 November 2004 [on file with the author] and E. Balibar, *We, the People of Europe?*, Princeton University Press, Princeton 2004.

34 The binding force of the common political culture becomes progressively more 'abstract' and 'neutral' as subcultures reduce it to a common denominator, without losing its bind-ing force of integrating a multicultural society (J. Habermas, 'The Nation, the Rule of Law, and Democracy', in: Habermas, *The Inclusion of the Other*, p. 146.)

35 The cultural fibres of that thread may not be equally 'strong': 'Since cultures are not equal in their vitality and richness, their respective contributions might not carry equal convic-tion with others and find an equal space in the common culture that eventually emerges from their dialogue.' (Parekh, *Rethinking Multiculturalism: Cultural Diversity and Political*

Theory, p. 221.)

36 This is in a sense similar to Arendt's notion of a deliberate, impartial solidarity or civic friendship which is the political virtue of the public realm, since they alone 'make political demands and preserve reference to the world' (H. Arendt, *Men in Dark Times*, Harcourt Brace, New York 1968, p. 25). Therefore Arendt insists that the spaces within persons – or the spaces of unshared meaning in the *gebrochene Intersubjektivität* – must not be closed. This is why the inner multiplicity of the self and the plurality of the public realm are conditions of action and politics.

37 In a different way, Jodi Dean has argued for a model of 'dialogical' solidarity based on dissent in which participants addressing one another invoke a 'situated hypothetic third' as the position of the differend that may always be there but silenced (J. Dean, *Solidarity with Strangers: Feminism after Identity Politics*, University of California Press, Berkeley, CA, 1996, p. 174). I share with her the emphasis of critical reflection which is in-built in the notion of dialogical solidarity, but stress the importance of actual participation of concrete thirds, i.e. the fact that we cannot put ourselves in the shoes of others and paternalistically 're-place' their voice, but have to engage in practical dialogue *with* them.

38 J. Habermas, 'Individuation through Socialization: On Mead's Theory of Subjectivity', in: J. Habermas, *Postmetaphysical Thinking: Philosophical Essays*, MIT Press, Cambridge, MA, 1992.

39 Habermas, *Between Facts and Norms*, p. 496.

40 The fact that constitutional principles are only accessible through interpretation constitutes the pragmatic-hermeneutic circle of democratic discourse. See: A. Wellmer, 'Conditions of a Democratic Culture', in: A. Wellmer, *Endgames*, MIT Press, Cambridge, MA, 1998, p. 45.

41 'Only when agents distance themselves from their practical dealings with the world and enter argumentation or rational discourse, objectifyng the situation "ready to hand" in order to reach understanding with one another about something in the world, does a perception that challenges reality and shakes up behavioural certainties become a "reason" that as a criticism gains entry into the *conceptual* balance and the semantic reservoir of potential inferences attached to existing views, setting in motion revisions, if necessary.' (J. Habermas, 'From Kant to Hegel: On Robert Brandom's Pragmatic Philosophy of Language', in: *European Journal of Philosophy* 8:3, 2000, p. 339.)

42 Along similar lines Kostakopoulou argues: 'Acknowledging the particularistic anchoring of constitutional principles … is a good reason to expose them to critical exchanges by other interpretative communities, not to insulate them from the very forces and challenges that could allow them to operate in a more universalist context. Critical exchanges and collisions enhance the possibility for reflexive self-awareness by showing the limits and relativity of one's political culture. Exposure of the limits leads to a better understanding of the whole and its potential. A strong democracy needs strong critique.' (D. Kostakopoulou, 'Is There an Alternative to "Schengenland"?', in: *Political Studies* 46, 1998, p. 898.)

PART III

European identity without a *demos*?
Empirical perspectives

The question of EU legitimacy should not only be posed at the level of juridico-political theory, but should also consider the potential commitment of people to Europe, their collective identity and their understanding of citizenship. It is only when viewed against the background of a particular social context that the language of political theory becomes less abstract. Thus, we ask: is the concept of 'situated constitutional patriotism', as formulated in Chapter 6, an armchair theory, or is it supported by empirical evidence of peoples' sense of belonging?

If we want to explore this question, we should listen to those who we can reasonably expect to be knowledgeable 'political theorists',[1] that is, those who live and work between nations, cultures and languages. Under today's condition of societal denationalization,[2] such 'intercultural identities' are far more common than we might assume and are certainly not limited to underprivileged migrants or an elite of 'global players'. As we will soon learn, the increasing mobility of Europeans has led to the emergence of a broader mental 'map', or a 'transnationalized space' where growing numbers of individuals are going through experiences in their professional and everyday lives that transform their sense of belonging.

In Chapter 7, I will briefly present the material, setting and methodology of my fieldwork. Chapter 8 starts with stories of four individuals – excerpts which illustrate the principle themes in, and the development of, their lives. I will then conduct a systematic analysis of all the empirical material, tentatively relating it to the theoretical discussion elaborated in Part II. The last part of Chapter 8 explores the collective identities of individuals and their understanding of citizenship with regard to the European Union.

7

Self and citizenship: a qualitative approach to European identity

A person has no sovereign internal territory, he is wholly
and always on the boundary; looking inside himself,
he looks into the eyes of another or with the eyes of another.

Mikhail Bakhtin[3]

If we are to talk about collective identities at a time of Europeanization, we need to move beyond theory and listen to people. Before discussing at length the narratives that make this possible, I would like to first offer a glimpse into my case studies with two brief extracts.

Annalisa Corradi, a small, delicate, neat woman in her thirties, greets me in her immaculate apartment. She came to Frankfurt at the age of six and worked for many years as a hairdresser before marrying an Italian waiter who has recently taken over his own pizzeria. She is now a housewife and mother of two children. Initially, Annalisa is somewhat doubtful of the purpose of the interview, and she is very much under control. Her story is one of success, of moving up the ladder step by hard-earned step. One of the signs of her ambitions lies in the fact that she has sent her children to a private school in order to learn 'good German', which in state schools is 'impossible because of the huge number of foreign kids'. Indeed, the use of perfect German is evidently very important to her and she excuses herself repeatedly, embarrassed when she thinks she has made a mistake. Annalisa's German and Italian personae come to the fore at different times. During the course of the interview, she sadly remarks about her parents' decision to return to their village in Basilicata:[4]

> I never felt like a foreigner … I don't live according to the motto of my parents: 'Work here, save money, and then go back'. In fact, we don't actually live like that … Our future is here … I can be an Italian; I can be a German … What am I? Everything [short laughter], everything, I am surely an Italian … but ah, when I have to play the German role, then I play the German role, no problem.[5]

Riccardo Dente gives a rather different impression. Big, well-dressed and jovial, he breaks into a fleeting smile when he finds something funny about the stories he tells me. At forty, he has a law firm with twenty employees in one of the most elegant streets in Frankfurt, but he evidently prefers to be 'one of the boys', rather than play the role of the 'big boss'. He moved to Germany with his father, a physician from Friuli, when he was five years old, after the death of his mother, a Neapolitan musician. Riccardo is now married to a German woman and has four children. He clearly enjoys being at the centre of attention, underlining his self-consciously Italian savoir vivre with somewhat theatrical gestures, even though he speaks German with a strong Hessian accent. In the middle of recounting his life story he says:

> Well, as an Italian at school I always felt somewhat special ... I have sold being an Italian well [here]; it has, as we say, gone down well ... And today? Okay, I would say, I am an Italian and a German ... But, ah, if I had either the fortune or the misfortune of ... making a clear choice: ... I am certainly an Italian, I am a German, then I would also say 'yes' [I am] politically European, [and] culturally German.[6]

Theoretical background: self and public

The modern era has been described as a time of increasing individualization, of weakening customs, of the thrusting of new choices on the individual, and, above all, of the atrophy of the pre-established social bonds that provide clear social identities. With regard to national identity, however, political theorists have always built on the methodological fiction of societies with closed borders and clear boundaries between members and non-members.[7] By emphasizing the 'sameness' of its members and suppressing the differences amongst them, a collectivity creates boundaries which exclude non-members. Nationhood, for instance, is a political and cultural construct which privileges one set of characteristics over another; it calls on the self to identify with those characteristics, and is then established as an identity. If we conceive of national (or European) identity in these holistic terms, we overlook the fact that there is always a plurality of cultural and political meanings of 'nation' (or 'Europe') that are negotiated 'within the margins of the nation-space and in the boundaries in-between nations and peoples'.[8] Moreover, contemporary processes of societal denationalization undermine the sense of belonging to a national community. Where a person may once have found a ready-made social and national identity, she must now 'interpret' or construct her identity from a range of much more ambiguous material. The current changes in our social world force us more than ever before to assume a sociological scepticism about concepts of identity – essentializing or homogenizing conceptualizations of collective identity, ideas which can be understood as typically modern and which arise from a need to fight against ambivalence.[9]

If we want to address the question of political and cultural belonging in contemporary Europe, normative considerations should be informed by sociological analysis. Scholars of linguistics, cultural studies, and critical social psychology assume that people construct their identities rather than 'hold' or 'possess' them, and that a key agent for these constructions is language.[10] Adopting such a perspective, political theory can no longer conceive of collective identities as given (and static) entities but has to account for the *process* of identity-formation which is shaped by complex societal, cultural and economic conflicts. The formation of collective identities is a *cross-categorizing* process and, as such, is intrinsically ambivalent: it blurs categories like nation and culture. Taking this view, European identity is formed in a continuous struggle between different socio-cultural and national 'voices' (e.g. between local Germans and Italians, as well as Turks). Identity-formation is best studied through the temporal and multilayered narratives which form its basis. A life story is dynamic, containing elements of temporality, spatiality and emplotment, and describes interaction with others. It therefore displays the processual and intersubjective constitution of identities,[11] avoiding the conventional array of fixed, essentialist, singular categories, such as those of nation, culture or gender. When people narrate a story, 'their accounts contain many different voices that are not entirely controllable by the speaker's more conscious held attitudes'.[12]

By studying autobiographical narratives, Chapters 7 and 8 aim at shedding light on the new identities that emerge as a result of denationalization and the disintegration of the demos (i.e., a national or cultural group based on shared values, concerns and knowledge). Such an approach transforms the subject-object dualism of modern social theory into numerous matrices of patterned relationships, social practices, and institutions mediated by narratives. For Hannah Arendt, narratives are crucial for the construction of collective and individual identities, and provide a useful method and source for exploring the self as a potential player in the public sphere. They contain a normative argument: a person's story, told in the first person, invariably defines what kind of moral agent she is and reveals her view on the values embodied in the practices of a society, that is, the individual's attitude toward the network of expectations and obligations in which she is situated.[13] Arendt underscores the inner multiplicity of the self – the self as a site of agonistic struggle.[14]

We are all aware that there are social forces pushing towards increasing fluidity and complexity in the way in which maps of both personal and collective identities are drawn. What kind of concept of the self is able to capture these conditions? The underlying assumption of my case studies is that the self is a sort of piecemeal construction formed in a process of ongoing dialogue *between* rather than *within* interlocutors (Bakhtin, Mead), whether real or imagined. Such a dialogical theory of the self challenges the supremacy of the interiority of selfhood by reinterpreting the concept of 'boundary'. Rather than being something which excludes otherness, it becomes the active site of dialogue and definition of self. Selfhood is less a property of mind than it is a joint (intersubjective) production, a dialogue between selfhood and otherness. Accordingly, the biographical narrative of a dialogical self is not seen as a fixed text, but is a multitude of situated, dialogical re-interpretations, re-ordered with each telling and hearing in concrete social contexts. Such a self is non-conventional since it goes through life without basing itself essentially on a *demos*. It interacts with other individuals, not necessarily sharing definitions of the situation or meanings, but learning by encountering individuals who have other ideas about or interpretations of the social world and negotiating 'shared' meanings with them.

The more an individual's self is de-centred, the more that one has to counter-balance inner multiplicity by 'reflexivity' directed at particular roles, identities, and senses of belonging.[15] Individualism in personal life and socio-cultural/ethical pluralism in collective life both call for a non-conventional ego identity with a high level of autonomy. This kind of 'postconventional' identity, characterized by a principled moral consciousness, is a precondition for post-traditional forms of public justification.[16] What is needed, however, is a different conceptualization of agency that is suitable for decentred selves that are plural, differentiated and conflicted because they are constituted by multiple lifeworlds and identities: 'The social dimensions of the self's formation as a subject-citizen require and generate an openness to its continual renegotiation of its boundaries and affiliations in relation to a variety of (often incommensurable) groups, networks, discourses, and ideologies, both within its "home" state and abroad'.[17] As I argue in Chapters 5 and 6, if we are to conceive democratic politics as a process of deliberation, such identities must be accompanied by high levels of 'multicultural literacy' or 'interpretative charity' which cut across cultural and national boundaries.[18] Research in the field of social psychology has demonstrated the importance of empathy among strangers, or 'the more general quality of being able to put yourself in the place of another as an important ingredient of democratic man'.[19] From this perspective, we can study the private processes of self-description as resources for political practices. New identities may enrich democratic politics with innovative interpretations of the social world or, for that matter, an emerging transnational polity such as the European Union. If politics is seen as contention among linguistically encoded self-understandings, sensibilities or 'vocabularies' (genres), then the political extends into the private realm and vice versa: The motives driving epistemic political contention or the 'exploration of difference' are peoples' diverse interpretations of the same social world, that is, they express their perspectives on interest and situation, need and possibility.

In *The Structural Transformation of the Public Sphere,* Habermas documents how the 'self-fashioning' nature of autobiographies and letters reveals new forms of subjectivity which broaden and transform the reading public. In a similar way, I aim tentatively to explore, through autobiographical interviews, whether contemporary conditions of denationalization have transformed the formation of collective identity and the idea of belonging. If so, I ask whether this has led to the emergence of a socio-cultural substratum of European citizenship practices. In other words, do the processes of societal denationalization encourage people to develop a postconventional solidarity and trust, or do they produce un-centred, detached and morally impoverished selves?

Identities and citizenship

Personal identity generally refers to the image an individual constructs of and for herself[20] whereas collective identity is what situates the individual in society, specifically in relation to others. Collective identities, the focus of the present study, are expressions of individuals' sense of belonging, or of their self-categorization[21] as members of certain collectivities (e.g. a local community, a nation, Europe, the EU, a profession, class, gender etc.). According to this perspective, national identity is understood as a repertoire of cultural tokens, which largely refer to a state-bound society. Identifications with social groups are represented in collective self-images and interpretations of the past, which are enacted through social practices and public communication (in media or official discourses as well as in everyday life discourse).[22] These communicatively generated definitions of membership may entail processes of inclusion and exclusion; there are different narrative (or ideological) patterns of picturing the unity of a social group and of constructing its boundaries, or of expanding solidarity beyond these boundaries. Of interest here are the questions, do interviewees narrate tales which legitimate the exclusion and intolerance of 'others', or do their stories leave space for critical reflection, the inclusion of 'others' and mutual learning?

Discourses on citizenship make ideologies[23] of belonging and political loyalties explicit, and reveal peoples' normative ideals with respect to collective identification (boundaries of legitimacy and solidarity, of inclusion and exclusion).[24] The case of Germany, considered as a destination for both high- and low-skilled migrants, invites questions about societal and political membership as framed in specifically cultural terms: German identity is traditionally built on the idea of *Kulturnation* (German for 'cultural nation') and until 1999, citizenship, an essential element for the constitution of collective identities,[25] was mainly based on *ius sanguinis*.[26] After the SPD/Greens won the Bundestag elections in September 1998, a heated and widespread debate focused on the desirability of granting German (or dual) citizenship to long-standing resident guest-workers. In the Hessen Landtag elections of February 1999, the CDU/CSU based their whole election campaign on their opposition to the 'dual passport' – and won. The campaign even extended to gathering signatures on the streets of Frankfurt for a petition against the citizenship law reform project. In the context of this public debate,[27] during which my interviews took place, the question of being a European citizen or a non-European 'Ausländer' had indeed become increasingly relevant. As I was looking for the emergence of a specifically European dimension in collective identity – as opposed to a national/regional/local or cosmopolitan dimension – it made sense to focus my inquiry on migrants with European citizenship.[28]

The case study of one group – Italian migrants – is, of course, insufficient empirical evidence for my general argument that 'multicultural literacy' is conducive to the construction of an interdiscursive European public sphere. However, this single case study may provide the methodological groundwork for further research on other groups of migrants, as well as on persons who spend their entire lives living within the same community[29] and those who generally feel threatened by Europeanization and who reject intercultural dialogue. Thus far, empirical studies on European identity and Euro-scepticism focus on survey data and on parties rejecting European integration.[30] Eurobarometer data has shown, for example, that negative attitudes towards immigrants are a key variable that is highly correlated with hostility toward European integration.[31] However, what is perhaps more interesting, is that data has shown that even during the period in which support for the EU dwindled (after about 1990), the majority of those surveyed by Eurobarometer identified with Europe: an attachment which grew throughout the 1990s.[32] As it stands today, citizens of the original member countries and Southern Europe are more likely to identify as Europeans than those of either the Scandinavian countries or the United Kingdom – but even in these traditionally Euro-sceptical countries, an increased attachment to Europe on the part of citizens has been observed.[33] In fact, maintaining a European identity does not erode one's feelings towards a nation. Contrary to traditional Euro-sceptic discourse in the political science literature, respondents with high levels of national identity are more likely to identify with Europe than respondents who display weaker levels of political identification.[34] It has also been shown that living in another European country, speaking foreign languages and travelling makes respondents more likely to feel European and to support European integration.[35] At the same time, younger and better-educated respondents are more likely to orient themselves towards Europe.[36]

Though these findings are significant, qualitative research is still needed in order to understand how attitudes and variables such as age, linguistic abilities, education etc. play a part in the creation of a European identity or anti-Europeanism. Furthermore, it is still unclear as to what people actually mean when they say that they are either European or 'anti-European'. According to Eurobarometer survey data, a critical factor involved in mitigating prejudice towards 'outsiders' seems to be adopting a sense of collective identity that is not exclusively national.[37] Therefore, it might be safe to hypothesize that people with a highly circumscribed sense of collective identity may be more hostile to 'outsiders' than those with heterogeneous and decentred identities. In other words, people who identify, at least in part, with Europe should have fewer negative feelings towards people of different backgrounds. Moreover, the more Europe is identified in 'civic-political' rather than in 'cultural-ethnic' terms, and the more cultural diversity is welcomed, the less exclusion and categorization of others (fellow European citizens or immigrants) takes place.[38]

While the present study investigates one particular group of migrants, the methodology developed here (unlike survey data such as Eurobarometer) could also be applied to other social groups (e.g. 'non-mobile' persons), making it possible to identify the obstacles to European identity formation by asking two fundamental questions: Under which conditions do individuals perceive Europeanization as a threat to their national culture? And why do some individuals tend to categorize others into out-groups and others not? Further qualitative research is needed in order to explore the exact relationship between European identity, openness to intercultural dialogue (or translation) and tolerance for fellow Europeans and immigrants.

Methodology and setting

In my case study, I have taken a group of migrants with European citizenship as a 'proto-type' for exploring how individuals negotiate their own multiple identities (German, Italian, European). The material providing the principal evidence for Part III is a set of extended interviews with twelve Italian migrants living in Germany. The interviews were recorded and transcribed to form twelve texts, varying in length from four pages (e.g. the story of Veronica Costanzo, a fifteen-year-old school girl) to twenty-seven pages (e.g. Riccardo Dente's story). The entire corpus of interviews consists of 143 pages of verbatim transcripts in German and Italian (translated for the purposes of this book). The authors of these autobiographical works were Italian denizens[39] from different occupational backgrounds (computer engineer, secretary, construction worker, greengrocer, school student, etc.) residing in Frankfurt am Main.

Frankfurt is a multicultural city in the region or *Land* of Hessen with a population of over 600,000. A centre of international finance and labour mobility (high-skilled as well as low-skilled immigration),[40] it ranks fifth among the world's 'global cities'[41] and offers many transnational and intercultural spaces for professional, as well as everyday life experiences. At 30%, the proportion of non-German inhabitants in Frankfurt is higher than in any other German city. After Turks and nationals of the former Yugoslavia, Italians are the third-largest group of foreigners and the largest group of nationals from any EU member-state (13,500 residents).[42]

I began my field research by gathering information about Italian migrants in Frankfurt, including statistics about their occupations, education and other biographical characteristics, as well as their membership of voluntary associations and so on. Thirty potential interview candidates were randomly selected from a list provided by the Italian consulate. Using the technique of minimal and maximal contrasting[43] I drew a 'theoretical sample' of fifteen from the shortlist, ensuring that the selection was balanced in terms of sex, age, occupation, education and time spent in Germany (I established a minimum of five years).[44] When I contacted these fifteen people, twelve agreed to be interviewed about 'how migrants live and think today'.[45]

At their convenience, I interviewed the subjects in their familiar private or professional surroundings. With the assurance of anonymity – an assurance honoured here by the usage of aliases in place of real names[46] – these men and women talked freely and apparently without inhibition about their lives, their experience of living in Germany, their ideas about citizenship, their sense of belonging and so on. The interviews were open-ended and exploratory. They were driven not by the need to test hypotheses but by an interest in the interviewees' views of the world, with a particular focus on the issues of citizenship, identity, sense of belonging and Europe. Since the interviews are autobiographical, we are in a position to relate life experience to the meaning of these topics.[47]

Most subjects were flattered and eager to participate, but two were markedly reluctant, and agreed only after some persuasion: Maria Luisa di Boggio, a thirty-six-year-old secretary at the Banco di Napoli, originally from a middle-class family in Rome, who came to Frankfurt in 1994; and Franco Baratta, who came from Messina at the age of twenty-one, earning his living for many years as a worker at Höchst AG but now, at the age of sixty-two, the owner of a well-known detective agency. I would argue that the reluctance of these two interviewees supports the claim that the group was not arbitrarily 'self-selected'. In order to become familiar with the specific socio-cultural world of the interviewees, I attended a few events held by associations[48] of which they were members and also conducted informal conversations with a number of prominent members of the Italian community in Frankfurt.[49]

During the interviews, I allowed the subjects to follow their own trains of thought and association, leaving scope for anecdote and argument, moral comment and rationalization. Since I was interested in *their* reference system, e.g. if and in what discursive context 'belonging to two cultures', 'citizenship' and so on becomes relevant to *them*, I first asked my interviewees simply to tell me their life stories. I then added some questions regarding any identity issues mentioned in their narrative. Only at the end did I ask whether or not they would apply for German (or dual) citizenship if it were to become available. In fact, none of them were interested in becoming German citizens, but almost all spontaneously brought up the subject of their *European* identity and European citizenship, although I had myself been careful never to mention 'Europe' or 'European citizenship'.

The younger interviewees were a little more inhibited, and so in these interviews the second part was necessarily more structured: I took the opportunity to probe personal understandings of concepts such as national identity, attempting to clarify the interviewees' own thinking by posing a series of more specific questions (about their friends, marriage, school, future, football, etc.). My aim was to conduct the interviews as 'dialogically' as possible, that is, I tried to listen with 'interpretative charity' in order to understand the outlook of my interviewees and to see things as they saw them. It helped to conduct all interviews under circumstances that were familiar to the subjects such as in their home or workplace.[50] Immediately after each interview, I made ethnographic notes on the setting and social background. I also listened to the recording to capture the overall sense of the person and his or her life story.

In analyzing the texts of the interviews, I began by identifying the common themes and concepts that described the interviewees' 'identity-constructions' and their attitudes towards people with different cultural backgrounds. In doing so, I was looking particularly for systematic variations depending on age, gender, social background etc. in their understanding of whether, for example, they understood 'European' to mean 'Euro-culture' or 'international' or 'cosmopolitan'. The second step was to classify each page of each transcript thematically in order to perform a systematic analysis of all the themes and concepts as well as the relationship between them. Was there, for example, a link between cultural identity and citizenship? In doing so, I approached the interviews as texts, as data against which my theoretical questions were to be explored.[51]

There were two principal questions which guided the analysis of the narratives: First, is the nation-state or national citizenship implicated in the formation of identity? (that is, do interviewees display pre-discursive exogenous self-understanding or do they form an endogenous or 'post-conventional' self-understanding on the basis of multiple national and socio-cultural references?) Second, what is the pluralizing effect of 'transnational' spaces of professional and everyday life experience? Or, more specifically, does this effect produce a sense of rootlessness and 'anomie' or does it creates an upward drift of reflexivity and moral consciousness?

What emerged from my enquiries were a number of indicators common to all of the interviewees that would allow me to structure the final interpretation of what I had heard, and how it relates to a theory of transnational citizenship practices. The ethnographic research was itself a process of translation. It involved not only the discovery of the world views of the informants – getting inside their language and thinking, embracing their meaning system – but also the process of relating their vocabularies and concepts to those of political theory. For Part III, I have selected some excerpts from my own interviews with Italian migrants, setting these alongside quotations from interviews with Turkish ('non-EU') migrants in Germany taken from the extensive literature that already exists on this group.[52] Seeing as the present methodology relies heavily upon the usages of language, interviewees are often quoted at length.

Although the interviews form the basis for the argument presented in the next chapter, I will often go beyond the empirical material to formulate modest interpretative constructs that relate this material to theory. The aim of Chapter 8 will be to establish a link between the theory of 'multicultural literacy' and a European intercultural or 'pastiche' identity. Most of my conclusions can be supported by other recent quantitative and qualitative research.[53] In the discussion of interviews, wherever I make a comment which applies to 'most' of the interviewees or where some causal connection is inferred, it is on the basis of a significant number of supporting statements, albeit unreported. I would invite the reader to consider whether the following narratives, or 'eyewitness evidence', sufficiently support the socio-cultural presuppositions of a 'Europe without *demos*' put forward in Part II.

Notes

1 See the social psychology of political life by R. Lane, *Political Ideology: Why the American Common Man Believes What He Does,* The Free Press, New York 1962.
2 M. Beisheim, S. Dreher and G. Walter, *Im Zeitalter der Globalisierung? Thesen und Daten zur gesellschaftlichen und politischen Denationalisierung,* Nomos, Baden-Baden 1998; M. Zürn,

Regieren jenseits des Nationalstaats, Suhrkamp Verlag, Frankfurt am Main 1998.

3 M. Bakhtin, 'Toward a Reworking of the Dostoevsky Book, Appendix 2', in: M. Bakhtin, *Problems of Dostoevsky*, Minnesota University Press, Minneapolis 1984, p. 293.

4 In order to facilitate the reading, I do not cite the interviews according to transcription rules.

5 Annalisa Corradi displays a self-conscious ability to play different identity roles and to switch between them autonomously. Accordingly, she has no essentializing conception of cultural and national self-understandings and seems rather aware of their 'constructedness'.
   Original transcript follows: 'Ich hab' mich nie als Fremde gefühlt. ... Ich lebe nicht nach dem Motto wie meine Eltern: 'hier arbeiten, sparen und wieder nachher zurückzugehen'. So leben wir nicht. ... Unsere Zukunft ist hier. ... Ich bin hier, äh, ja, ich kann hier Italienerin sein, ich kann hier Deutsche sein. ... Was ich bin? Alles (kurzes Lachen), alles, ich bin schon Italienerin, klar logisch, aber äh, wenn ich heute die deutsche Rolle spielen soll, dann spiel' ich die deutsche Rolle, kein Problem.' (Translation by Lorraine Frisina.)

6 Original transcript follows: 'Also, ich hab' mich als Italiener in dieser Schule eigentlich immer als etwas Besonderes gefühlt, ja? ... Gut, hab' ich das [hier] noch gut verkauft, das Italienersein, das ist ja auch, sagen wir mal, gut angekommen. ... Und heute? Okay, ich würde sagen, ich bin Italiener und deutsch, ich bin, ich bin vielleicht für Leute wie wir können sagen, sie sind vielleicht Europäer, nicht, weil sie sich als Europäer fühlen, sondern weil sie sich irgendwie nicht entscheiden können, ob's eins oder das andere ist. Aber, äh, wenn ich das Glück oder das Pech hätte, wie man's nimmt, ja, 'ne klare Zuweisung zu haben, zu sagen, ich bin deutlich Italiener, ich bin Deutscher, dann würde ich 'ja' dazu sagen, politisch Europäer, kulturell Deutscher.' (Translation by Lorraine Frisina.)
   Most poignant about this statement is Riccardo's caution when using identity-categories, as well as his unproblematic (even slightly positive) view on apparently conflicting sentiments: he 'is' Italian, politically European and culturally German.

7 S. Benhabib, *Kulturelle Vielfalt und demokratische Gleichheit: Politische Partizipation im Zeitalter der Globalisierung*, Fischer Taschenbuch Verlag, Frankfurt am Main 1999, p. 93.

8 H. K. Bhabha, 'DissemiNation: Time, Narrative, and the Margins of the Modern Nation', in: H. K. Bhabha (ed.), *Nation and Narration*, Routledge, London/New York 1990, p. 140.

9 Z. Bauman, *Modernity and Ambivalence*, Polity Press, Cambridge 1991.

10 See for example: U. Meinhof and K. Richardson (eds.), *Text, Discourse and Context: Representation of Poverty in* Britain, Longman, London 1994; S. Hall, 'Who Needs "Identity"?', in: S. Hall and P. du Gay (eds.), *Questions of Cultural Identity*, Sage, London 1996, pp. 1–17; M. Billig, 'Socio-psychological Aspects of Nationalism: Imagining Ingroups, Others and the World of Nations', in: K. v. Benda-Beckmann and M. Verkuyten (eds.), *Nationalism, Ethnicity and Cultural Identity in Europe*, European Research Centre of Migration and Ethnic Relations (ERCOMER), Utrecht 1995, pp. 89–106.

11 M. R. Somers, 'Narrating and Naturalizing Civil Society and Citizenship Theory: The Place of Political Culture and the Public Sphere', in: *Sociological Theory* 13:3, 1995, pp. 229–274.

12 U. Meinhof, 'Europe Viewed from Below', in: R. H. Herrmann, T. Risse and M. B. Brewer (eds.), *Transnational Identities: Becoming European in the EU*, Rowman & Littlefield, New York 2004, pp. 161–185.

13 H. Arendt, *The Human Condition*, Chicago University Press, Chicago 1958, pp. 187–198.

14 Arendt rejects the idea of personal autonomy, arguing that the self is in fact fragmented apart from action and speech. However, if we conceive of the self as intersubjectively or dialogically constituted (Bakthin, Mead), personal autonomy does not mean self-sufficiency but rather is a fragile condition for self-determination and self-development that is enormously dependent on external care, dialogical practices of recognition, juridical support and stable socio-economic conditions (Sen, Nussbaum). See: G. H. Mead and C. Morris (eds.), *Mind, Self and Society: from the standpoint of a socialbehaviorist*, Chicago University Press, Chicago 1934).

15 Or as Habermas argues, 'the internalizing processing of ... conflicts leads to an

autonomization of the self' (J. Habermas, *Postmetaphysical Thinking*, MIT Press, Cambridge, MA, 1992, p. 152).

16 'What self-legislation and moral autonomy signifies in the sphere of personal life corresponds to the rational natural-law interpretations of political freedom, that is, interpretations of democratic self-legislation in the constitution of a "just" society.' (J. Habermas, *Between Facts and Norms. Contributions to a Discourse Theory of Law and Democracy*, MIT Press, Cambridge, MA, 1996, p. 98.)

17 B. Honig, 'Difference, Dilemmas, and the Politics of Home', in: S. Benhabib (ed.), *Democracy and Difference*, Princeton University Press, Princeton 1993, p. 273.

18 Symbolic boundary-drawing refers to the process by which individuals define their identity in opposition to that of others. In contrast, boundary-crossing indicates the process by which social actors blur social and cultural categories. See for instance Michèle Lamont's inspiring study on the boundary work of the French and the American upper-middle class (M. Lamont, *Money, Morals, and Manners: The Culture of French and American Upper-Middle Class*, Chicago University Press, Chicago 1992).

19 Lane, *Political Ideology*, p. 405.

20 It includes (a) her self-awareness, that is, the degree to which she is attentive to and aware of the wide range of phenomena that take place in her mind, (b) her self-description, i.e. the characteristics she thinks describe her and which are important features of her personality and (c) her self-esteem, that is, the value she places upon herself and her ideas. The classical definition reads as follows (I will not discuss the later critiques): 'This sense of identity provides the ability to experience oneself as something that has continuity and sameness, and act accordingly' (E. Erikson, *Childhood and Society*, Norton Press, New York 1951, p. 38).

21 By this I mean the particular reference that people make when enacting collective identities and do not intend to allude to the 'Theory of Social Categories' by Henri Tajfel (H. Tajfel, *Human Groups and Social Categories*, Cambridge University Press, Cambridge 1981).

22 The imaginary process of creating traditions and activating collective memories extends through time. The dark side of memory is, of course, amnesia regarding historical conflicts or catastrophes (e.g. the Holocaust). Collective identities also have a spatial dimension, although this need not always conform to a model of territorial concentration and juridico-political order (e.g. the Basques).

23 'Ideology' is used here without any moral or judgemental intent. Rather, it is intended to point to social structures which are reflected in peoples' narratives about themselves and society. Ideologies are the result of historical processes and social events and thus exist independent of any single individual (T. W. Adorno, E. Freskel-Brunswik and D. Levinson et al., *The Authoritarian Personality*, Harper, New York 1950; K. Mannheim, *Ideology and Utopia*, Harcourt Brace, New York 1949). Ideologies are 'latent' insofar as they are not well-developed arguments of 'experts' but loosely structure our discourses in everyday life.

24 For the relation of immigration policies and citizenship see: R. Koslowski: *Migrants and Citizens: Demographic Change in the European State System*, Cornell University, Ithaca 2000. For an interesting micro-sociological account of how people in contemporary France experience citizenship see: S. Duchesne, *Citoyenneté à la Française*, Presse de Science Politique, Paris 1997. For a comparative historical account see: T. K. Oommen, *Citizenship, Nationality and Ethnicity*, Polity Press, Cambridge 1997. In opposition to D. Miller (*On Nationality*, Oxford University Press, Oxford 1995), Oommen concludes that citizenship must be detached from the cultural idea of nation if it is to serve as an inclusionary concept with all its emancipatory potential. For an insightful philosophical account see J. Shklar, *American Citizenship: The Quest for Inclusion*, Harvard University Press, Cambridge, MA, 1991.

25 Y. N. Soysal, 'Changing Citizenship in Europe. Remarks on postnational membership and the national state', in: D. Cesarani/M. Fulbrook (eds.), *Citizenship, Nationality and Migration in Europe*. Routledge, London/New York 1996, pp. 17–29.

26 In 1999 the Social Democratic government passed a new citizenship law which cut the link

between German blood and nationality and thereby paved the way for 'guestworkers' to seek citizenship. The new Act gives automatic citizenship to children born in Germany to foreign residents. On the reform of German citizenship law see: 'Gesetz zur Reform des Staatsangehörigkeitsrechts v. 15.7.1999' (in: BGB1 1999 I, p. 1618 Art. 1 Nr. 3).

27 W. Grenz, 'Die Ausländer- und Asylpolitik der rot-grünen Bundesregierung', in: C. Butterwege and G. Hentges (eds.), *Zuwanderung im Zeichen der Globalisierung. Migrations-, Integrations- und Minderheitenpolitik*, Leske+Budrich, Opladen 2000, pp. 105–119. For an account of the debate until the early 1990s see: K. Schönwälder, 'Migration, Refugees and Ethnic Plurality as Issues of Public and Political Debates in (West) Germany', in: D. Cesarani and M. Fulbrook (eds.), *Citizenship, Nationality and Migration in Europe*, Routledge, London/New York 1996, pp. 159–178.

28 European citizenship was formally established through the Maastricht Treaty of 1992. This innovative development extended civil, and some political rights to all individuals who were members of EU countries. Citizens of EU member states can also vote to send representatives to the European Parliament and are encouraged to engage in new forms of political participation in the multi-level governance system (e.g. closer cross-national collaboration between political parties, pressure groups and social movements). Unfortunately, the opportunity to sever the link between nationality and citizenship was not taken at the time the treaty was drawn up. According to EU law, member states can still assert their right to determine citizenship of their own communities and, in turn, EU citizenship is limited to those individuals who are legitimate citizens of member states. This exclusive aspect which sets cultural as well as legal limits to the expansion of citizenship to immigrants from Europe's third countries was confirmed by the Amsterdam Treaty of 1997 which asserted that EU citizenship was to complement and not supersede national citizenship. A. Favell, 'European Citizenship and the Incorporation of Migrants and Minorities in Europe: Emergence, Tranformation and Effects of the New Political Field', in: *Paper of the European Forum (European University Institute)*, 1997, pp. 1–57; M. Martiniello, 'The Development of European Union Citizenship: A Critical Evaluation', in: M. Roche and R. Van Berkel (eds.), *European Citizenship and Social Exclusion*, Ashgate, Aldershot 1997, pp. 35–47; U. K. Preuss, 'The Relevance of the Concept of Citizenship for the Political and Constitutional Development of the EU', in: U. K. Preuss and F. Requejo (eds.), *European Citizenship, Multiculturalism, and the State*, Nomos, Baden-Baden 1998, pp. 11–28.

29 There is extremely little qualitative research. For a recent study on people who spent their entire lives in the same communities at the German–Polish border, see: U. Meinhof, 'Europe Viewed from Below', in: R. H. Herrmann, T. Risse and M. B. Brewer (eds.), *Transnational Identities: Becoming European in the EU*, Rowman & Littlefield, New York 2004, pp. 161–185.

30 According to the Eurobarometer of 2000, 44% of the sample fears the loss of the language and 48% fear the loss of national identity or culture (see: J. Citrin and J. Sides, 'More Than Just Nationals: How Identity Choice Matters in the New Europe', in: Herrmann, Risse and Brewer (eds.), *Transnational Identities*, pp. 176–177); on Euro-scepticscism see: P. Kopecký and C. Mudde, 'Two Sides of Euroskepticism. Party Positions on European Integration in East Central Europe', in: *European Union Politics* 3:3, 2001, pp. 297–326; P. Taggart, 'A Touchstone of Dissent: Euroscepticism in Contemporary Western European Party Systems', in: *European Journal of Political Research* 33, 1998. pp. 363–388.

31 Interestingly, citizens do not distinguish between the potential threat of immigration from current EU countries or future EU members or non EU-countries (L. McLaren, 'Immigration and the New Politics of Inclusion and Exclusion in the European Union: The Effects of Elites and the EU on Individual-Level Opinions Regarding European and Non-European Immigrants', in: *European Journal of Political Research* 39:1, 2001, pp. 81–108).

32 J. Citrin and J. Sides, 'More Than Just Nationals: How Identity Choice Matters in the New Europe', in: Herrmann, Risse and Brewer (eds.), *Transnational Identities*, pp. 166–167.

33 *Ibid.*, p. 167 fo.

34 If individuals hold multiple identities, we can reject zero-sum conceptions of national or regional versus European identity. See: M. Bruter, 'Civic and Cultural Components of a European Identity: A Pilot Model of Measurement of Citizens' Levels of European Identity', in: Herrmann, Risse and Brewer (eds.), *Transnational Identities*, p. 204.

35 *Ibid.*, p. 207.

36 Citrin and Sides, 'More Than Just Nationals: How Identity Choice Matters in the New Europe', in: Herrmann, Risse and Brewer (eds.), *Transnational Identities*, pp. 172–173.

37 *Ibid.*, p. 182.

38 Bruter, 'Civic and Cultural Components of a European Identity', pp. 186–213.

39 That is, non-German citizens legally resident in Germany.

40 B. Freund, 'Frankfurt am Main und der Frankfurter Raum als Ziel qualifizierter Migranten', in: *Zeitschrift für Wirtschaftsgeographie* 42:2, 1998, pp. 57–81.

41 S. Sassen, *Cities of a World Economy*, Pine Forge Press, Thousand Oaks 1994.

42 For sociological accounts of Italian immigration, see: S. Haug, 'Soziales Kapital. Migrationsentscheidungen und Kettenmigrationsprozesse. Am Beispiel der italienischen Migranten in Deutschland', Dissertation, Universität Mannheim 1999; I. Philipper, *Biographische Dimension der Migration. Zur Lebensgeschichte von Italienerinnen in Deutschland*, Beltzverlag, Weinheim 1997; L. Novi, 'Lebenswelten italienischer Migranten', in: J. Motte, R. Ohlinger and A.v.Oswald (eds.), *50 Jahre Bundesrepublik – 50 Jahre Einwanderung. Nachkriegsgeschichte als Migrationsgeschichte*, Campus, Frankfurt/New York 1999, pp. 243–258.

43 For Grounded Theory, see: A. Strauss and J. Corbin, *Basics of Qualitative Research: Grounded Theory, Procedures and Techniques*, Sage, London 1990.

44 Of these fifteen people, seven were men and eight women; four were under twenty years old, eight were between thirty and forty-five years old, and three were over sixty years old; eight came to Germany in their childhood or were born there, and seven went to Germany when they were over eighteen; six were professionals (five of whom had a university degree). Of the three subjects who did not want to be interviewed, one was unavailable. The others, over sixty years old, came to Germany after the age of eighteen (first-generation immigrants). One was a retired worker (female), and the other a retired craftsman (male).

45 Since patterns of discursive identity-constructions began to repeat within this sample and little new material was generated, I decided to conduct no further interviews.

46 In order to be consistent, I invented also the last names of the Turkish interviewees taken from the literature.

47 W. Fischer-Rosenthal and G. Rosenthal, 'Narrationsanalyse biographischer Selbstpräsentationen', in: R. Hitzler and A. Honer (eds.) *Sozialwissenschaftliche Hermeneutik*, Leske+Budrich, Opladen 1997, pp. 133–165. F. Schütze, 'Biographieforschung und narratives Interview', in: *Neue Praxis. Zeitschrift für Sozialarbeit, Sozialpädagogik und Sozialpolitik* 13:3, 1973, pp. 283–293.

48 A couple of meetings of the Italian trade union CGIL, an evening event held by the *Associazione Famiglie Italiane Sport e Cultura*, and the celebration of the first transnational certificate for ice-cream producers (*Gelatieri in Europa*) awarded by the *Handelskammer* and the *Camera del Commercio di Belluno e Treviso*.

49 The conversations were with Valeria Tomasselli (in charge of social affairs at the Italian consulate); Carlo del Prete (a journalist on *Il Corriere D'Italia*, the biggest Italian newspaper in Germany, based in Frankfurt and founded in the 1960s with Church money, for migrants); Carlo Bastasin (correspondent for the Italian financial newspaper *Il sole 24 ore*); the priest Don Giovanni de Florian (*Comunita' Cattolica Italiana*); Anna Liguori Pace (*SPD-Stadträtin* and high school teacher); Marina DeMaria (*Grüne/Bündnis 90-Stadträtin* and director of the Italian-German Kindergarten); Liana Novelli-Glab (historian, involved in an Italian women's group); and Carmela Castronovo (member of the Italian trade union CGIL).

50 Perhaps it helped that I am myself half Italian and was raised bilingually in Germany. To

make interviewees comfortable, I let them choose the language in which to talk and revealed the fact that I have an Italian mother and that I was raised in Germany. However, I tried to maintain a blurred social and cultural identity in order to minimize the danger that the interviewees would be affected by what he or she presumed were my opinions, values and expectations.

The reflexive turn in the social sciences has drawn our attention to the fact that external factors may influence the data-gathering process. The researcher's own educational and national background, sex, age and social difference, language problems etc. can effect the responses elicited, as well as the interview situation itself. Thus, I tried at least to be aware of my own subjectivity and of the 'non-shared' between me and the interviewees in order to minimize such distorting factors. See: P. Bourdieu, 'Epilogue: On the Possibility of a Field of World Sociology', in: P. Bourdieu and J. S. Coleman (eds.), *Social Theory for a Changing Society*, Westview Press, Boulder/San Francisco 1991, pp. 301–335; P. Bourdieu (ed.), *La misère du monde*, Seuil, Paris 1993.

51 On this kind of methodology, see: H. Rubin and I. Rubin, *Qualitative Interviewing: The Art of Hearing Data*, Sage Publications, London 1995.

52 S. Sauter, *Wir sind 'Frankfurter Türken': Adoleszente Ablösungsprozesse in der deutschen Einwanderungsgesellschaft*, Brandes & Apsel, Frankfurt 2000; H. Tertilt, *Turkish Power Boys. Ethnographie einer Jugendbande*, Suhrkamp Verlag, Frankfurt am Main 1996; N. Tietze, *Islamische Identitäten: Formen muslimischer Religiosität junger Männer in Deutschland und Frankreich*, Hamburger Edition, Hamburg 2001; U. Bielefeld, *Inländische Ausländer: Zum gesellschaftlichen Bewußtsein türkischer Jugendlicher in der Bundesrepublik*, Campus, Frankfurt am Main/New York 1988; and the biographical interviews in: Deutsche Shell (ed.), *Jugend 2000*, vol. 2, Leske+Budrich, Opladen 2000. The transcriptions of the autobiographical interviews have been rewritten by the editors of the Shellstudie and are therefore more fluent than the interviews transcribed verbatim.

53 See for instance: Deutsche Shell (ed.), *Jugend 2000, vol.2*; B. Parekh, *The Future of Multi-Ethnic Britain. Report of the Commission on the Future of Multi-Ethnic Britain*, Profile Books, London 2000; A. Ong, *Flexible Citizenship: The Cultural Logics of Transnationality*, Duke University Press, Durham 1999.

8

Voices of migrants

> One language, one person –
> two languages, two people.
> Turkish proverb[1]

The aim of this chapter is to find out whether societal denationalization, which is to say the absence of a single *demos*, undermines socio-cultural presuppositions of trust and solidarity among the people of a polity (see Chapter 2) or whether it instead fosters the 'multicultural literacy' (see Chapter 5) necessary for postnational and intercultural 'constitutional patriotism' (see Chapter 6). Whereas in Part II I posed this question within the field of social and political theory and offered my own perspective on it, I will now situate the same thematic discussion within the ethnographic field of everyday life understandings of actors.[2] I will consider the same question at a strictly descriptive level, looking at the phenomenon of societal denationalization 'from below'. The aim of this exploratory research is to yield further material for reflection within the field of political and social theory. The central question is whether there is any evidence that citizens in our contemporary world have developed a postconventional identity and morality; whether they suppose a 'kingdom of ends here and now as a context of interaction and as a communication community in which everyone is capable of taking the perspective of everyone else and is willing to do so'[3] even when they do not share a 'we-identity'?

Multiple belongings and patriotism

There are two stages to what follows. First, I will present the autobiographical narratives of four interviewees (more or less) as they were told to me,[4] mainly using the interviewees' own words in order to explore what kind of 'patriotism' or sense of belonging they have developed in the course of their lives. Second, I will conduct my analysis systematically across all of the interviews according to a number of indicators developed here.

Four life stories

Francesco

Francesco Foraccio is a vigorous man in his early thirties, with the nervous energy typical of many journalists. Beside him during the interview in his office at the *Hessischer Rundfunk* (Hessian radio) sits his somewhat grim German girlfriend. Quite a bit older than he is, she works for the *Hessische Ausländerbeirat*. Francesco's German is better than his Italian, and he speaks with a strong Hessian accent and a tendency to use multi-kulti (multi-cultural) rhetoric typical of well-meaning leftist schoolteachers, public servants and journalists. When he was six years old, his parents, both of whom had already been working for some years for a Frankfurt construction company, finally decided to bring him and his two older sisters from Sicily (where they had been living with their aunt in order to get an 'Italian education'). The decision, apparently, was made 'when they were told that their eldest daughter was dating a boy from the village'. From early on, Francesco was very ambitious at school. He underlines his conscious decision to better his circumstances through studying and mastering the German language:

> Though I didn't stand out because of my skin colour, due to language problems, hum, one just sensed – up until the fifth grade – that I was a stranger. From about the sixth grade on, something worked in me; I really thought about it: You don't need these stupid (laughing) classmates harassing you. And this was the phase … in which I tried somehow to better myself … You have to try to not always be the victim … the best way [to improve yourself] is through language and learning. But then suddenly I was left out [by classmates] not because I was just a foreigner, (laughing) but because I was then called 'an eager beaver'.[5]

Francesco had to struggle to gain the acceptance of his peers, to be allowed to belong to the 'same group', and made great efforts to improve his German and his results at school. While in the interview he adopts the rhetoric of victimization (the Italian foreigner as *Spaghettifresser* or 'Spaghetti-eater')[6] at the same time he denies his victimhood through relativization ('this could happen to anybody', i.e. not only to foreigners) and by reference to his own success. When he made it known that he wanted to go to the Gymnasium, or advanced high school, he started quarrelling with his father, a quasi-illiterate worker who did not want his son to get a higher education. In this conflict with his father, Francesco used a German rights discourse which a young man in Italy, and particularly in Sicily, would have been very unlikely to use: he threatened to tell the 'official administration' about his father's misuse of state child benefits or *Kindergeld*. He speaks very positively about the German school system and especially about his experiences in high school, as if it were the school and the teachers who 'gave' him the opportunity to improve himself and broaden his mind. He feels that what counted at his school was not where you came from but whether you were intelligent, whether you could argue and formulate your ideas well. It is clear that he places great trust in the state system, which he sees as a guarantor of his (and others') rights – in contrast to his father's more Sicilian trust in relying on networks of acquaintances and favours.

> Well, till tenth grade there was this problem ... My father had argued about it with me, [I could attend school up to] the sixth grade ... [But] then up to the tenth grade ... [in order to get to school] I had to go somewhere, somewhere far away, and he had to finance my monthly transportation. [But] this didn't work ... I then said that I would go to an official and report that [he] misused my state child benefit [laughing] ... And then everything was ok ... It was a very open school and there were no great hurdles for foreigners. Yeah, and there I started to develop a bit of a political awareness, you could say, and there was no longer this constant conflict about where I came from, or where I didn't come from; instead, the only thing that counted was the question: What have you got in your head?[7]

In telling his story, Francesco continually emphasizes his ongoing learning and self-improvement. However, after some reflection on whether his personal development is a matter of simple assimilation, he concludes with an ambivalent statement: his thinking is German (and we might note here that at a different point he also says that his political identity is German), but for a long time he has been unable to feel German. He also seems to have difficulties in switching between cultures, something that the younger interviewees do with ease, and unlike them, does not display an ambivalent 'pastiche' identity at a linguistic level.

> Well, I could somehow adjust myself in such a way that I didn't think about my roots anymore; but for a long time I couldn't quite feel things as a German. I could analyze in German, I could think in German [laughing], but 'the feeling' was missing.[8]

His description of regular trips back to his village in Sicily tends to points to this. Although he claims a sense of belonging, and that he is just like the young men he left behind, he views those same young men as having in some sense 'stood still' (*stehengeblieben*) and as less advanced than 'we are here' (i.e. in Germany). Francesco seems to be the interviewee who has gained most from the school system, and who has put most social, occupational and educational distance between himself and his parents. As well as placing great emphasis on the quality of the German education system, he believes it unlikely that he would have become 'politically awoken' or a journalist had he stayed in Sicily. At the same time, Francesco is the interviewee who makes most reference to his foreign status, albeit in a clichéd, multi-kulti, identity-politics manner, and it is clear from his career path that his difference has played an important role in his professional life. He regrets not having finished his studies (political science, journalism and French), which he justifies by saying that he was troubled by his father's death (Francesco's father took his own life after his wife left him) and by having started, at the age of nineteen, to work for the *Corriere d'Italia*, the biggest newspaper for Italian migrants in Germany (based in Frankfurt). During the last few years, he has contributed articles to the *Taz*, a left-wing newspaper, and has worked for the Associated Press news agency, as well as for the foreigners' programme (*Ausländerprogramm*) of the *Hessischer Rundfunk*. Today he is a freelance journalist working chiefly for the *Hessenschau*, a regional television news programme. He tells me that he is proud to have recently commented on the regional (*Landtag*) elections, although – and he smiles at the irony – being an Italian citizen, he himself was unable to vote.

Armando

I interview Armando Guerri in the back room of the tiny food shop run by his parents in Bockenheim. Short of stature and solidly built, the nineteen-year-old apprentice hotelier with a friendly face calls himself a 'typical third-generation immigrant brat' (in fact, Armondo is only first-generation German). He talks quickly, swallowing his words while his lively dark eyes wander around. Although he occasionally switches to Italian, his German is better. Unlike Francesco, he seems at ease with a 'hyphenated' or 'pastiche' Italian-German identity, an identity which extends even to his gestures and way of talking. There is no sign of the discourse of victimization adopted by Francesco. Armando's parents came to Germany at an early age. Being from the same Sicilian village, and attending the same secondary school in Frankfurt, their meeting was almost inevitable. Armando himself was born in Frankfurt, but spent two years at an elementary school in Sicily, where he stayed with his grandmother. When he returned to Frankfurt at the age of eight, he had forgotten his German and felt isolated in class (where there were many other foreigners). At the beginning, as he did not understand German, he mistook his classmates' friendly manners for something rather more threatening, but his openness finally won over and he caught on quickly, making friends with his classmates.

> Because I didn't understand any German at the time, whenever someone said something to me, I thought it was negative … Later I noticed that the other kids … were really nice [short laugh] … I have many international friends, the smallest number of which is German [short laugh] … A few of them have also got German citizenship, because they've had problems in … their homelands [short laugh] … In my case … Italy is in the EU … [so] I have no problems. I don't know why I should want German citizenship when I have … just as may rights as a German. That is, aside from voting[9]

Armando is keen to emphasize that his friends are 'international'. When he goes back to his village in Sicily during the summer, he feels just as at home as he does in Frankfurt, but then, as he points out with a smile, more than half of the other guys are also migrants and normally live in Germany or Holland. He believes that non-EU immigrants can benefit from German citizenship, but he himself, being Italian (i.e. an EU citizen), does not need it, even if this means that he cannot vote in the national elections – he is happy with his right to vote in the local Kommunal elections. Armando's discourse on European citizenship is based on rights and 'legal advantages', not on some idea of a shared essentialistic identity or common

European culture which non-Europeans do not share. In his narrative, there are no such boundaries between 'us' and 'them', between 'friends' and 'enemies'. For him, 'European' seems to mean 'international' or 'intercultural'. He feels 'one hundred per cent European', and can see himself living in other European countries – but also beyond, for example, in America. He can also see himself having an African or Moroccan girlfriend. Indeed, rather than excluding non-EU migrants from his European discourse, he tends to place a high value on encountering different cultures. He is also able to put himself in the shoes of non-EU migrants (reflexivity – see indicator 3 below). For example, he tells me that if he were Turkish, he would want German citizenship because non-EU migrants have fewer rights. For Armando, what counts is how someone is as a person, regardless of his national or cultural identity. This is a theme which repeatedly recurs in all the interviews.

> Well, if I were from Turkey ... I would want to have German citizenship ... because I know, as a Turk ..., one doesn't have as many advantages as an Italian in Germany. I feel 100% European [short laugh] ... I see advantages in that, because I also have interest in other countries ... How about a girlfriend from another country? Well, for me it depends only on what the person is like ... It's all the same to me whether she is African or Moroccan or whatever ... It matters only what the person is like.[10]

Armando's own identity is more of a 'pastiche'. He feels quite happy with the plurality of co-existing national identities and seems aware of their dynamic constructedness (see indicator 1 below):

> Well, really, I don't know, I'm somewhere in between [short laugh]. Well it's very hard, because ... the Italian ways are well known to me, as well as the German... There are things that are not so good in Germany but better in Italian ... and vice versa.[11]

Depending on the context, he can navigate, now as the 'third-generation immigrant in Frankfurt' (focusing on common intercultural experience); now stressing his Germanness (for example, when he is with someone from his Sicilian village who hasn't gone abroad); now his Italian origins (for example, when he watches football with his friends – they all 'play' with their own and each others' different origins).[12] In his everyday life Armando draws on his knowledge of different cultures and languages, mixing them and picking out the good elements from both (see indicator 2 below).

Teresa

Teresa Pedrini is a pretty, stylish nineteen-year-old, full of energy, but seemingly uneasy about her life. She left the Gymnasium a year before taking the Abitur school examinations, a decision she now regrets. She works part-time in a clothes shop and plans to go back to the Gymnasium and then to Italy to carry on her studies. She is very articulate, speaking an almost artificially 'clean' Italian. My interview with Teresa takes place in the living room of her parents' house, with her younger sister sitting beside her.

   Teresa's life story is one of transnational coming and going, a pattern more typical of Italian than, say, Turkish or Spanish migrants.[13] She was born in

Frankfurt, where she went to school for two years, winning a prize for her Italian. (It is common for mother-tongue language courses to be held in schools where there are many immigrants). Just after her eighth birthday the whole family returned to Lecce. It was here that Teresa spent what she calls her 'important years' in terms of socialization. After seven years, however, her father lost his job and the family decided to go back to Frankfurt, where he found work at a McDonalds restaurant. Having been a 'good pupil' in Lecce, Teresa had expected the Gymnasium to be easy scholastically, but instead she found it extremely difficult. This was, she says, because, her 'German grammar' was not perfect and her linguistic style, interrupted at the age of eight, when she left Frankfurt, was too 'colloquial'. Despite this, she felt immediately socially accepted in her class, where the majority of students were also foreigners.

> At the beginning everyone looked at me a bit strangely ... then it stopped. On the part of the students, it wasn't a problem and I quickly made friendships ... with everyone ... No, no, no, there was no real difference between students ... You can say that we were all Germans, no matter whether one was [also] a foreigner, Italian, Spanish, Portuguese ...[14]

Teresa, like many of the other interviewees, tells me that her friends are 'Germans, Spaniards, Moroccans, Turks, French and English'. While she emphasizes that there were no differences between them and that they were all fundamentally 'Germans' regardless of background, at the same time Teresa's narrative underlines cultural diversity, stressing in particular her own Italian identity, but also the fact that encountering all these different cultures was an enriching experience (see indicator 2 ii below).

> When we had a free hour perhaps the entire class would meet up and we'd speak about my country, their country, the differences, the similarities, and also a bit ... about politics ... above all about questions that one wants to hear about in order to feel more at home, even if we weren't all from one country ... speaking about one's country made us feel at home talking amongst friends, you know?[15]

At school, she and her classmates would often discuss what was happening in their different countries of origins. By adopting various parts of the different ways of life, cultures, religions of others, they broadened their own cultures and horizons. She describes this as important for her 'personal learning processes' (see indicator 2 iii below). Although she otherwise speaks highly of her friends in Lecce, she criticizes them for their lack of curiosity about foreigners, telling me, for example, of their surprise when a Moroccan friend called her from Frankfurt. The people in Lecce, she suggests, have fixed, if not racist ideas about Albanians and Turks who arrive at the Italian coast. Although her words belie a degree of nostalgia for Lecce, she underscores the fact that she has no problem with living as a foreigner in Germany alongside the many cultures of her peers, as well as her own dualistic culture.

> You are in Germany, you live in Germany, for an Italian, [it's] no problem ... That is, personally speaking, nothing has ever happened to me to make me feel foreign,

> actually sometimes I feel more foreign in Italy …! It is enriching [in Germany…]
> because you have contact with Germans, Moroccans, Turks, and many other na-
> tionalities and from each nationality you derive a life, a lifestyle, a culture, a religion
> that enrich your own … and perhaps you don't remain as Italians living amongst Ital-
> ians. Ok, now there are even Albanians and Turks [in Italy] but no one is really interested
> in them … Two weeks ago when I was in Italy talking to some friends, a Moroccan friend
> of mine phoned (from Germany) … They couldn't imagine [why he was my friend] and
> it was useless, they had a fixed idea [about Moroccans] and I didn't.[16]

Teresa would like her friends in Lecce to have a more nuanced view of foreigners
and their cultures. For her and for all of those from her age group who were interviewed by me and other scholars, 'European' describes the mixing and encountering of different cultures which she experiences in her Frankfurt life. For her, the
unification of Europe was present all along in her classroom.

> Sincerely speaking, [European unification] is very significant … because before I
> ever distinguished between countries, for me Europe was already unified […When]
> you live in Germany, you have many friends of different races … therefore European
> unification for me was already happening on a small scale [in class] … I hope that it
> continues in this way.[17]

Franco

Sixty-two-year-old Franco Baratta offers a contrasting view. A strong, loud and
energetic man, he is proud of his success and of his unquestioned male identity.
He is the owner of a detective agency with twenty employees, situated in the very
centre of Frankfurt. Our interview takes place in the agency's offices, where he
greets me with a firm handshake and tells me his story in slightly rusty Italian.

At the age of twenty he arrived in Germany from Messina where his family
owned a butcher's shop. He had to leave because, in his own words, he was too
'quarrelsome' and 'would be in prison or long under the earth if … [he] had stayed
in Sicily'. His first job in Germany in the 1960s was in a Höchst AG factory where
he experienced a lot of discrimination. The Italians were primarily viewed as the
'traitors' in World War II. At one point, when he could no longer bear to be called
'dirty Italian', he jumped onto a conveyor-belt, lowered his trousers and shouted
at the other workers: 'Look, I change my underpants every day, show me yours'.
From that moment on, he was respected, although he tells me that he thinks the
new generation of Germans has changed for the better, that they are less 'chauvin-
istic'. Little by little he worked his way up, finding a job at the reception of the
Frankfurter Rundschau, a newspaper, and then by chance becoming a detective in
the *Kaufhof*, a big department store. During our interview, he smiles as he tells me
of the many times he caught German lawyers or other 'respectable figures' steal-
ing items from the shop.

Franco Baratta is divorced from his German wife and has a son. Although his
son is, obviously, half German and half Italian, he does not have dual citizenship,
and travels on an Italian passport. Franco is very keen that his son adopts the
Italian identity of which his father is so proud. (In fact, if his son were to be in

some sense insufficiently Italian, he would 'break his head'.)

> I remain Italian; I am proud to be Italian. Although I no longer live in my city, I am proud. Our culture is of another kind, no? Our roots are much more profound, no? ... I remain Italian ... I would not suggest to anyone leaving their city, their things, their people, no I would not recommend it to anyone, because today I [must] sit on the fence, no?[18]

Franco is clearly happy with both his private and professional lives. He owns a house in the Taunus area, has friends from different origins and seems well-integrated into German society. He is perfectly able to understand what the Turks ('who replaced the Italians') and asylum seekers, for whom he has much sympathy, are going through (see indicator 3 below). Notwithstanding his positive experience of intercultural mixing in his own circle of friends, Franco's idea of citizenship is bound to an identity which seems pre-given and stable. He is the only interviewee who finds it difficult to switch between two cultures – indeed he sees himself in a dilemma, and describes his position as 'sitting on the fence' – a situation which he would not recommend to another. Franco has some difficulty with accepting ambivalence, the fact that 'there are pros and cons' to living in both Italy and in Germany, and he feels uneasy about the fact that he is not be able to live in Sicily. His age and the fact that his socialization took place entirely in Italy set him apart from the other interviewees. That he cannot live happily between two cultures may be due to this and to the fact that it was for social, and not primarily for economic reasons that he left Messina. He was also the only interviewee who excluded the possibility of returning to Italy. The overriding sense that one gets from this interview is that Franco is somehow stuck. While he has friends and experiences that cut across nationalities and cultures, he does not apparently want to learn from them. Things are as they are, so to speak. It is unsurprising then, that in contrast to all the other interviewees he is not interested in Europe, it does not matter to him: 'Europe? If it has to come, then let it'.[19]

Perspectives of the self: three indicators

From initial readings and analysis, three main indicators emerged that were common to all of the interviews that would allow me to make a systematic interpretation of the narratives and assess the empirical plausibility of a 'constitutional patriotism' beyond the nation-state. The indicators refer to the preconditions which enable or inhibit the development of trust and solidarity across national and cultural boundaries. These preconditions are found within the relationships between the self and society, the self and others and the self towards itself. Naturally, all three are interrelated. The indicators follow below, together with the questions that I applied (for each) to the interview material:

1) Self towards society: constructed vs. ready-made self-understanding (Endogenous and autonomous vs. exogenous and conventional.)

Do the interviewees understand their identity to be dialogically constructed or as something pre-discursively defined by categories such as nation, region etc.? To what degree can they deal with ambivalence?

2) Self towards others: mixing, encounter and learning
(Degree of openness to and curiosity about other cultures and nations; solidarity and trust vs. constricted empathy and fear.)

To what extent do the interviewees mix with those from other cultures, and how willing are they to engage with and learn from them?

3) Self towards itself: degree of reflexivity and relativization
(Dynamic vs. static self-understanding.)

To what degree are the interviewees self-reflexive i.e.: Do they see their own perspectives as partial and are they willing to see the world through the eyes of others?

(1) Constructed vs. ready-made self-understanding

Frankfurt-born Sonia Rossiello, a vivacious seventeen-year-old, daughter of a working-class family from Cosenza:

> Strange, when I'm here, then I feel German, I speak German, I listen to German and German is the [language of] school lessons. When I'm in Italy, I feel more Italian … I have Italian friends, the atmosphere is very different and … I wear different clothing …[20]

Reyhan Sener, a fifteen-year-old school girl from Frankfurt:

> I am a German Turk. In Turkey they call me a foreigner, because I come from [Germany], and here I am also a foreigner. I don't know where I belong. It's good the way that I am. If I were only a Turk, I wouldn't find it good. I don't know how it would feel … I prefer to stay just as I am … half German and half Turkish.[21]

Eighteen-year-old Fatih Yildirim, member of an Azeri folklore group based at the *Casa di Cultura*, begins his self-presentation like this:

> My name is Fatih and I am a Frankfurter Turk. I was born in Frankfurt, but I have Turkish citizenship … Yeah, this means that I have two cultures. That's how I feel because I was born and raised here [in Germany]. I was never in Turkey as a small child … I've got something from the German culture, and I've got something from the Turkish culture. And this means that I'm a Frankfurter Turk: Frankfurter and Turk![22]

Sonia's use of the term 'strange' (in German, 'komisch') suggests that this young woman perceives her multiple belongings as anomalous compared to the 'norm' of the supposedly unequivocal identities of local Germans (or Italians). Nevertheless, she seems to be quite happy with the plurality of coexisting national identities – depending on the context, she can feel either German or Italian. Sonia, Reyhan and Fatih are not 'uprooted', but are rather rooted within two cultures. This is perhaps the most striking feature of the interviews and of the literature:

the ambivalence of the interviewees' sense of belonging and their awareness that their identities are multiple and constructed, not ready-made or pre-given by any national or cultural bond.

Apart from Franco Baratta (see the section 'Four life stories' above), they all reject the either/or classifications of collective identity which are typical of ready-made conceptions (e.g. the underlying idea of a pre-given identity, which was an important feature of the German debate about dual citizenship). Having developed a certain predisposition to perceive themselves from an intercultural and transnational perspective,[23] migrants are 'betwixt and between'. As we can also see from the literature, second and third-generation migrants display many different kinds of 'positive' enactment of their ambivalent or 'in-between' national and cultural status.[24] Migrants underline the fact that they are both foreign (Italian, Turkish) and German, and most express an ambivalent but strongly-situated idea of citizenship and identity.[25] The plurality of belongings – arising from family, socialization in German schools, work environment, or everyday life in a certain neighbourhood – calls for a complex subjectivity which does not allow migrants to maintain clear, unambiguous social and cultural identifications. However, almost all of my interviewees see this kind of plural belonging as a resource rather than a burden, and move freely between two or more identities.

To conclude this section, I would like to cite an extract from the autobiographical narrative of a young Turkish man who sees the essentializing ideas of a ready-made or pre-given identity (e.g. 'the' Turks, 'the' Germans, 'the' Italians) as a coping strategy adopted by people who cannot deal with ambivalent belongings. Ayberk Yilmaz is a twenty-three-year-old student at the *Hanseatischen Akademie für Medien*.

> In kindergarten there were some problems […] There was, that is, [the expression] 'you shitty foreigner, you Turk!' But this had nothing to do with my being Turkish, rather, it was simply an expression like any other such as 'you're ugly, you're poor'. Expressions which mean really nothing … [One] could've just easily said to me 'you idiot'.[26]

Even when Ayberk was called a 'shitty foreigner' (or '*Scheißausländer*' in German) by children at his kindergarten, he did not feel victimized. He took the insult not as discrimination due to his nationality, but rather as an expression of anger that could easily have been substituted by the term 'idiot', or any other insult that could have been directed at anyone. This theme of young migrants in a multicultural setting using the idea of 'difference' to insult their peers in a more or less serious way also emerges in my own interviews, but we can argue that since in this context 'difference' is distanced from any form of essentializing meaning, the migrants are able to 'play' with these distinctions.[27] Later, in his adolescence, Ayberk discussed with his German peers their 'reservations' about foreigners, but the very fact of being prepared to discuss, he says, meant that they were already recognizing him as an equal human being. He believes that a person develops through his or her experiences and through interactions with others in the course of his or her life; in other words, that individuals are relatively independent of traditions and nationalities:

> Naturally I won't raise my children as Turkish or as German, rather I will raise them
> as Ayberk. My personality is not led by some nationality ... All that I've experienced,
> the people that I've met, the experiences that I have had have all formed my charac-
> ter, my personality ... That has very little to do with tradition or nationality ... I am
> proud to be Turkish or to be German or to speak Turkish or German – for me
> [language] is a technique, a communications technique [laugh] ... I believe that
> when people want to know where you come from or where you belong, this is more
> of a protective function.[28]

Ayberk's ambivalence leads to a dynamic self-understanding. He is certain that
his identity has been 'constructed' through his life's experiences and the people he
has met, epitomizing the dialogical self we have formulated above. He stresses his
'in-between' national status, and rejects essentializing classifications of nationhood, a rejection that is often accompanied in his and others' interviews by an
emphasis on being 'international' and a 'human being' (or 'Mensch' in German).[29]
Ayberk believes that only 'weak' individuals, those who are afraid of encounters
with people of different origins and experience, cling to the shelter of a *demos*, of
a known territory, language and society. He believes that the ability to circum-
navigate around these false but comforting categories of nationhood and culture
is a sign of strength and autonomy, and is accordingly against a patriotism based
on ethnic or cultural bonds or any sort of attitude endorsed by identity-politics.[30]

  In sum, the evidence from my own and other interviews suggests two things:
first, that most migrants, particularly the younger ones who have grown up in
multicultural cities, seem to have little difficulty in dealing with ambivalent belongings and do not need to adopt coping strategies which assign them to clear-
cut national or cultural categories; and second – perhaps more positively – that
migrants find the experience of intercultural interaction enriching.

(2) Mixing, encountering, learning

(i) Mixing: 'Multi-kulti' as a marketplace
Annalisa Corradi (see also the beginning of Chapter 7):

> [I]n my household it is not the case that my children only speak Italian or [read]
> only Italian books or [watch] only Italian films ... In my house, anything goes ... If
> I feel like hearing an Italian song, then I listen to an Italian song. If I feel like hearing
> a German song, then I listen to a German song ... I am happy to have been raised in
> the two cultures, [and] clearly I also would like my children to be raised in the two
> cultures as well. And if possible, even a third![31]

All my interviewees apart from Franco Baratta see their ambivalent belonging –
belonging to two or more cultures – as a resource. Some of them understand it in
terms of 'intercultural competence' or professional know how,[32] others in terms
of deliberate boundary-crossing as a device for distinguishing their particular
lifestyle. For Annalisa, identities are contextually situated, and she is conscious of
being able to switch between them at will, like playing different roles (as she says

at the beginning, 'I can be an Italian, I can be a German'). Accordingly, the link between personal self-understanding, national identity and citizenship is decoupled. Asked whether there would be advantages to having German or dual citizenship, she, like many others, says that she is who she is, and remains so, regardless of citizenship.[33]

Many of the interviewees, for example Armando Guerri (see the section 'Four life stories' above), argue that one should pick and choose the best of the available cultures and mix them together. Or, as Deniz Yücel, a twenty-two-year-old apprentice from Wilhelmsburg remarks:

> As a Turk living in Germany, I must see what's good in the other culture. And I take what's good into my life. But I also see what's good in my own culture and I bring it altogether. That's how it's got to be![34]

(ii) Encounter: friends

Chiara Gambaro is a small, lively greengrocer at the *Kleinmarkthalle*, a huge multicultural food and vegetable market that mixes the exotic with more run-of-the-mill fare. At thirty-eight, she seems uninterested in her appearance, but emanates warmth and a quick intelligence. She talks very fast with a slight Sicilian accent. When she was twelve years old, she came to Frankfurt with her parents, both workers from Agrigento. After a difficult period when she first arrived at school – she spoke not a single word of German – her teacher, 'the kind Herr Wittig', sat her next to another Italian girl who translated for her. In this way she gradually learned to read and write in German. At twenty she married a Sicilian and now has two sons. During our interview she expresses a strong interest in both Italian and German politics (although she has never voted in her life), telling me that she reads an Italian newspaper and regularly watches the German television news 'because one has to know what is going on in the country in which one lives'. Certain of the fact that she has the 'same rights' as a German citizen (apart from national voting rights), she, like all other interviewees, is uninterested in German citizenship. Her idea of citizens' rights is detached from questions of identity.[35] Several times she underlines the fact that she likes working in the multicultural context of the *Kleinmarkthalle* and is especially fond of her Kurdish friends, for whose political troubles in Turkey she expresses much sympathy. She told me that her son has many 'international' friendships, but that he feels perfectly at home when he goes back to Sicily. Chiara too feels at home in Sicily, but also dislikes the fact that people of different social status are treated differently there when they go to an office, a bank or to the doctor, and the fact that women are less free.[36] As we will see below, Chiara mentions 'equality' between men and women, as well as among all persons regardless of where they come from, as a distinctive quality of European citizenship.

> I get along, that is, I feel comfortable with anyone whether they are African, Italian, or Greek; I don't see any difference, none at all ... No, I am Italian and remain Italian in my style, I don't want double citizenship, I don't want German citizenship, I am Italian ... Seeing as I have the same rights as Germans, why should I change my nationality?[37]

Let us recall again Tino Esposito, a high school senior, who says that after their arrival in Germany, his parents eventually made an effort to 'integrate', that is, to 'open up' their culture and language to the Germans, having learnt to trust what is different, and not to be afraid or suspicious of people who did not share the same origins. Tino sees himself as a 'modern man' for whom the boundary between the shared and 'unshared' does not represent any kind of limit for interaction. Put more positively, the unknown is challenging, exciting. What counts when it comes to fighting prejudice and fostering curiosity is intercultural exchanges and experiences and the meeting of different nationalities at school:

> My parents only wanted to stay here for a few months. This turned into more than 30 years … [At first] they didn't want to integrate. Once it was clear to them that they would be living here, then they started … to venture towards the 'unknown'. That was the problem: Too much fear of the unknown, of others' traditions, of others' languages … In my opinion, the only thing that can help is … education. The bringing together of different nationalities must be done through school … For this reason, I support every school exchange [programme], because one can talk and talk, but if a person hasn't had any contact with others, the conversation will go nowhere![38]

Of the questions that prove most revealing of the symbolic drawing or crossing of boundaries is that of the interviewee's friends. All say that they have friends from different national and cultural backgrounds: Italians, other foreigners (both European and non-European) and Germans. As we have already seen in the narratives of Armando Guerri and Teresa Pedrini, they frequently use the term 'international' and 'mixed' without this involving any sort of boundary-drawing.[39] For many, this has the same meaning as intercultural and 'European' and, as Teresa Pedrini commented, a united Europe is already a reality for many migrants. This finding is supported by the literature on Turkish migrants: to them, the contrast between the multicultural setting of school and the cultural practices of the family home seems greater than that which Italian migrants have to face. Fatih Yildirim, the eighteen-year-old member of the Azeri folklore group in Frankfurt says:

> Yeah, because the social environment was [actually] two environments: … at school, it is not purely German, I have Albanian, Yugoslavian, Italian and German friends. This is another culture … a European culture. And at home, it is a Turkish culture that operates according to Turkish principles. The two [environments] are difficult to connect.[40]

(iii) Learning

My own interviewees and those whose narratives are reported in the literature emphasize that people with different origins can go beyond encounters with others and mixing with them interculturally by actively learning from one another. While they recognize that such encounters can involve conflict or other difficulties, all seem to agree that attempts at mutual understanding and learning are enriching experiences which contribute to one's development as a person. Such an open and dialogically constructed self is a crucial presupposition for participation in a transnational public sphere. As we have seen in Chapter 6, the idea of intercultural (and inter-societal) learning[41] is very important in the development of the theory of 'situated' constitutional patriotism. Using a dialogical approach, plurality is understood as a source of new perspectives when interpreting the social world or constitutional principles in the give and take of political deliberation.

Before we look at more extracts from the interviews, it is useful to first briefly consider some quantitative results from a series of attitude surveys conducted in 2000 as part of the well-respected *Shellstudie*. This major social research project covered more than 5000 adolescents in Germany from different educational and social backgrounds. Overall, the findings of the *Shellstudie* 2000 suggest strongly that hostility towards foreigners (or *Ausländerfeindlichkeit* in German) does not result from personal experience. On the contrary, the more contact or interaction with foreigners that people have, the higher the chances that they do not display discriminatory attitudes towards foreigners. Boundary drawing, the sharp distinction of 'us' and 'them' (inclusion and exclusion) seems to be the product of discourses 'about' foreigners in general, not of a 'situating' experience of communicative interaction 'with' foreigners. The evidence, therefore, seems to suggest that a European politics 'without *demos*' could, in principle, be fostered by cross-national and intercultural deliberation.

There are three particular findings of the *Shellstudie* 2000 (the focus of which was the views of adolescents on multicultural society) that are of interest here. First, it was found that, among respondents, Germans were the most pessimistic about the future: 36% of male and 37% of female Germans surveyed agreed that the 'future was rather gloomy'. Of the foreigners, 35% of male Turks and 26% of female Turks agreed with the statement, while 26% of male Italians and 23% of female Italians agreed. These foreigners in Germany see the future more positively than Germans, and among the foreigners, Italians are more optimistic than Turks, and women more optimistic than men.[42] This supports the impression given by my own interview material that migrants feel that they roughly enjoy the same opportunities as the indigenous population. They feel free to navigate between their different identities, something that a society in which identity politics or a 'multicultural politics of difference' would be unlikely to foster.

Second, Germans, Turks and Italians all recognized more similarities between each other than differences. Over 50% of those surveyed responded that in almost all their activities (eating, buying clothes, watching television, listening to music, education, work, choosing friends, partners and lovers, sports, going out at night, politics, travel) they 'behave similarly'. Exceptions to these categories of activity were family life (only between 20 and 30% reported that their family life was similar to that of those from different cultural backgrounds) and religion.[43]

Finally, and most importantly, a strikingly high percentage of respondents said that Germans and non-Germans could learn from each other. Participants in the survey were given four options from which to choose: (a) Yes, they can learn from each other, but Germans can learn more from foreigners than vice versa; (b) yes, they can learn from each other, but foreigners can learn more from Germans than vice versa; (c) yes, Germans and foreigners have an equal amount to learn from each other; (d) no, they cannot learn from each another. The results are set out in the table below.

		% of respondents choosing each option			
		A Germans learn more from foreigners	B Foreigners learn more from Germans	C Both learn equally from each other	D Neither can learn from the other
Germans	Male	2.3	13.9	69.5	14.4
	Female	2.3	11.5	76.7	9.5
Italians	Male	8.1	4.5	81.8	5.6
	Female	4.9	1.8	87.7	5.5
Turks	Male	8.2	4.5	77.9	9.4
	Female	7.2	2.3	83.3	7.2

Source: Deutsche Shell (ed.), *Jugend 2000*, vol. 1, Leske+Budrich, Opladen 2000, pp. 245–247.

Among those choosing response 'C' were the more educated and politically interested (nearer to the SPD, PDS and Grüne than to the CDU/CSU and FDP).[44] Let us now return to the insights of my interviewees.

Maurizio Albertini is thirty-two years old, just beginning to thicken a little around the midriff. He is polite and courteous, always careful to try to conform to the expectations of others, the sort of person who one would not be surprised to discover is a civil servant. In fact, he is a computer engineer who studied in Milan and Tokyo and who since 1994 has worked at the European Central Bank. He comes from a middle-class family in northern Italy and presents himself as an open-minded person who from an early age has been curious about foreign cultures. In our interview, Maurizio complains about his Italian colleagues who keep to themselves instead of mixing with people from other countries and 'learning' from them. It may take years, but, he says, it is worthwhile.

> One of the things that interest me is that those Italians don't mingle … they always stay amongst their own kind … they always visit other Italians, and many times they don't even realise … this attachment … but one can also learn [to change], this is a bit of my … vision.[45]

Similarly, Maria Luisa di Boggio, a neatly-dressed thirty-six-year-old secretary at the Banco di Napoli, insists that working with people from different cultural backgrounds and ways of thinking provides an opportunity for mutual learning, and that such learning leads to 'personal development':

> It broadens you mentally, in my opinion … you notice the differences of mentality [amongst people] but … not only the defects … you also value some things; therefore, this certainly makes you grow … as a person … In my opinion it is positive … being in contact with different people can only help individual development.[46]

As we have seen above, the younger generation of interviewees who grew up in the multicultural environment of inner-city schools spontaneously underline the enriching experience of encountering people from different countries and 'learning' about their culture, history and political situation. Not one of them thinks that intercultural differences inhibit mutual understanding or that it is not worth making the effort involved in 'interpretative charity'. This is true even of Ali Karabulut, a nineteen-year-old man who came from Turkey to Frankfurt only three years ago, and who might reasonably have been expected to have had more difficulty with intercultural interaction due to his poor German and lack of shared socialization:

> I came here [to Frankfurt] and they had a whole other culture. And I also had a whole other culture. But if someone wants with all their heart, then one can live together [with] … the two cultures. It is not easy, perhaps … But it can be done. I even had a German girlfriend … Yes, yes, it's another culture, but if you … understand each other, then both can learn. [47]

(3) Reflexivity: dynamic vs. static self-understanding

At the age of thirty-three, Luisa Mangani works in a glass-encased skyscraper in front of the city opera house for one of Germany's biggest law firms. Dressed in a dark blue suit, she greets me in a huge conference room with a ten-metre-long table. Asked about her life, she refers to her meteoric career and repeatedly underscores the 'global player' status of her company. Clearly used to public performances, her narrative is precise and matter-of-fact. Born in Venice to a bourgeois family, she studied law in Bologna, and has worked in Brussels and Frankfurt, where she has been for the last five years. She much preferred Brussels for its 'more flexible 360-degree vision of the world', while she views Frankfurt as a more circumscribed and merely European setting. She is married to a half-Italian, half-German bank manager and has no children. Asked whether her national identity has been transformed by living abroad, she replies that her view on both Italy and Germany has become more 'objective':

> Perhaps I have more of an objective vision of Italy and Germany … Concerning Italy, I have realized that, by living abroad … I have become more patriotic, more attached to Italy, but I also see [the country's] defects, the disorganization, the immense political chaos which, in my opinion, also exist in other states … before [while in Italy] I was on the inside, therefore I had, without question, a less detached view … more emotional and less objective. [48]

Luisa was surprised to find that, in living abroad, she has become 'more attached' to and 'patriotic' about Italy, but at the same time 'more detached' and 'less emotional'. This, along with other interviews, shows that exposure to a plural situatedness somehow relativizes the attachment to one's roots. Multiple belongings do not seem to lead to a sort of abstract postnational identity but to a more reflexive, although situated, sense of belonging. The processing of inner multiplicity seems to foster an 'autonomization' of the self: the collective identity of migrants is ambivalent and relativized, while their personal identity is strong but flexible – and not at all 'morally impoverished' or 'non-committed' as *demos*-theorists might assume.

All my Italian interviewees display a 'postconventional' identity, here understood as the capacity to move between multiple identities at will, according to the context of social interaction. With the sole exception of Marco Cimino (discussed in the next section) who includes only people with a 'European culture', this capacity is accompanied by a striking willingness (spontaneously expressed in the narratives) to change perspective in order to try to see the world through others' eyes (multicultural literacy or interpretative charity). Some, for example, say that if they were Turkish (i.e. if they did not have EU citizenship), they too would ask for German citizenship in order to have the same rights as Germans or migrants from EU member states (see for instance Armando Guerri in the section 'Four life stories'). Similarly, they underline (like Franco Baratta and Chiara Gambaro) that today the Turks or the asylum-seekers in Germany or the Albanians and Kurds who arrive on the coast of Puglia are like the Italian migrants of the 1960s.[49]

In all my data, we find evidence of the upward drift of a moral consciousness in which the terms 'us' and 'them' – 'friend' and 'enemy' according to the idea of belonging to primary or primordial communities – have no basis. Rather, under conditions of multiple senses of belonging, cultural and national identities become more 'relativized' and reflexive. Reflexivity, that is, the insight that one's own perspective is partial and that the perspective of others is potentially equally valid, is crucial for the idea of dialogical solidarity across national or cultural boundaries. The idea of solidaristic redistribution to reduce natural or economic inequalities, which found its expression in the modern welfare state, need not be based on a pre-political 'we-identity' – as argued in Chapters 2 and 6 – but can be based on universalistic norms (interpreted in dialogical deliberation) arising from different perspectives. For the European polity this would mean surrendering the idea that solidarity and trust presuppose boundaries that define whose welfare is to be counted and whose resource position is to be equalized with regard to a certain national group. My data provides some evidence that the socio-cultural presuppositions for democratic politics and for (dialogical) solidarity across national and cultural boundaries can already be obtained in many contexts, and can be fostered in others.

The creation of a European identity

In regard to the encounter of different cultures, Bakhtin noted:

> In the realm of culture, outsideness is a most powerful factor in (creative) understanding. It is only in the eyes of another culture that foreign culture reveals itself fully and profoundly … A meaning only reveals its depths once it has encountered and come into contact with another, foreign meaning; they engage in a kind of dialogue, which surmounts the closedness and one-sidedness of these particular meanings, these cultures. We raise new questions for a foreign culture, ones that it does

not raise for itself; we seek answers to our own questions in it; and the foreign cul-
ture responds to us by revealing to us its new aspects and new semantic depths ...
Such a dialogic encounter of two cultures does not result in merging or mixing.
Each remains its own unity and open totality, but they are mutually enriched.[50]

As seen in our analysis of the European public sphere (Chapter 3), a plurality
of cultural and ideological perspectives on Europe are 'invented' and negotiated
among a variety of fragmented, sometimes overlapping or contending, discourses:
the official discourse of the EU,[51] the discourse of social scientists, the media discourse of intellectuals and opinion-leaders (in television, newspapers, books), but
also in the informal discourse of people in everyday life. Since there are no a priori
criteria (language, territorial unity, socialization, etc.) for the formation of collective identities, empirical research can only reconstruct the socio-historical con-
figurations of their emergence.[52] In my case studies, I focus on the role of those
who live and work between two or more countries as agents of the formation of
collective identities. The previous part of this chapter revealed that contemporary
Europeans are in fact evolving as a result of the variegated reality of Europe in a
way that undermines and supersedes conventional theoretical considerations of
European identity.

Theories of European identity are rarely based on sociological research, and
if so they are almost always limited to the analysis of 'hard' societal and institutional structures or quantitative analysis of attitudes towards Europe (through
opinion polls like that of Eurobarometer). It has been shown, for example, that
there are a declining number of people who identify exclusively with a nation-
state. Europe has become a viable and positive identity for many people who see it
as supplementing rather than eroding national identity.[53] However, the often suggested idea that Europeanness is expressed in the form of a pyramid of identities,
whereby the European component is at the top, is an all too simple account of
identities. The various components of individual identity 'cannot be neatly sepa-
rated on different levels'.[54] Rather, it seems that the self-understanding of being
German, French or Italian inherently contains aspects of Europeanness. Interestingly, this differs in the case of the British, where being 'English', for example, is
seen in stark contrast to being 'European'. However, seeing as the British case is
more the exception than the rule within Europe, this point will not be further
elaborated here.[55]

In piecing together the various findings available regarding European identity, it may be concluded that there is, as of yet, no comprehensive research-base
which explores 'l'Europe vécue' – that is, how people actually make sense of European identity and citizenship under conditions of societal denationalization.[56] My
argument here is that the increasing mobility of Europeans has produced
transnational spaces for professional and everyday life experience that transform
the understanding of national identities by facilitating the mixing of elements
from different cultures. The interviews show that this results in increasing awareness, at individual and collective levels, of the 'constructed' (or dialogical) nature
of identity.

We will now carry on with the analysis of interview data, at this stage looking for answers to the following questions: first, what kind of European identity do the interviewees assume (converging or 'pastiche')? Second, do they stress a 'cultural-ethnic' or a 'civic-political' ideology of European citizenship, which is to say, how do they conceive the boundaries of Europe? Thirdly and finally, is there any evidence in contemporary Europe for the existence of a 'situated' constitutional patriotism as a postnational form of identity – an identity without cultural unity or *demos* and, therefore, without enemies?

European identity: converging or pastiche?

My interviewees spontaneously mention Europe, displaying a transnational (rather than post-national) European identity, although often carefully underlining that they want to 'keep' their Italian and/or German identity. Maria Luisa del Boggio, the thirty-six-year-old secretary at the Banco di Napoli wants her son to grow up in an 'international' environment but at the same time, to keep his 'Italian identity'. This, she says, is easy: 'I do not feel that I have left my country … or am isolated from it'. On the contrary, her emotional and cultural connection to Italy is nourished by the media. She feels that she has total 'freedom of movement', while living abroad has made her aware of the differences between people and world views, whose interactions create what she calls 'the real European spirit'. She thinks that Europe will one day be united.

> I would like my son to maintain … let's say, be an Italian … In my opinion, it is important to maintain one's own roots, one's own identity … But I believe that freedom of movement … gives one the sense of physical closeness and… contact with … different worlds: Inevitably there are differences, and perhaps there will always be; it's correct that there are … This, in my opinion, is the real European spirit.[57]

Together with other interviews, Maria Luisa's statements show that collective identities are a jumble of heterogeneous narrative elements, that Europe is experienced as an intercultural pastiche which embraces difference (see too the interviews earlier in this chapter with Toni Esposito and Chiara Gambaro) and the production of highly differentiated spaces of social experience in which a variety of identifications and self-categorizations can be (and are) enacted. In their daily lives, people negotiate local, regional, national and supranational, as well as political, ethnic, religious and socio-cultural patterns of identification. The exact combination of factors involved depends on the concrete situation (and the other people present), as well as the larger socio-political context, that is, how these collective identities are framed by public discourses.

Thus, it would seem that viewing Europeanization solely in terms of convergence[58] is empirically narrow and historically flat. Like globalisation, Europeanization, in our socially fragmented and pluricultural societies, does not mean cultural unification,[59] and the emerging European identity is unlikely to reflect a

supranational overarching ideal which neatly packages national, regional and local identities like a Russian doll. To be European is not to identify with a common
identity comparable to a national or regional identity. It is not premised upon the
fictive myth of a *demos*. Rather, as Gerard Delanty has pointed out, Europeanness
is to be found in critical and reflexive forms of self-understanding: 'To be European is simply to recognize that one lives in a world that does not belong to a
specific people'.[60] And as my interviews demonstrate, it also means assuming a
high degree of cognitive openness and curiosity towards other cultures, as well as
a willingness to actively learn from one another.

Where are the boundaries of Europe?

In a world where collective identities are not erased by an all-encompassing European identity, but rather co-exist with it and one another in a fluctuating network
of socio-cultural and national identities, do people still distinguish between 'members' and 'non-members'? In this section, I will explore the multiplicity of latent
ideologies as discursive strategies of boundary-drawing between 'us' and 'them'.
Different ideological constructions of national and European identity and citizenship correspond to different, more or less rigid forms of symbolic boundary-
drawing[61] and thus to different politics of inclusion/exclusion.[62]

My interviews show how Italian migrants, especially those who attended school
in Germany, enact ambivalent self-understandings (simultaneously Italian, German and 'international'), but – and in this they differ from their Turkish peers –
often spontaneously deem themselves 'European' when asked about citizenship
issues. Unlike Turkish migrants, they are citizens of an EU member state and say
that because of the 'legal advantages' of being an EU citizen they 'do not need'
German citizenship. All narratives stress a 'situated patriotism' that goes beyond
cultural and national boundaries, a fundamental element of the socio-cultural
preconditions for a European polity without a *demos*.

Veronica Costanzo, a fifteen-year-old born in Frankfurt:

> PN: Would you like to have German citizenship or dual citizenship or …?
> VC: Nah
> PN: Neither nor?
> VC: No, I don't need it. I'm European.
> PN: And what does that mean?
> VC: That I don't need dual nationalities. I can't be thrown out of Germany.[63]

Veronica proceeds to draw boundaries between herself and her Turkish peers;
however this boundary-drawing remains relatively 'neutral' as she understands
citizenship in juridical, not ethnical-cultural terms.[64]

The only interviewee whose boundary-drawing is firmly based on cultural
and ethnic criteria (and who as a consequence displays a sort of federalist Euro-
nationalism) is Marco Cimino, a clumsy thirty-nine-year-old. We meet in his rather
neglected apartment, where he is keen to show me his new TV which can project

a picture onto the living room wall – currently RAI television news. He is extremely eager to chat and speaks quickly, although sometimes a little distractedly, with a heavy Pugliese accent. He came to Germany at the age of eighteen because he wanted to earn money (working at Höchst) to buy a house in Foggia. In fact, Marco remained in Germany, marrying a Portuguese woman and eventually becoming an electrician at the Historical Museum of Frankfurt. As an EU citizen, he tells me he could even become a *Beamter* (civil servant). He is also very proud that he is the vice-president of the AFI (*Associazione Famiglie Italiane*), an association which organizes feasts for Italian communities (although Spanish and German families often join), and also recently became a *Kommunaler Ausländervertreter*, that is, a representative for all foreigners in the city of Frankfurt. When talking about his first job, Marco describes his Turkish colleagues in negative terms. He was happier once he had changed jobs and found himself working with Spaniards, Portuguese, and Greeks (also Germans). It is they, with whom he has lived and worked since, that he views as 'European foreigners'. He says that the Turks simply 'think differently'.

> When the Turks have feasts there's always a mess … they kill each other, they disturb the neighbours and because of them, we are forced – Italians and others who organize feasts – to pay … for their damages; that is, here they believe that they can do whatever they want because they are in a foreign land, let's say … many years ago, perhaps when our fathers came [to Germany] they would say 'Well we're here only for a short while and then we'll go back and so it doesn't interest me what goes on' and this I'm actually witnessing now with the Turks … They don't adapt … I see that they don't care …[65]

Marco proceeds to remark that everyone should behave respectfully towards the Germans and other nations. Asked about the meaning of 'Europe' (something which he spontaneously and extensively mentions), he says it means self-government of the people who live in Europe, bringing together all the 'good things' from the different countries, which would become like regions (e.g. Germany would be like Bavaria today). Marco emphasizes that one ought to 'adapt' to the habits of others, to 'enter' into their culture. In his view, everyone should learn from the way people from other countries do things, how they tackle problems. He could bring things he has learnt in Germany and Italy to the Portuguese, for example, just like his children do when they go back to Italy or to Portugal to visit relatives. The 'exchange of ideas' through European newspapers and television and the formation of European political parties (he imagines something like a big SPD) would foster European unification.[66] Asked about citizenship, he says he will wait for a 'European passport and a European constitution'. For his three daughters (who speak German, Italian and Portuguese), he paints a very positive picture of their future in the 'new Europe'.

> One has to adapt to where one lives; that is, if I go to Portugal, I can't live as though I were in Italy, or as I do in Germany … I would have to force myself to enter into their ways, the culture they have … I could offer in exchange those ideas, those things that I learned in Germany or Italy … If you speak of Europe and then of

constituting a European constitution, it means that it would be the same regardless of whether you are in Italy – in the North or South – [or anywhere] in Europe ... I believe it will be this way ... [for the children] who will have many more opportunities ... than we do.[67]

Like most of the other interviewees, Marco stresses his in-between national status, but when confronted with issues of citizenship (which asks for unequivocal identification), he is the only interviewee who takes on a 'thick' European identity, which he defines by drawing an ethnic-cultural boundary that excludes 'Turks'.[68] This positive identification (e.g. between Italian and Spanish migrants in Germany), which refers to processes of inclusion among Europeans and the creation of a European citizenship, goes hand in hand with negative identification (e.g. of Turkish migrants), which involves the drawing of (more or less rigid) boundaries and processes of exclusion of 'non-European' foreigners. If we conceive of European citizenship in cultural or ethnic terms (a European *demos*), we risk providing the criteria for a common delimitation of the outside.[69] This forces a new dichotomy into public discourse, that is, between intra-European migrants and extra-EU immigrants (or 'extra-comunitari' or 'extra-communitarian residents').[70]

Nevertheless, all interviewees apart from Marco, especially the younger ones, emphasize EU citizenship in civic-political terms (see for example Armando Guerri in the 'Four life stories' section), thus boundaries become arbitrary or 'constructed'. Remember also Maurizio Albertini, the computer engineer at the European Central Bank who describes himself as a 'cittadino del mondo' (citizen of the world) and who sees Europe as a forum for exchange across cultural boundaries that 'could extend to the "Arab" world', for example. My question about whether he would apply for the German/double citizenship surprises him: Europe is what is already 'happening' in his bank and somehow an 'arbitrary' circumstance. His international experience goes well beyond Europe.[71]

Let us end this section with an extract from the interview with Chiara Gambaro, the greengrocer in the *Kleinmarkthalle*, who stresses equality (by which she means equality of legal rights), freedom and democracy as the important features of a European identity. Her idea of Europe is 'situated' or rooted in her German and Italian cultures, as well as that of the intercultural Frankfurt in which she lives and works. At the same time, her Europe reaches out and can include 'threatened' Kurds, 'oppressed' Indian women and non-Europeans ('extracomunitari'); thereby blurring boundaries drawn by European citizenship between individuals from member states and individuals from 'third' states:

We are all European, no? I think so ... In my opinion, feeling like a European is feeling free, independent, not like in some nations of the world like India where [people] have no rights, as women, for example [....] We are democratic ... We are international, we are truly Europeans, and even non-Europeans living here have adapted a bit as well.[72]

Conclusion

The interview material shows that there is little evidence for the existence of a converging (cultural) European identity even for people who live different cultures at the same time. Rather, they display a pastiche self-consciousness and a transnational idea of citizenship which does not identify the 'other' as enemy or alien, but rather as an interlocutor whose difference is a resource and a wealth. Moreover, the political and cultural elements of a collective identity are intertwined: intercultural exchanges occur in everyday Frankfurt-life that potentially reinforce loyalty to the practice of a situated constitutional patriotism beyond the nation-state. If dialogue goes across national or cultural boundaries, and dialogue generates trust and solidarity, it follows that trust and solidarity can also move across those same boundaries – negating the need for a European *demos*. Increasing numbers of people with multiple sense of belonging or a pastiche European identity seem ready to develop identities which are less parochial (or in other words, more universalistic), yet they are 'situated' in their everyday (intercultural) life experience. These are socio-cultural presuppositions for deliberative politics beyond the nation-state which can be fostered by institutionalized citizenship practices promoting cultural self-reflexivity, openness to diversity and cross-national political dialogue.[73] In the multicultural and transnational context of a new Europe, such arrangements would 'empower' citizens by allowing them to participate actively in a 'horizontal' political/constitutional dialogue instead of being observers within a benign social democratic pluralism that is delegated to an elite. Such 'active' citizenship practices undermine the monopoly of representation and social dependency assumed by the political class. Rather than understanding individuals as authoring politicians through voting practices, the idea of democracy as genuine self-rule demands participation in collective action and public discourse as a good in itself.

Notes

1 In Turkish: 'Bir dil bir insan; iki dil iki insan'. It means that if you have one language you are one person, but that if you have two languages you are 'worth' two people.

2 I use the term 'everyday life' in Peter Berger and Thomas Luckmann's sense, i.e. as the ordinary reality of social life. They argue that the social world is constructed by processes of thinking in everyday life (P. L. Berger and T. Luckmann, *Die gesellschaftliche Konstruktion der Wirklichkeit: eine Theorie der Wissenssoziologie*, S. Fischer Verlag, Frankfurt am Main 1969).

3 J. Habermas, *Postmetaphysical Thinking*, MIT Press, Cambridge, MA, 1992, p. 185.

4 For the sake of brevity and clarity, interviews had to be condensed in some instances. Also, due to linguistic differences, English translations presented here do not always represent the – word for word – statements made by interviewees. However, original language transcripts are provided in corresponding endnotes.

5 Original transcript follows: 'Ich fiel durch meine Hautfarbe zwar nicht auf, aber immer noch durch sprachliche Probleme, ähm, da hat man schon gespürt, dass du, immer noch bis zur fünften Klasse, dass du eigentlich ein Sonderling bist. So hatte ich jedenfalls immer

das Gefühl. … Also ab der sechsten ungefähr, hat es in mir gearbeitet, ich hab' mir wirklich überlegt, ähm, du hast es irgendwie nicht nötig, ja, dich ständig von diesen blöden, äh, [lachend] Klassenkameraden da anmachen zu lassen. Und das war … ähm, so 'ne Phase, in der ich in dieser Zeit nachgedacht habe, ähm, wie ich irgendwie mich selber verbessern kann. … *Man muss ja auch irgendwie, man hat ja auch versucht, irgendwie nicht immer nur als Opfer dazustehen …, über die Sprache und über's Lernen geht's am besten.* … Dann waren plötzlich wieder die Leute da die deswegen ausgegrenzt haben. Also nicht nur, weil man Ausländer ist, sondern es fing dann an [lachend], so nach dem Motto "Streber, du machst ja immer alles besser". Ja, und dann war man wieder in irgendeiner Ecke. Aber das kann, das passiert anderen auch.' (Translation by Lorraine Frisina).

6 Derogatory term assigned to Italian immigrants in Germany.

7 Original transcript follows: 'Also, bis zur zehnten gab's diese Probleme, … mein Vater hat mir gegenüber argumentiert, sechste Klasse und dann noch bis zur zehnten, und dann muss ich irgendwo hin, was weit weg ist, und er muss mir dann, ähm, die Monatskarte finanzieren, das geht nicht. … Ähm, ich hab' dann gesagt, dann werd' ich, äh, irgendwelche offiziellen Stellen, äh, anschreiben und sagen, dass du mein Kindergeld falsch verwendest, ja? Die haben ja immerhin Kindergeld dafür bekommen [lachend]. Und dann, dann war's klar, ne. …Es war 'ne sehr offene Schule, die also keine großen Hürden gesetzt hat für Ausländer. Die hatte, die wurden aufgenommen. Ja, und da hat sich ja so'n bisschen politisches Gewissen bei mir geformt, kann man schon sagen und es gab nicht immer diese Konflikte darüber, wo ich herkomme, wo ich nicht herkomme mit den anderen Schülern, äh, sondern da ging es wirklich nur darum: Hast du was im Kopf?' (Translation by Lorraine Frisina.)

8 Original transcript follows: 'Also, ich könnt' mich ja irgendwie so stark angepasst haben, dass ich nicht mehr so an meine eigenen Wurzeln gedacht hab', aber ich hab' echt, äh, 'ne ganze Weile lang nie so richtig deutsch empfinden können, ich konnte deutsch analysieren, deutsch denken [lachend], aber das Empfinden hat sich nie eingestellt.' (Translation by Lorraine Frisina.)

9 Original transcript follows: 'Weil ich halt kein Deutsch verstanden hab', also, ich dachte halt, ich hab' das immer als negativ aufgefasst, wenn man mir was gesagt hat. … Nein, also später hab' ich's halt so bemerkt, die andern Kinder waren halt, haben sich nicht verändert, und als ich dann begriffen hab', was die mir halt immer gesagt haben, die waren halt supernett [kurzes Lachen], ich bin halt immer noch mit denen gut befreundet, mit meinen alten Grundschul-, äh, -mitschülern. … Ich hab', äh, internationale Freunde halt, der wenigste Teil ist deutsch [kurzes Lachen], also, ich hab' viele, da gibt's, was weiß ich, aus Sri Lanka, aus Kroatien, was hab' ich denn noch? Aus Türkei hab' ich viele Freunde, also schon international. … Wir sind fast alle halt so "*Dritte-Generationsmässig*", und ich hab' halt, ich hab' so, äh, leicht eingebürgert, kann man sagen. Paar von denen haben jetzt auch die deutsche Staatsbürgerschaft angenommen, weil die sind, die haben halt Probleme mit, äh, ihrer Herkunft, mit ihrem, äh, mit ihrem Herkunftsland [kurzes Lachen] … der eine Kroate wegen wegen was weiß ich, wenn er halt ins Ausland möchte, muss er halt Visum und so was, hat er halt jetzt auch deutsche Staatsbürgerschaft angenommen. … Bei mir, bei mir ist es halt, Italien ist halt in der EU, und ich hab' halt keine Probleme, ich wüsste auch nicht, warum ich, äh, die deutsche Staatsbürgerschaft annehmen sollte, ich hab' … ich hab' genauso viele Rechte so gesehen als wie die Deutschen. Also, außer das mit den Wahlen, aber ansonsten, find ich, hab' ich keine Benachteiligung als, äh, EU-Staats, also Mitbürger.' (Translation by Lorraine Frisina.)

10 Original transcript follows: 'Also, wär' ich, was weiß ich, aus der Türkei oder so […] würd' 'ich dann schon die, äh, die deutsche Staatsbürgerschaft annehmen wollen. Weil, äh, ich weiß nicht, als Türke hat man, ich weiß nicht, nicht so viele Vorteile wie wenn man Italiener ist in Deutschland. Ich fühl' mich als Europäer, also hundertprozentig [kurzes Lachen] … Ich seh' nur Vorteile darin, weil ich hab' mich jetzt halt mittlerweile für die anderen Länder auch interessiert, und ich find' das halt gut … der eine erzählt mir halt von Kroatien, es ist

schön dort und so was, und jetzt fahr' ich halt bald mit dem in Urlaub dort nach Kroatien und schau's mir das halt dort an und so. Und der eine Türke meint halt: "Komm mal mit nach Türkei, schau'n wir uns", also solang, also ich seh' da keine, äh, irgendwie negativen Aspekte, dass man da anderen, andere Länder kennenlernen sollte. … Ne Freundin aus 'nem anderen Land? Also, es kommt halt drauf an, wie sich eine Person anstellt. … das wär' mir ganz egal, was weiß ich mit 'ner Afrikanerin oder Marrokanerin oder sowas, das, nee, also, mir ist das ganz egal. Es kommt halt immer auf die Person drauf an.' (Translation by Lorraine Frisina.)

11 Original transcript follows: 'Also, eigentlich, ich weiß nicht, ich lieg' irgendwie dazwischen, also [kurzes Lachen] das ist jetzt ganz schwer, weil ich kann mich da nicht, ähm, also identi-, identifizieren mit irgendwie deutsche Kultur, italienische Kultur, ich, ich wüsste, also schon, die italienischen Bräuche sind mir schon bekannt und auch die deutschen. Da gibt's halt das eine, was in Deutschland halt weniger gut ist und Italien vielleicht besser, und dann gibt's halt das andere, was wiederum andersrum, äh, verläuft, also das in Italien schlechter ist und in Italien bes-, äh, in Deutschland besser.' (Translation by Lorraine Frisina.)

12 Armando reflects on the ways in which he and his friends poke fun at one another's national origins within the context of football (original transcript follows): 'Ja, da, da ist dann halt [kurzes Lachen], da sind dann halt hat man öfter Konflikte und so mit meinen' Freunden [lachend], "Ach, ihr Italiener", was weiß ich so mit Foul … was weiß ich, zum Beispiel da geschieht gerade ein Foul, und der Schiedsrichter sieht das nicht, und dann heißt es halt "Ihr Italiener foult da rum" und so, und da streitet man sich halt des öfteren: "Ach, ihr Kroaten" und so, "Ihr mit euren Rentnern dort auf 'm Spielfeld", also … [kurzes Lachen] oder was weiß ich, der eine verschießt ein Elfmeter halt in der Weltmeisterschaft und dann heißt es dann halt wieder "die Italiener können kein Elfmeter schießen", also es passiert dann halt oder was weiß ich, ich mach' die halt blöd an, was weiß ich, "Türkei macht die und so und jenes oder Kroatien halt immer" oder "Ihr habt gar keine Fußball-Nationalmannschaft aus Sri Lanka" oder so [kurzes Lachen].'

13 This to-ing and fro-ing is supposedly one of the reasons why Italian children are less successful at school than the children of other migrants. (In fact, Teresa Pedrini's brother and sister attend a special needs school, the *Sonderschule*.)

Italians were the largest group to immigrate to Germany at the end of the 1950s; their image of 'integrated' European migrants, however, contrasts with the fact that, compared with other groups, third-generation German-Italians have shown a remarkably low level of social mobility in terms of education and entry into the professions (A. Cavalli-Wordel, *Schicksale italienischer Migrantenkinder. Eine Fallstudie*, Beltzverlag, Weinheim 1989; A. Lanfranchi, *Immigration und Schule. Transformationsprozesse in traditionellen Familienwelten als Vorraussetzung für schulisches Überleben von Migrantenkindern*, Westdeutscher Verlag, Opladen 1995; see also: Projekt zur Förderung des Schulerfolgs italienischer Kinder in Deutschland e.V., *Informationsblätter,* Frankfurt am Main 1998).

14 Original transcript follows: 'All'inizio tutti mi guardavano un pochettino così strano no, italiana, la curiosità degli altri, poi niente, da parte dei ragazzi è stato senza problemi ho iniziato subito a instaurare un rapporto di amicizia, però…Con tutti, cioè io non, non faccio differenze ormai. … No, no, no, non c'era nessuna distinzione cioè proprio tra ragazzi questo non esisteva, cioè non esiste proprio, tutti sono si può dire tutti tedeschi, è uguale se adesso sei straniero, italiano, spagnolo, portoghese …' (Translation by Lorraine Frisina.)

15 Original transcript follows: 'Quando si ha le ore libere magari ci si incontra con tutta la classe, si parla del mio paese, del loro paese, cosa c'è di differente, cosa c'è di uguale, cosa, cosa manca nel loro paese, cosa manca nel mio paese, anche un pochettino sul, sul campo politico si parla anche, perché la maggior parte delle volte tutto deriva anche dalla politica del proprio paese, no? … Si parla più che altro della politica che c'è nella Turchia momentaneamente con i curdi. … più che altro questione che ci si vuole sentire un pochettino come se si stesse a casa, anche se non siamo tutti di un paese ma di tanti, di diversi paesi, però ci sentiamo poi casa, parlando del proprio paese, come se stessimo a

casa parlando con i nostri amici, no?' (Translation by Lorraine Frisina.)

16 Original transcript follows: 'Tu sei in Germania, vivi in Germania, da italiano, nessun problema ... Cioè a me personalmente non è mai successo di sentirmi straniera, anzi alcune volte mi sento più straniera in Italia, per dirti! ... E' un arricchimento sì, assolutamente, perché stai a contatto con tedeschi, con marocchini, con turchi, con tante altre nazionalità e da ogni nazionalità prendi un vivere, un modo di vivere, una cultura, una religione cioè ampli anche il tuo, la tua cultura, la propria cultura personale perché non rimani poi magari come tanti ragazzi italiani tra italiani, magari poi, ok adesso ci sono anche gli albanesi e i turchi ma più di tanto cioè non gli interessa nemmeno, loro non hanno un'idea ben precisa, ... invece da noi non è così, io per dirti il mio migliore amico è un marocchino cioè non è che, non c'è distinzione [...] loro vivono esattamente come noi, l'unica cosa che li differenzia da noi è la religione ma più di tanto non c'è. ... Due settimane fa sono stata giù in Italia, e parlando con un paio di ragazzi lì, perché mi chiamò un amico, un marocchino mi chiamò, allora dissero ma chi era, chi non era, e allora raccontai un pochettino, "No io con gente così no, ma manco se mi sparassero", cioè per dirti, cioè proprio il razzismo si sente, poi magari spieghi un pochettino la situazione, un pochettino come vivono nel loro paese [...], e loro non se lo possono immaginare è inutile cioè loro hanno un'idea ferma ed io no.' (Translation by Lorraine Frisina.)

17 Original transcript follows: 'Io sinceramente, [European unification] ha un grande significato, si, assolutamente, però che adesso abbiano unificato l'Europa per me già prima, cioè per me personalmente, no adesso per me come paese, ma per me personalmente, perchè prima non avevo mai fatto queste distinzioni tra tutti questi paesi per me era già unita l'Europa ... Eh si, perchè, perché tu vivi in Germania, vivi in Germania, hai tanti amici di tante razze, quindi per te ormai ... quindi l'unificazione dell'Europa per me c'era già, nel piccolo naturalmente. ... sperando che continui in questo modo.' (Translation by Lorraine Frisina.)

18 Original transcript follows: 'Io resto italiano, sono orgoglioso di essere italiano, neh? Perché non riesco a vivere più nella mia città, però sono orgoglioso, la nostra cultura è un'altra, neh? Le nostre radici sono molto più profonde, neh? Ecco è un'altra cosa, io resto italiano ... Io non consiglierei a nessuno di abbandonare la propria città, i propri, i loro nativi, non lo consiglio più a nessuno, perché oggi siedo tra due sedie, neh?' (Translation by Lorraine Frisina.)

19 Franco's statement in Italian: 'Se è che Europa venga che venga pure'.

20 Original transcript follows: 'Komisch, wenn ich hier bin, dann fühle ich mich halt deutsch, ich rede deutsch, ich höre deutsch und deutsch ist der Unterricht und so. Wenn ich in Italien bin, also dann fühle ich mich mehr italienisch, halt weil ich dann italienisch rede, ich habe italienische Freunde, die Atmosphäre ist dann dort ganz anders und ... der Unterschied ist dann halt, daß ich halt andere Klamotten an habe, oder so, als die anderen.' (Translation by Lorraine Frisina.)

21 Original transcript follows: 'Ich bin eine *deutsche Türkin*. In der Türkei sagen sie zu mir Ausländerin, weil ich von hier komme, und hier bin ich auch Ausländer. Ich weiß gar nicht, wo ich hingehöre. Es ist gut, wie ich bin. Wenn ich jetzt nur Türkin wäre, ich würde das nicht gut finden. Ich weiß jetzt nicht, was das für ein Gefühl wäre, weil ich ja noch nie richtig Türkin war, aber ich würde lieber so bleiben wie ich bin, weil ich das so besser finde: *Halb Deutsche und halb Türkin*.' (Deutsche Shell (ed.), *Jugend 2000*, vol.2, Leske+Budrich, Opladen 2000, p. 20. Translation by Lorraine Frisina.)

22 Original transcript follows: 'Ich heiße Fatih, und *ich bin ein Frankfurter Türke*. Bin in Frankfurt geboren, habe aber die türkische Staatsbürgerschaft. ... Ja, das heißt halt, daß ich zwei Kulturen hab. Daß, so fühle, halt weil ich hier geboren, hier aufgewachsen bin. Ich war nie nur als ich ganz klein war ein Jahr in der Türkei. ... Ich hab halt etwas von der deutschen Kultur bekommen, und ich habe auch etwas von der türkischen Kultur, also ich hab beides. Und das heißt halt, daß ich Frankfurter Türke bin: Frankfurter und Türke.' (S. Sauter, *Wir sind 'Frankfurter Türken'*, Brandes & Apsel, Frankfurt am Main 2000, pp. 209–210. Transla-

tion by Lorraine Frisina.)

23 'Kreuz und Quer'/'Criss-cross' (1996), the last film of a five-part documentary series (by Hans A. Guttner) called 'Europe, a transnational dream' looks at the life of an extended family from Naples who since the late 1960s has migrated back and forth between Southern Italy and Germany. It shows that at the end of the twentieth century migrants to whom a 'Europe without border' is no longer a question of choice, but of vital necessity, have developed a 'European' sense of belonging as a frame for their transnational existence.

24 We can, for example, also observe more subversive ways of coping with double belonging: by enacting a mix of cultural (and often linguistic) tokens in daily interaction, young immigrants blur the boundaries of socio-cultural and national identities within the space of a nation-space. By emphasizing their 'Turkishness', for example, 'Ethnic' hip-hop groups of the 1990s subvert their 'otherization' as 'Turks'. Similar to the use of 'nigger' in Black American Hip-Hop lyrics, they for instance transform the contemptuous term *Kanake*, which Germans use to insult Turks, into a discursive weapon against discrimination and marginalization. They combine elements of global youth rebellion, like rap music, 'cool' modes of dressing and aggressive (macho) behavior with expressions of 'Turkishness' as a device against demands for assimilation: 'I'm not the black man/I'm not the white man/ I'm just the type between them/I'm a Turkish man in a foreign land' (rap song in English by the 'Turkish Power Boys' in Frankfurt, see: H. Tertilt, *Turkish Power Boys*, Suhrkamp Verlag, Frankfurt am Main 1996). They don't designate themselves as 'foreigners', instead declaring Germany a 'foreign land' to them. This artistic cultural mixage has also become a leitmotiv of the poetry of the so-called *Ausländerliteratur*. However, the Italian migrant literature seems more defensive than the artistic expressions of German Turks. See, for instance, the poem by Giuseppe Giambusso, *Il funambolo*: 'Sul filo intrecciato/Delle mie lingue/E vite/vado/Palpando die Fremde/In alto/Fra spettatori assenti/e pseudopatrie/i miei io/si snodano in un ballo/senza fine'. Or in German, *Der Seiltänzer*: 'Auf der geflochtenen Schnur/meiner Sprachen/und Leben/laufe ich/und betaste die Fremde Oben/zwischen abwesenden Zuschauern/und falschen Vaterländern/entknoten sich meine Ichs/in einem Tanz/ohne Ende'. (Cited from: G. Chiellino, 'La nascita della memoria biculturale', in: G. Scimonello (ed.), *Cultura Tedesca/Deutsche Kultur: Letteratura e immigrazione*, vol. 10, Donzelli Editore, Rome 1998, p. 27.)

25 See, for example Osman Zaimoglu, a young German Turk who works in a travel agency in Wilhelmsburg, who seems to subvert the argument against the dual passport according to which people cannot be loyal to two countries: 'Ich will Deutscher und Türke sein. Man darf seine Identität nicht aufgeben. Denn wer einmal seine Identität aufgibt, kann sie auch ein zweites Mal aufgeben. Die Jugendlichen, die vergessen, daß sie Türken sind, können auch keine guten Deutschen werden.' (N. Tietze, *Islamische Identitäten*, Hamburger Edition, Hamburg 2001, p. 384.)

26 Original transcript follows: 'Im Kindergarten gab es einige Konflikte, aber rein persönlicher Natur. Da gab es zwar "du Scheißausländer, du Türke!", aber das hatte nie etwas mit meinem Türkentum zu tun, sondern war einfach nur ein Argument für die wie "du bist häßlich, du bist arm". Also ein Argument, was eigentlich keines ist. Das war nie so gemeint, d.h. er haßt mich nicht, weil ich Türke bin, sondern der haßt mich, weil ich sein Auto zertrümmert habe. Er könnte genauso gut "Blödmann" zu mir sagen.' (Deutsche Shell (ed.), *Jugend 2000*, vol. 2, p. 195. Translation by Lorraine Frisina.)

27 See Armando Guerri when he watches football with his friends.

28 Original transcript follows: 'Natürlich erziehe ich meine Kinder nicht als Türke oder als Deutscher, sondern ich erziehe sie als Ayberk. Ich als Persönlichkeit bin nicht geleitet durch irgendwelche Nationalitäten. Ich bin so, wie ich bin! ... All das, was ich erlebt habe, die Menschen, die ich getroffen habe, die Erfahrungen, die ich gemacht habe, haben meinen Charakter, meine Persönlichkeit geformt, wie ich heutzutage bin. *Das hat mit irgendwelchen Traditionen oder Nationalitäten nur gering zu tun. Es ist für mich nur natürlich! Ich habe das Gefühl, ich bin dazwischen irgendwo und will mich nicht da festhalten, wo andere Leute sich*

überall festhalten. Da schwimme ich halt drum herum. Leute, die sich so fest halten, verurteile ich nicht, aber ich bemitleide sie ein bißchen. Denn im wirklichen Leben spielt das weiß Gott keine Rolle. … Mein bester Freund war ein Jugoslawe. Dann war es ein Deutscher, dann war es ein Iraner, dann war es ein Türke, und jetzt ist es ein Pole. Also ein Mixtur. Der Aspekt einer Nationalität hat nie eine Rolle gespielt in Bezug auf Freundschaften. … Ich bin weder stolz, Türke zu sein oder Deutscher zu sein oder die türkische Sprache sprechen zu können oder die deutsche – das ist für mich Technik, Kommunikationstechnik (lacht). … Ich glaube, wenn Menschen gerne wissen wollen, woher sie kommen oder zu wem sie gehören, das ist mehr eine Schutzfunktion. Weil sie die Sprache sprechen, weil sie ethnisch und territorial da groß geworden sind und dazu gehören, man kennt das Land und weiß, wie bestimmte Abläufe sind. Deswegen sehe ich das mehr als Schutzfunktion und nicht unbedingt als Zeichen von innerer Stärke. Vielleicht ist es ja Schwäche [lacht]. Mein Stärke kommt daher, weil ich weder deutsch noch türkisch bin, vollständig.' (Deutsche Shell (ed.), *Jugend 2000*, vol.2, pp. 193–194. Translation by Lorraine Frisina.)

29 This is expressed even more strongly by Ali Karabulut, a nineteen-year-old man who came from Turkey to Frankfurt three years previously: 'Wenn jemand sagt, zum Beispiel, wenn ein Lehrer fragt: Wo kommst Du her? Ich hab nicht geantwortet. Ich hab gesagt: Hauptsache bin Mensch. Sie hat gelacht, ich weiß, daß Du Mensch bist, aber wo kommst Du her? Ich hatte gesagt, ich komme aus der Türkei, aber ich fühle mich nicht Türke, ich fühle mich auch nicht deutsch. Habe ich weitergeredet, hat sie gesagt, das darfst du nicht sagen. Ich hab gesagt: ich bin ein internationaler. Sie hat gesagt, das darfst Du niemals sagen! Entweder bist Du Türke oder Deutscher oder Italiener oder was weiß ich. Also wenn jemand sagt, ich bin internationaler, ist das schlimm? So gemischt.' (S. Sauter, *Wir sind 'Frankfurter Türken'*, pp. 242–243.)

30 Maurizio Albertini, a thirty-two-year-old computer engineer at the European Central Bank, says that he does not see the need to seek the company of other Italians. He found it much more interesting to interact with people from different parts of Europe than with the people from his home town or country: 'Incontrare un italiano solo perché è italiano non è abbastanza per me, non trovo, non trovo questa necessità. … Il fatto di avere contatti con gente che viene da tutte le parti d'Europa a me francamente appaga molto di più che non il trovarmi con il prossimo milanese che comunque avrei comunque incontrato a Milano, o comunque un altro italiano così come ne ho visti tanti nella mia vita.'

31 Original transcript follows: 'Und, ähm, wie soll ich sagen, äh, bei mir zu Hause gibt's nicht, dass meine Kinder nur Italienisch sprechen oder nur italienische Bücher oder nur italienische Filme oder, das gibt's nicht. Bei uns wird alles gemacht, also mal so mal so, wie es kommt. Hab' ich Lust, italienische Lieder zu hören, hör' ich italienische Lieder, hab' ich Lust auf deutsche Lieder, hören wir deutsche Lieder. Also … ich bin froh, dass ich mit zwei Kulturen aufgewachsen bin, klar, ich möchte auch, dass meine Kinder mit zwei Kulturen aufwachsen, wenn es geht, noch 'ne dritte dazu. Das hat überhaupt nicht geschadet.' (Translation by Lorraine Frisina.)

32 Listen, for instance, to Armando Guerri (original transcript follows): 'Also, ich hab' noch, also jetzt, äh, in diesen Hotelfachmann, also, was ich gerad' erlerne, hat es eigentlich nur Vorteile, wenn man halt mehrere Fremdsprachen kann und durch mein Italienisch, äh, versteh' ich auch, ähm, 'n bisschen Spanisch und, ähm, Fremdsprachen haben mich sowieso schon immer fasziniert. Ich hab' in meiner Gesamtschule auch schon Französisch gehabt und Englisch, und wenn ich jetzt halt noch die Wahl hätte in meiner Berufsfachschule für noch eine Fremdsprache, würd' ich sofort noch mit 'ner anderen Fremdsprache anfangen.'

See also the narrative of Riccardo Dente, the lawyer quoted at the beginning of this chapter, who reasons as follows: 'Wir stehen für die neuen, die Italiener, die nicht nur als Last empfunden werden, sondern im Gegenteil, wir haben hier ein Know-how gebaut … weil wir eben eben über das Potential verfügen, ja, was, was hier auf europäischer Ebene entwickelt werden kann'.

33 'Keine. Es gibt kein Vorteil und kein Nachteil, denk' ich mir. Es bleibt, wie es ist. Ich als

Mensch bleibe so wie ich bin.'

34 Original transcript follows: 'Wenn ich also Türke bin und in Deutschland lebe, dann muß ich sehen, was ist gut an der anderen Kultur. Und ich nehme das Gute auf in mein Leben. Aber ich sehe auch das Gute an meiner Kultur und setze das dann zusammen. So muß das sein.' (N. Tietze, *Islamische Identitäten*, p. 368. Translation by Lorraine Frisina.)

Similar comments were made by Cemal Erol, an eighteen-year-old man from Frankfurt: 'Alles hat seine Vor-und Nachteile. Wir kennen Deutschland. Wir kennen die Türkei. Wir nehmen uns die Vorteile von Deutschland und die von der Türkei. Wir verbinden das irgendwie. Die Nachteile gehen davon nicht weg.' Deutsche Shell (ed.), *Jugend 2000, vol.2*, p. 21). Or listen to Ismael Yagmur, aged eighteen, who lives in Frankfurt: 'Die Türken können vor allem Ordnung von den Deutschen lernen. Auch die Menschenrechte, wie man Politik macht, was man für die Ärmeren der Bevölkerung tun sollte. Die Kopftuchpflicht sollte abgeschafft werden. Die Deutschen könnten sich die Gastfreundschaft abgucken, mehr Spontaneität, könnten spendabler sein, sollten nicht so mit Vorurteilen an andere Menschen rangehen' (*Ibid.*, p. 19).

35 Listen also to Annalisa Corradi, the housewife and mother from Basilicata. When I asked her whether she would accept German citizenship – not if she would ask for it – she said that if the German state would ask her to get German citizenship she would have no problem; but this would not mean that she would no longer feel Italian: 'Ja, warum denn, warum soll ich sagen "Nee, um Gottes Willen, nein." Und, ähm, ich hab' mir auch die Frage gestellt, ob eines Tages, wenn der Staat hier äh, uns ruft und sagt: "Hier Deutsche Angehörigkeit", ja, kein Problem, geben sie sie mir, nehm ich gern an, ich lebe doch hier, warum soll ich sie nicht nehmen? [energisch] Das heißt noch lang net, dass ich dann keine Italienerin mehr bin oder das bisschen Italienisch, was in mir ist, dann abgeschaltet wird, überhaupt nicht. Also, wenn ich mit einem in Deutschland leben muss, und ich muss eine deutsche Staatsangehörigkeit nehmen, dann ist kein Grund, Leute anzuziehen, also wirklich nicht.'

36 Original transcript follows: 'Qua [in Germany] vai negli uffici sanitari, vai dai dottori, vai in banca, vai in un ufficio, sei trattata uguale di una tedesca cioè non c'è nessuna differenza se sei una straniera: arrivi e vieni servita, per bene. … Quando sono andata in Sicilia da sola perché avevamo incominciato a costruire una casa, saranno ma un otto anni forse, anche di più, allora sono dovuta andare io da sola, e un amico di mio marito è venuto a prendermi alla stazione e poi con lui sono andata ad Agrigento, ho girato per sbrigare dei documenti e la gente "Eh mamma mia e come fai, vai da sola, con un uomo, fuori paese?!" e dico che cavolo, che cavolo devo fare, cioè è quella la differenza, capisce?'

37 Original transcript follows: 'Io vado d'accordo, cioè mi trovo bene sia con un africano che con l'italiano o con un greco, non ci vedo differenza, nessuna. … No, *io sono italiana e rimango italiana nel mio modo, non voglio doppia cittadinanza*, non voglio cittadinanza tedesca, sono italiana, ci rimango … C'ho gli stessi diritti dei tedeschi, perché cambiare la mia nazionalità? Assolutamente!' (Translation by Lorraine Frisina.)

38 Original transcript follows: 'Meine Eltern wollten nur für einige Monate hier bleiben. Daraus sind über 30 Jahre geworden. Sie werden nie mehr zurückkehren. … Die wollten sich nicht integrieren. Erst nachdem ihnen klar geworden ist, daß sie nun mal hier leben, haben sie damit begonnen, indem sie gegenüber den Deutschen nicht mehr so verschlossen waren. Sie sind mehr auf das Andere, das Unbekannte zugegangen. *Da liegt das Problem: Zu viel Angst vor dem Unbekannten, vor der anderen Tradition, vor der anderen Sprache. Was aber, finde ich als moderner Mensch, gar kein Hindernis ist, im Gegenteil, das ist gerade das Reizvolle.* … Meiner Meinung nach hilft nur ein erhöhtes Bildungswesen. Es muß schon in der Schule versucht werden, die verschiedenen Nationalitäten zusammenzuführen, damit die Vorurteile abgebaut werden können. Deshalb unterstütze ich jeden Schüleraustausch, weil, man kann viel reden und reden, aber wenn man den persönlichen Kontakt zum Anderen nicht hat, bringt das Reden gar nichts.' (Deutsche Shell (ed.), *Jugend 2000*, vol. 2, p. 142 fos. Translation by Lorraine Frisina.)

39 When asked what kind of friends she has and where they come from, Veronica Costanzo

says: 'Gemischt, international.'
40 Original transcript follows: 'Ja, weil das gesellschaftliche Umfeld sind ja zwei Umfelder.
    Also einmal ist es so, daß man in der Schule ist, da hat man halt mehr – es ist nicht rein
    deutsch dann, ich habe Freunde Albaner, Jugoslawen, Italiener, Deutsche, es ist halt alles
    gemischt. Das ist halt eine andere Kultur. Solange ich – ich sag mal europäische Kultur.
    Und zu Hause, da hat man halt die türkische Kultur, das geht noch nach alten türkischen
    Prinzipien zu, diese beiden kann man schwer verbinden. Damit irgendwann klarzukommen,
    das war halt auch meine Schwierigkeit.' (S. Sauter, *Wir sind 'Frankfurter Türken'*, pp. 219–
    220. Translation by Lorraine Frisina.)
41 Several years ago the European Union (Federal Ministries for Labour and Social Affairs,
    and Education) began to promote the idea of 'continuous learning' for all European citi-
    zens throughout their working lives. 'Lifelong learning' presupposes a 'flexible' self with a
    constant openness to new experiences. (See: http://europa.eu.int/comm/education/life/
    memoen.pdf)
42 Deutsche Shell (ed.), *Jugend 2000*, vol. 1, p. 27.
43 *Ibid.*, p. 249.
44 *Ibid.*, pp. 245–247.
45 Original transcript follows: 'Delle cose che invece sono molto interessanti secondo me, è
    che quegli italiani che non si mescolano, … che stanno sempre nel loro brodo, per dire
    così, si frequentano sempre tra italiani, tante volte non si accorgono neanche di questo, di
    questo atteggiamento … ma puoi anche imparare, questa è un po' la mia, la mia visione.'
    (Translation by Lorraine Frisina.)
46 Original transcript follows: 'Ti porta un'apertura mentale, secondo me, … noti le differenze
    di mentalità però … non noti soltanto i difetti … delle altre mentalità magari apprezzi
    anche alcune cose, quindi sicuramente questo ti fa crescere, insomma come persona …
    sicuramente ecco è un apertura mentale il fatto di venire a contatto con persone diverse,
    culture diverse … Secondo me è positivo comunque perché, sì, probabilmente sarà anche
    diciamo fonte di conflitti ma, secondo me, *il fatto di essere a contatto con persone diverse non
    può che aiutare diciamo la crescita dell'individuo.'* (Translation by Lorraine Frisina.)
47 Original transcript follows: 'Bin ich dorthin (nach Frankfurt) gekommen und die haben
    ganz andere Kultur gehabt. Und ich hab auch eine ganz andere Kultur gehabt. Aber wenn
    jemand will, von Herzen, dann kann man zusammenleben und die zwei Kulturen auch
    leben. Das ist nicht einfach, vielleicht, ich weiß das schon … Aber des kann man doch so
    machen. Ich hab auch eine deutsche Freundin gehabt. … Ja, ja, das ist die andere Kultur,
    aber wenn jemand sich … ja, gegenseitig verstehen kann, dann können beide lernen.' (Sauter,
    Wir sind 'Frankfurter Türken', pp. 240 and 245. Translation by Lorraine Frisina).
48 Original transcript follows: 'Forse ho una visione più obiettiva sia dell'Italia che della
    Germania, senz'altro … Per quanto riguarda l'Italia mi sono accorta che, stando all'estero,
    cosa che non pensavo di me stessa, sono diventata senz'altro più patriotica, più legata
    all'Italia, però mi saltano agli occhi i difetti, la disorganizzazione, i grossi caos di politica
    che secondo me esistono anche in altri stati e però non vanno a finire a grossi titoli sui
    giornali o cose del genere, queste cose le vedo di più, mi saltano di più agli occhi, prima
    probabilmente ci ero dentro quindi avevo una visione senz'altro meno distaccata forse più
    emotiva ecco e meno obiettiva.' (Translation by Lorraine Frisina.)
49 Tino Esposito, the high school senior from Southern Germany, like Teresa Pedrini, relativizes
    any sort of victimization discourse on behalf of his Italian peers, asking them to reflect on
    the discrimination and exclusion of foreigners in Italy: 'Es gibt natürlich Angst vor Fremden
    in Deutschland, und es werden immer Sündenböcke gesucht. … Wenn ich über dieses
    Thema mit meinen italienischen Mitbürgern spreche, sage ich denen, daß viele Naziskins
    in Italien sich genauso verhalten wie hier. Nur sind wir Ausländer hier halt in der dumpfen
    Position der Sündenböcke. In Italien sind es die Albaner oder die Nordafrikaner' (Deutsche
    Shell (ed.), *Jugend 2000*, vol. 2, p. 143).
50 M. Bakhtin, 'Response to a Question from the Novy Mir Editorial Staff', in: M. Bakhtin,

Speech Genres and Other Late Essays, Texas University Press, Austin 1986, p. 7.
51 Hobsbawm shows how 'mass-produced invented tradition' is created by bureaucratic elites
    in order to foster people's respect and loyalty (E. Hobsbawm and T. Ranger, *The Invention
    of Tradition*, Cambridge University Press, Cambridge 1983). In this sense, the Directorate
    of the EU Commission responsible for 'Audiovisual, Information, Communication and
    Culture' (DG 10) invokes a European identity through common values and a coherent
    tradition (such a cultural heritage lists Greek thought and Roman law, Christianity, the
    Renaissance, the Age of Reason, the Industrial Revolution, the protection of civil rights
    and Social Democracy): see P. Schlesinger, 'From Cultural Defense to Political Culture:
    Media, Politics and Collective Identity in the European Union', in: *Media, Culture & Society*
    19:3, 1997, pp. 369–391; C. Shore, 'Governing Europe: European Union Audiovisual Policy
    and the Politics of Identity', in: C. Shore and S. Wright (eds.), *Anthropology of Policy: Criti-
    cal Perspectives on Governance and Power*, Routledge, London/New York 1997, pp. 165–192.
52 P. Wagner, 'Fest-Stellungen, Beobachtungen zur sozialwissenschaftlichen Diskussion über
    Identität', in: A. Assmann and H. Friese (eds.), *Identitäten: Erinnerung, Geschichte, Identität
    3*, Suhrkamp Verlag, Frankfurt am Main 1998, pp. 44–72.
53 J. Citrin and J. Sides, 'More Than Just Nationals: How Identity Choice Matters in the New
    Europe', in: R. H. Herrmann, T. Risse and M.B. Brewer (eds.), *Transnational Identities: Be-
    coming European in the EU*, Rowman & Littlefield, New York 2004, pp. 161–185. Neverthe-
    less, studies do indicate that only 11% put Europe before the nation as a reference point for
    their identity (see: M. Kohli, 'The Battlegrounds of European Identity', in: *European Society*
    2:2, 2000, p. 125).
54 T. Risse, 'European Institutions and Identiy Change', in: R. H. Herrmann, T. Risse and M. B.
    Brewer (eds.), *Transnational Identities: Becoming European in the EU*, Rowman & Littlefield,
    New York 2004, p. 251.
55 *Ibid.*, pp. 265–266.
56 René Girault reminded us of the important analytical distinction between 'L'Europe pensée'
    or 'l'Europe voulue' and 'l'Europe vécue' (R. Girault (sous la direction de), *Identité et con-
    science européennes au XX siècle*, Hachette, Paris 1994, p. 25), between cultural representa-
    tions or ideas of Europe and European identity as a form of consciousness.
57 Original transcript follows: 'Io vorrei che mio figlio mantenesse – cioè, si, mantenesse
    diciamo, fosse un italiano …. Secondo me è importante mantenere comunque le proprie
    radici, la propria identità. … Ma, penso la libertà di movimento ecco, … si ha proprio
    insomma il senso di vicinanza fisica e questo poter venire a contatto con real- con mondi
    diversi, inevitabilmente ci sono differenze forse ci saranno sempre, è giusto che ci siano,
    però ecco questo poter, cioè avere questo contatto diciamo facilitato con culture diverse e,
    … , questo qua secondo me è lo spirito europeo ecco.' (Translation by Lorraine Frisina.)
58 Listen again to Annalisa Corradi, the housewife and mother in Frankfurt who, when asked
    about the meaning of the unification of Europe, revealed an enthusiasm for the widening
    of borders and boundaries between states, but a skepticism regarding the transformation
    of European identities (original transcript follows): 'Also, eine Bedeutung teilweise. Ich
    denke mir, wenn wir keine Grenzen haben, ist es natürlich schön und jeder kann verreisen
    wie er möchte, aber ähm, das, was wir sind, ja, ähm, wird uns niemand wegnehmen. … Ja,
    wir werden alle die gleiche Geldwährung haben, wir werden, aber wir werden immer
    verschiedene Sprachen haben, ja? Und wir werden auch immer die verschiedenen
    Meinungen haben. … Ich bin das, was ich bis heute war. Halb deutsch, halb italienisch.'
59 It seems clear that under conditions of cultural pluralism and societal denationalization,
    the culturalist theory of European integration, which emphasizes the process of conver-
    gence of European societies after the end of World War II and which is still prominent in
    the discourse of federalists, is inadequate. Theorists of this (bottom-up) approach – which
    is implicit in the identity politics of the European Union – assume that increased contact
    and socialization at popular and elite levels will strengthen the sense of community which
    drives European integration. An increasingly dense network of affiliations criss-crossing

the European space will gradually turn the EU into an 'integrated field of communication' within which will be generated a common and overarching European identity or *demos*. (K. W. Deutsch, *Nationalism and Social Communication: An Inquiry into the Foundations of Nationality*, MIT Press, Cambridge, MA, 1966.) In brief, this model of a supranationalizing Europe assumes that increasing social contact necessarily creates a relatively homogeneous, common European identity; a pool of shared experiences which is understood as the prerequisite of civic commitment and democratic legitimation. This approach can be understood as part of modernization theory, which is resurfacing with a new communitarian twist: culture is constructed around the idea of a community as a homogenous discourse that somehow provides the glue which binds society together. It echoes Ferdinand Tönnies' idea of a 'socio-psychological community' (*Gemeinschaft*) with a sense of solidarity based on shared values. Such a theory of social integration takes for granted that cultural cohesion exists in national societies and then simply transfers the idea of state-formation to a supranational, European level. But even on the level of nation-states a culturally integrated community was always a constitutive myth rather than a sociologically accurate depiction of collective identities.

60 G. Delanty, 'What Does it Mean to be a "European"?', in: *Innovation* 18:1, 2005, p. 19.

61 Listen to how Nesla, a young woman from the folklore group in Frankfurt, reflects on the 'identity' labels which are chosen or imposed: 'Also du heiratest jetzt einen Deutschen – da frag ich mich manchmal, wo ist denn da der Unterschied? Ich hab heutzutage ein Problem mit meinem Arbeitsplatz, ich hab einen super Arbeitsplatz, aber ich weiß ganz genau, daß mein Chef gegen Ausländer ist. Und ich bin der einzige Ausländer in der ganzen Firma. Und ich bin trotzdem da! Und wenn er zu mir sagt, du bist ein Deutscher, sag ich: Stop! Ich bin Türkin. Ich bin als Türkin geboren – in Deutschland. Aber es gibt Momente, wo ich sage: Heh, Leute, ich bin Deutsche, ich bin Frankfurterin … ja? Das sag ich auch. Aber es gibt Momente, wo du das benutzen kannst – wenn man dir was sagt, als Beleidigung, dann sag ich dagegen was. Und des isses Problem. Ich kann zu mir selbst Kanake sagen, aber kein anderer kann zu mir das sagen – kein anderer hat dazu das Recht.' (Sauter, *Wir sind 'Frankfurter Türken'*, p. 246.)

62 See P. Nanz, 'In-between Nations: Ambivalence and the Making of European Identity', in: B. Stråth (ed.), *Europe and the Other and Europe as the Other*, Peter Lang Verlag, Brussels 2000, pp. 279–309.

63 Original transcript follows:
'PN: Hättest du gerne die deutsche Staatsbürgerschaft oder die doppelte Staatsbürgerschaft oder …?
VC: Nee.
PN: Weder noch?
VC: Nö. Die brauch' ich ja nicht, ich bin ja Europäerin.
PN: Und was heißt das?
VC: Ja, dass ich die nicht brauche, die doppelte Staatsangehörigkeit. Ich kann ja nicht rausgeschmissen werden aus Deutschland.' (Translation by Lorraine Frisina.)

64 'VC: 'Ja, zum Beispiel werden bei uns an der Schule die Türken voll fertiggemacht und so…. Von den Deutschen, von Spaniern, Italienern und äh … Die machen immer Witze über Türken. [Lachen]
PN: 'Und da meinst du ist der Unterschied, das ist echt, also da ist der Unterschied wirklich zwischen Europäern und Nichteuropäern?'
VC: 'Ja, bei manchen schon. Da gibt's viele, die das machen bei uns an der Schule…. Also für mich macht das eigentlich keinen Unterschied … Wir sind ja alle Menschen.'

65 Original transcript follows: 'I turchi fanno delle feste succede sempre casino, mmh, si ammazzano e disturbano ai vicini e per colpa di questi siamo costretti noi, italiani o altri che organizzano feste, a pagare le loro, le loro, i danni che fanno, cioè qua loro si credono di fare quello che vogliono perché stanno in terra straniera, diciamo è una cosa che penso che tanti anni fa, diciamo *cinquant'anni fa, lì facevano forse i nostri padri, prima venivano dicevano*

"Tanto noi stiamo là di passaggio poi dobbiamo tornare quindi non ci interessa cosa succede", è questo io sto notando attualmente con i turchi … Loro non si adattano alla vita diciamo, se io vivo in Germania adesso attualmente, cerco di vivere nella zona dove vivo e di attenermi a quello che si vive, rispetto agli altri, rispetto a me, rispetto ai tedeschi e delle altre nazioni, come potrebbero fare, potrebbero funzionare pure i turchi così o altre nazioni, solo che per me io vedo che loro se ne infischiano cioè dicono "Tanto noi stiamo di passaggio, un domani me ne vado là", finito là.' (Translation by Lorraine Frisina.)

66 Original transcript follows: 'E politicamente fare non so, cioè bisogna portare una politica e poi votare, mettere delle persone diciamo che sono i candidati politici, di formarsi fra l'Europa, se c'è la sinistra, di formarsi una sinistra, sinistra in collaborazione con D'Alema, con l'SPD di qua, diciamo Schröder, qualsiasi socialista e mettersi uniti e di fare una riforma socialista europea.'

67 Original transcript follows: 'Dove vive si deve adeguare a vivere, cioè se io vado in Portogallo non è che posso fare una vita di come stavo in Italia, o di come sto in Germania, io per attenermi agli altri, ai portoghesi, all'ambiente portoghese, *mi devo sforzare io a entrare a vedere le usanze che c'hanno, la cultura che c'hanno per io entrare nella stessa cultura portoghese, io potrei dare delle idee, delle cose che io ho appreso sia in Germania sia dal Italia che c'ho porterei là*, gli spiegherei, farei, farei assieme un piccolo aggiuntivo, ma no che posso imporre io a tutti gli altri quello che io c'ho in testa, io devo imparare e poi mettere piano piano delle piccole cose che io posso aderire a mettere, se, se gli piace, se acconsentono, con la forza non si, non si, non si ricava niente uguale. … Se si parla dell'Europa si parla poi di costituire una costituzione europea quindi è come tu stessi in Italia così stai al nord o al sud, così stessi in Europa sto nella parte italiana, nella parte spagnola, nella parte, cioè penso che verrà così penso, mi auguro di andare in questo campo, per loro [for the children] avere molto più scelta e più, molto migliore delle nostre diciamo.' (Translation by Lorraine Frisina.)

He thinks that his children, who speak very good German, and who are learning Italian, Portuguese and English will be able to 'learn', 'feel' and 'integrate' in other cultures: 'In questo momento i nostri bambini c'hanno un tedesco effettivo abbastanza bene, più studiano lingue italiano, inglese, quindi riescono molto a en- a entrare nelle lingue, nelle culture, e sforzano molto di più a imparare quello che succede in Portogallo, a sentire, a vedere, cioè si integrano molto, nella terza generazione io penso che sarà una delle migliori cose europee, che si troveranno nell'Europa molto bene, molto meglio di noi.'

68 René Girault points out that migrants play a double role in the development of a European consciousness: in the long run they promote a homogenization of the image of the Other insofar as the Other is European (this process of an intercultural formation of European identity is, of course, also supported by the increasing mobility of Europeans, by institutionalized student exchanges, town-twinnings, etc.). However, this homogenization of the image of European foreigners has emerged in opposition to the (negative) image of non-European migrants. We can see this phenomenon, for instance, in the discourse of the pro-European extreme right in France (Girault, *Identité et conscience européennes au XX siècle*, p. 52).

69 This is, however, challenged by the narratives of Turks who depict themselves as being Europeans. For example, consider the words of Alev Erdogan, a twenty-year-old judicial employee in Frankfurt: 'Ich wünschte, es wird so sein, daß Europa eines Tages ein Land wird und daß es keine Grenzen mehr gibt und nur noch eine Regierung für Deutschland, Frankreich, England und die anderen Länder. Wenn wir ein Land wären, dann gäbe es nicht mehr dieses Nationalgefühl, oder es würde zumindest eingeschränkt. Es gäbe es weniger Streitigkeiten und Kriege. … Eines Tages wird es dann heißen. Ich bin Europäer, und vielleicht irgendwann ziemlich weit in der Zukunft wird es auf der Welt keine Länder mehr geben, dann wird die ganze Welt zusammen gehören, und dann sind wir keine Türken, Deutsche oder Franzosen, sondern Menschen, und das wäre doch erstrebenswert.' (Deutsche Shell (ed.), *Jugend 2000*, vol. 2, pp. 364–365.)

70 This fact may accelerate the changing public perception of immigrants: it is no longer the European immigrant, who in Germany was of much concern during the period of intensive labour recruitment in the 1960s, but the non-European immigrant, who has become the focus of negative images in public life (M. Martiniello, 'The Development of European Union Citizenship. A Critical Evaluation', in: M. Roche and R. Van Berkel (eds.), *European Citizenship and Social Exclusion*, Ashgate, Aldershot 1997, pp. 35–47).

71 Maurizio, for example, discusses his experience with Arabs while living in Japan: 'No, non trovo, adesso non ci sono delle grosse ehm, dei grossi ostacoli a espandere questo tipo di, questo tipo di atteggiamento, non ho esper-si, ne ho un pochettino però, non ho esperienze nel mondo arabo per esempio, ben poco, ho conosciuto, anche quando eravamo in Giappone, avevamo, avevamo un amico egiziano, ma, e stavamo da dio insomma, eeh, e avevamo due amici, per esempio uno giordano e l'altro israeliano e tra l'altro, cioè sai come sono le cose, eppure erano amicissimi, si frequentavano benissimo, insomma, queste cose qua sì capitano però, ecco per esempio il mondo arabo nel senso proprio Arabia o insomma, o Iraq adesso, non so, o anche per esempio anche, boh, non lo so, non mi è capitato però, non ho esperienze in questo.'

72 Original transcript follows: 'Siamo tutti europei no? Io penso di sì, siamo europei. ... europei, secondo me, *sentirsi europei è sentirsi liberi, indipendenti*, non come certe nazioni del mondo come l'India che non c'hai nessun diritto, da donna ad esempio, e che cavolo, sembriamo nel 1600, nel 1500, noi europei abbiamo i diritti, abbiamo gli stess- cioè siamo democratici ecco, per me è quello ... Siamo internazionali, siamo europei veramente, e anche extracomunitari diciamo ... *vivendo qua si sono un po' adeguati anche loro.'* (Translation by Lorraine Frisina.)

Listen once again to Teresa Pedrini, who says, that Europe (including non-Europeans) is already united in her classroom: 'Prima non avevo mai fatto queste distinzioni tra tutti questi paesi per me era già unita l'Europa. ... Eh si, perchè, perchè tu vivi in Germania, hai tanti amici di tante razze, quindi per te ormai ... quindi l'unificazione dell'Europa per me c'era già, nel piccolo naturalmente. ... sperando che continui in questo modo.'

73 Cf. for instance the empirical research on EU political practices done by C. Sabel and J. Cohen, 'Sovereignty and Solidarity in the EU: A Working Paper Where We Face Some Facts', in: *Reconfiguring Work and Welfare in the New Economy: A Transatlantic Dialogue, A Conference at the European Union Center*, UW-Madison, 2001.

9

Conclusion: self and politics in the new Europe

At present, Europe is an emerging post-national normative order, but one which is unlikely to become a new, integrated super-state. Rather, it is a transnational decision-making space, sustained by a set of evolving institutions, in which the question of statehood and the boundaries of its political community can permanently be contested. Disputes about just and fair political procedures and institutions for Europe may continue indefinitely. To affirm the permanence of contestation and struggle about the meaning of principles and rights within an ordered collaborative setting is not to envisage or celebrate a world without stability, standards or clear decision-making. Instead, it treats rules and laws as an open space for constant interpretation in political deliberation, not as instruments of closure.

Within any political community there is always contestation arising not only from conflicting – particularly economic – interests, but also from competing ethical perspectives, world views or outlooks, and cultural identities. In a conflict in which passionate loyalties exist on both sides, it is only a commitment to engage in the 'mutual exploration of difference' which enables the participants to find the 'best' or most 'just' solution to a common problem, thereby generating dialogical solidarity across ethical, cultural and national boundaries. At the start of this book, the question was posed: What are the normative and empirical presuppositions for a European constitution and for a European-wide public sphere – that is, institutionalized arenas for transnational political participation and for the intercultural formation of collective identities?

In order to tackle these issues, we had to inquire into a conceptual paradigm of democratic deliberation under conditions of persisting national, cultural and ethical pluralism. Such a paradigm builds on theories of deliberative democracy: it insists on the universalistic core of democratic constitutionalism, that is, the justification of norms that merit intersubjective recognition because they express a common interest. A dialogical approach, however, stresses the pluralistic aspect of justificatory discourses understood as the process by which principles are co-operatively discovered. It keeps with the constructivist idea that democratic le-gitimation and solidarity can be generated through public deliberation, but also underscores the plurality of cultural and ethical perspectives and focuses on the mechanism of mutual translation among them – namely, a process of exploration of heterogeneous perspectives. Such an account of politics conceives of delibera-tion as a dialogical exchange of public reasons for the purpose of resolving com-mon problems that makes participants answerable and accountable to one another. According to this definition, deliberation is not so much a form of discourse or argumentation aiming at reaching a consensual understanding, but a joint, co-operative activity of mutual translation and justification of viewpoints in an on-going process of pragmatic experimentation in the search for positive-sum outcomes. By promoting continuous intercultural translation or inter-societal learning, this kind of citizenship practice could produce a European political com-munity which is not based on a *demos* or a common cultural heritage, but on the shared pursuit of the most just and efficient solutions to social problems or the best interpretations of constitutional principles: a polity based on a 'situated con-stitutional patriotism' beyond the nation-state.

In Chapter 2, I scrutinized current theories of European integration with re-spect to the role they do or do not assign to the European public sphere. We saw that the debate has been bogged down by the apparently irreconcilable mutual opposition of two positions. On the one hand, there is the view that a European public sphere is neither possible nor necessary, a perspective which arises princi-pally from the tradition of economic liberalism; on the other hand, there is the view of those I have referred to as *demos*-theorists, according to whom, a Euro-pean public sphere is necessary but impossible. Both with and against these theo-ries, I have argued throughout this book that a thicker and more situated version of the European public sphere is not only normatively necessary, but already an emergent characteristic of the new Europe.

In Chapter 3, I endeavoured to conceptualize a notion of 'the public' which neither draws on the idea of a cultural homogeneity among citizens, nor with-draws into a purely procedural conception of the public as an anonymous, unsituated network of communicative forms. Instead of simply containing or lim-iting pluralism, my conception of the public sphere actively values the everyday exploration of difference between strangers with heterogeneous cultural/ethical and national backgrounds. The associated dialogical conception of citizenship can account for the struggles that most of us experience living under conditions of radical pluralism and points to an image of a European political/constitutional identity with no 'cultural common denominator', but with multiple voices and innumerable perspectives on common problems (Chapter 4).

In order to spell out the idea of the exploration of difference, I drew on theo-ries of translation, specifically those of Davidson, Putnam and Bakhtin. Davidson's approach is important because it shows that each language splits into a multiplic-ity of idiolects which are nonetheless mutually intertranslatable (Chapter 5). The everyday practice of mutual translation presupposes speakers' interpretative charity. Putnam's argument adds to this the idea of 'idealizations' which must be shared by speakers in order for mutual understanding to be possible, and emphasizes the situatedness and contextuality of dialogue. Finally, Bakhtin's work is of particular importance because he conceptualizes this phenomenon of contextualized social languages as 'speech genres' that link dialogical procedures (the formal aspect) and everyday experience (the substantive/world-disclosing aspect). Furthermore, Bakhtin emphasizes that the 'centripetal' forces of language (shared meanings) are constantly complemented by 'centrifugal' forces, the reaching out for new voices and the inclusion of otherness in each new speech situation. My idea was that this complementarity between the centrifugal and centripetal forces of communication offers the key to understanding the new Europe as the ongoing exploration of difference. Constitutional patriotism, then, is equivalent to the principle of interpretative charity, making translation within a constitutional dialogue possible (Chapter 6).

In Chapters 7 and 8, I showed that in contemporary Europe there is a host of empirical evidence in support of the idea of an emergent intercultural dialogue. This provides some grounds for optimism about the emergence of solidarity, trust and learning across cultural/ethical boundaries and beyond national fragmentation. For the people, European identity is not a matter of convergence but of 'interdiscursivity'. They display a pastiche of self-understandings and a multilayered idea of citizenship, both of which serve as a basis for their engagement in transnational citizenship practices.

Throughout this book, I have endeavoured to establish that – in principle – 'translation' is at the heart of all forms of communication. However, in engaging in the processes of translation, we assume varying degrees of cognitive openness or 'addressivity' (i.e., the mutual exploration of difference for the purposes of perspective-taking). This idea has theoretical, as well as practical consequences for European integration, which – within the present text – arises in the form of three particular thematic perspectives – namely, the conceptual application of the 'public sphere' to new institutional arrangements; the interrelation between European law and politics, and finally self-understanding and European identity.

Firstly: The larger aim of *Europolis: Constitutional Patriotism Beyond the Nation State* is to extend the idea of constitutional dialogue within society itself to encompass not just existing socio-political units, but also new, transnational governance arenas conceived as sites of mutual learning. The idea of a European public sphere as a multiplicity of ongoing cross-cultural civic dialogues can serve as a conceptual tool for current research on new forms of European governance arrangements. They stand for a move beyond both territorial and functional integration and they provide forums for the recombination of conflicting views on issues concerning society as a whole (e.g. foodstuff regulation, product safety, environmental standards and risk regulation in general). My aim in this study has been to spell out the theoretical premises for the idea of the exploration of difference, which can be used to animate research on European governance arrangements. If we conceptualize the public sphere as a communicative network where different publics partially overlap, the emerging character of the EU as a multi-level system of policy-making can be seen as offering the opportunity for the creation of new communities of political action.[1] Such a 'pluricentric' view of European politics should, of course, explore whether these new modes of governance (e.g. the Open Method of Coordination which operates in the area of employment, pension, and social exclusion policy) ensure the democratic legitimacy of decision-making. In order to monitor and to hold governance arenas accountable, we would have to define notions of constitutionality in terms of transparency, access to deliberation, responsiveness and inclusion.[2]

The idea of democratic legitimacy of European governance can be summed up as follows: fostering extended deliberation among stakeholders over the nature of problems and the best way to solve them, participatory arenas produce a pool of (transnationally) shared arguments which – often disseminated by civil society organisations – contribute to the emergence of a wider public sphere in which political decisions are exposed to 'transnational' public scrutiny. Ultimately, governance arrangements should become sites of public deliberation between social actors (e.g. government officials from different national communities, scientific experts and the 'critical voices' of minority expertise, NGOs, advocacy and economic interest groups etc.) that generate democratic legitimation in a heterogeneous transnational polity. It should be underlined here that deliberative arenas also put 'justificatory burdens' on non-state or private actors: they have to justify their positions in light of substantive (public) values and are held accountable for the success of constitutional interpretation. In fact, constitutionalism is 'internalised in deliberative institutions',[3] whether local, national or transnational: at the very least, the participants of deliberative processes are constrained to show the coherence of specific decisions with basic norms or constitutional principles.

Secondly: from a dialogical approach, law, rather than the ensemble of formal (positive) legal norms which can be made precise once and for all by delegated third parties (e.g. courts), is conceived as a discursive space within which competing normative claims are debated and eventually negotiated by social actors. To embrace ambiguity means also to give up the illusion that politics can be contained by law, that the right laws or constitution will one day settle the ambiguity that haunts all understanding and interpretation and finally free us from the vicissitudes of politics.[4] This kind of alternative politics of public deliberation does not shrink from the conflicts and uncertainty of social and political reality. Rather, it treats the disruptions of the political order and procedure, and the decentralizing effect of applying constitutional principles to new contexts, as valued sites of democratic freedom. Political and civic institutions must therefore secure and foster these spaces, encouraging citizens to initiate political action. In this vision of the new Europe, a lively (internally pluralized) political culture is the lifeblood of robust democratic deliberation within functioning institutions and procedures. It is not, then, a common cultural or national identity that generates mutual trust and solidarity, but rather the common endeavour of solving the manifold and never-ending affairs of living together.

Accordingly, the public sphere is as much an arena for conflict and for the exploration of difference in the solution of social problems, as it is a set of procedures or institutions for political deliberation designed to achieve binding decisions. Thus, dialogical politics has two poles: the centripetal forces of sedimentation (e.g. the always fragile interpretation of laws and, in particular, constitutional principles), of self-consolidation and of administration; and the centrifugal forces of the innovative interpretation of rights, of unruly excess or demonstration (e.g. protests against the EU and other social movements) and of spontaneous, local developments. Politics (as with all meaningful social practices) moves dialectically between stabilizing conservatism and destabilizing change. The former facilitates the effective governance of the state; the latter empowers citizens to engage, resist or affirm the settlements of those who govern them, and thus to legitimize political decisions. The closures represented by law, norms and procedures are not static, never faits accomplis, but always in process. They are performative actions, maintained daily in political deliberation (*le plébiscite de tous les jours*). Dialogical politics opens up spaces for critical reflection, dissent and the exploration of new solutions to problems. It calls for the perpetual expansion and amendment of the constitution, as well as of the practice of politics.

Thirdly: drawing on Bakhtin's conception of the self as liminal, and of identity as a process of dialogical interaction with concrete others, I have tried to theorize politics as an always unfinished project, committed to the constant formation of identities, both personal and institutional; the centripetal and centrifugal forces which drive the mechanism by which all social practices are continuously settled and disrupted. Multiplicity or internal plurality of the self is the precondition for it to be open to otherness. The experience of the 'many-in-one' of thought enables us to match and to affirm outer plurality, that is, the existence of different world perspectives and moral/ideological disagreement. These are the preconditions for reflexivity, self-relativization and learning from other perspectives. Individuals are never self-sovereign, but it is precisely the ambivalent nature of our identity (i.e. its constitutive dependency on others) that provides the impetus to engage in the dialogical exploration of difference, and the motivation to participate in politics in order to get things 'right'. Since this view holds that there is no 'true' self, public discourse cannot be seen as the externalization of an internal 'authenticity', but rather as an ongoing process of negotiation or epistemic struggle over the meanings that constitute the reality of the person and the world. This give and take requires a lot of interpretative charity or multicultural literacy; but the willingness to cooperate to find the best solutions to common problems, and perhaps also the enjoyment of discovering unexpected combinations of perspectives, repays the effort involved.

To speak more concretely now of European identity, it can be said that the EU – as a political and cultural space – is characterized by unclear and overlapping boundaries. Its history has been one of constant negotiation of difference, ongoing encounters between cultures, the existence of borderlands (Etienne Balibar): the boundaries of Schengenland which include a non-EU member such as Norway, but not Great Britain; the euro-zone which includes twelve EU member states; the Council of Europe's 'Europe' which comprises the Ukraine and Russia etc. Europe's heterogeneity will not be eliminated by an overarching European identity; it can only be dialogically mediated by a politics of memory,[5] which has, on the one hand, to be sustained by rich historical narratives and, on the other hand, connected to trasnational political action. Thus, we should be cautious not to reify the concept of European identity or an 'imagined community' on the basis of a set of common values or a fixed legacy. Rather, the core of European identity must be found in the growing reflexivity within European collective identities. It is open for difference and permanent contestation and has no need to exclude the 'other' for its own stabilisation. This said, however, it has also been argued here that a thin, post-national identity is not enough to ensure intense transnational political participation and solidarity among Europeans. Rather, what is called for is a 'situated' notion of transnational constitutional patriotism that makes translation within a constitutional dialogue (and constant re-negotiation of the meaning of principles) possible. Such a conception of an 'intercultural' or pastiche European identity is not at odds with the various national identities, but enriches them while at the same time exploring Europe's shared specificity.

Increasingly, the EU has a distinct identity-shaping effect on both elites and ordinary citizens.[6] For Europe's political, economic, and social elites, the EU is certainly very real. For ordinary citizens, however, the EU remains a more distant political community. This said, the single market, the introduction of euro bills and coins, the borders of Schengenland, Eastern enlargement and, most recently, the debate about the Constitutional Convention have clearly increased the 'reality' of the EU in people's daily life. Much of the EU's political future will depend on whether current institutional practices and reforms by the Constitutional Treaty will, in the long run, foster the development of a European constitutional patriotism. Without citizen support for democratic practices and identification with political institutions, the EU risks – at best – creating an environment of post-political consumer loyalty.[7] At worst, public resentment will brew in response to the EU's shallow treatment of constitutional ideals.[8] And this may also result in nationalist backlashes in which people develop a defence mechanism against the conflictual character of transnational and intercultural citizenship practices.

A 'situated' transnational constitutional patriotism can allow for the necessary critical distancing from the EU's institutional practices and the Constitutional Treaty, as it presently stands. Such a conception of patriotism is focused not only on the EU as a polity, but also, more deeply, on the heterogeneous (national) cultures of Europe. The engagement in transnational public discourse – conceived as the mutual exploration of difference – entails a commitment to constitutional ideals, diverse historical narratives and the active inclusion of marginal voices. European citizenship practices, conceived as such, could effectively counter nationalism and xenophobic sentiment. But who would be the likely actors well-disposed to transform ready-made collective identities into critical, relativized and reflexive self-understandings? New transnational citizens need not only emerge in the form of political activists or members of non-governmental organizations, let alone professional elites or EU-bureaucrats, but also as ordinary citizens who increasingly work across borders and regularly interact with 'others'. Indeed, it is these ordinary citizens that ought to be the focus of any discussion of European integration and it is to their concerns that European institutional arrangements should turn. The nature of the political process at the European level should provide citizens with opportunities and incentives to engage in transnational constitutional dialogue. In any case, it is crucial that European arrangements for political participation are complemented by systems of mass education, which would teach the linguistic skills necessary for translation between different languages as a 'daily practice' (Zygmunt Bauman). With this book I hoped to show that 'mass multicultural literacy' is the key to creating a vibrant transnational public sphere and transforming Europe into a society of intercultural learning.

Notes

1 See: P. Nanz and J.Steffek, 'Global Governance, Participation and the Public Sphere', in *Government and Opposition* 39:2, 2004, pp. 314–335; reprinted in D. Held and M. König-Archibugi (eds.), *Global Governance and Public Accountability*, Blackwell, Oxford, 2005, See also my current research project with Jens Steffek at the University of Bremen 'Participation and Legitimation in International Organisations', which explores new governance regimes with a focus on the participation of civil society actors in the context of the EU and the WTO (B 5 within the Sonderforschungsbereich 'Staatlichkeit im Wandel', see: www.sfb597.uni-bremen.de).

2 See: P. Nanz and J. Steffek, 'Assessing the Democratic Quality of Deliberation – Criteria and Research Strategies', in: *Acta politica* 40:3, 2005, pp. 368–383.

3 J. Bohman 'Constitution Making and Democratic Innovation: The European Union and Transnational Governance' in: *European Journal of Political Theory* 3:3, 2004, p. 356.

4 See also: B. Honig, *Political Theory and the Displacement of Politics*, Cornell University Press, Ithaca 1993.

5 See: M. Kumm, 'The Idea of a Thick Constitutional Patriotism and its Implications for the Role and the Structure of European Legal History', in: *German Law Journal* 6:2, 2005, pp. 319–354.

6 M. Bruter, 'Civic and Cultural Components of a European Identity: A Pilot Model of Measurement of Citizens' Levels of European Identity', in: R. H. Herrmann, T. Risse and M. B. Brewer (eds.), *Transnational Identities: Becoming European in the EU*, Rowman & Littlefield, New York 2004, pp. 186–213.

7 See: U. Haltern, 'Pathos and Patina: The Failure of Constitutionalism in the European Union', in: *European Law Journal* 14:19, 2002, pp. 14–44.

8 See: Kumm, 'The Idea of a Thick Constitutional Patriotism'.

Bibliography

Abélès, M., *La vie quotidienne au Parlement Européen*, Hachette, Paris 1982.
—— *Anthropologie de l'état*, Armand Colin, Paris 1990.
—— 'A la recherche d'un espace public communautaire', *Pouvoirs* 69, 1994, pp. 117–128.
Ackerman, B., 'Why Dialogue?', *Journal of Philosophy* 86:1, 1989, pp. 5–22.
Ackermann, A., 'Ethnologische Migrationsforschung: ein Überblick', in: *Kea: Zeitschrift für Kulturwissenschaften* 10, 1997, pp. 1–28.
Adorno, T. W., E. Freskel-Brunswik, and D. Levinson, *The Authoritarian Personality*, Harper, New York 1950.
Agar, M. H., *The Professional Stranger: An Informal Introduction to Ethnography*, Academic Press, San Diego/London 1980.
Alexander, J., 'The Return to Civil Society', *Contemporary Sociology* 22, 1993, pp. 797–803.
Almond, G. and S. Verba, *The Civic Culture*, Princeton University Press, Princeton 1963.
Amid-Talai, V. and H. Wulff (eds.), *Youth Cultures: A Cross-cultural Perspective*, Routledge, London/New York 1995.
Andersen, S. S. and T. R. Burns, 'The European Union and the Erosion of Parliamentary Democracy: A Study of Post-parliamentary Governance', in: S. S. Andersen and K. A. Eliassen (eds.), *The European Union: How Democratic is it?*, Sage, London 1996, pp. 227–251.
Anderson, B., *Imagined Communities: Reflections on the Origins and Spread of Nationalism*, Verso, London 1983.
—— 'Exodus', in: *Critical Inquiry* 20:2, 1994, pp. 314–326.
Appadurai, A., *Modernity at Large*, Minnesota University Press, Minneapolis 1996.
Appiah, K. A., 'Identity, Authenticity and Survival: Multicultural Societies and Social Reproduction', in: C. Taylor and A. Gutman (eds.), *Multiculturalism and the Politics of Recognition*, Princeton University Press, Princeton 1992, pp. 149–165.
—— 'Culture, Subculture, Multiculturalism: Educational Options', in: R. K. Fullinwider (ed.), *Public Education in a Multicultural Society: Policy, Theory, Critique*, Cambridge University Press, Cambridge 1996, pp. 65–89.
Arendt, H., *The Human Condition*, Chicago University Press, Chicago 1958.
—— *Men in Dark Times*, Harcourt Brace, New York 1968.
—— *Vita activa oder Vom tätigen Leben*, Piper Verlag, München 1981.
—— *Was ist Politik?*, Piper Verlag, München 1993.
Baggioni, D., *Langues et nations en Europe*, Payot, Paris 1997.
Baker, K. M., 'Defining the Public Sphere in Eighteenth Century France: Variations on a Theme

by Habermas', in: C. Calhoun (ed.), *Habermas and the Public Sphere*, MIT Press, Cambridge, MA, 1992, pp. 181–211.

Bakhtin, M., 'Discourse in the Novel', in: M. Bakhtin, *The Dialogic Imagination: Four Essays*, University of Texas Press, Austin 1981, pp. 259–422.

—— *The Dialogic Imagination: Four Essays*, University of Texas Press, Austin 1981.

—— 'The Characteristics of Genres and Plot', in: M. Bakhtin, *Problems of Dostoevsky*, Minnesota University Press, Minneapolis 1984, pp. 101–180.

—— 'Toward a Reworking of the Dostoevsky Book, Appendix 2', in: M. Bakhtin, *Problems of Dostoevsky*, Minnesota University Press, Minneapolis 1984.

—— 'Notes made in 1970–71', in: M. Bakhtin, *Speech Genres and Other Late Essays*, University of Texas Press, Austin 1986, pp. 132–172.

—— 'Response to a Question from the Novy Mir Editorial Staff', in: M. Bakhtin, *Speech Genres and Other Late Essays*, University of Texas Press, Austin 1986, pp. 1–9.

—— *Speech Genres and Other Late Essays*, University of Texas Press, Austin 1986.

—— 'The Problem of Speech Genres', in: M. Bakhtin, *Speech Genres and Other Late Essays*, University of Texas Press, Austin 1986, pp. 60–102.

Bakke, E., 'Towards a European Identity?', in: *Working Papers IUE (Oslo: ARENA)* 10, 1995, pp. 1–26.

Balibar, E., 'Europe as Borderland, Lecture Presented in Human Geography', University of Nijmegen, 10 November 2004 [on file with the author].

—— *We, the People of Europe?*, Princeton University Press, Princeton 2004

Balke, F., R. Habermas, P. Nanz, and P. Sillem (eds.), *Schwierige Fremdheit: Über Integration und Ausgrenzung in Einwanderungsländern*, Fischer Taschenbuch Verlag, Frankfurt am Main 1993.

Barber, B., *Strong Democracy: Participatory Politics for a New Age*, University of California Press, Berkeley, CA, 1984.

Bauman, Z., 'On Glocalization: Globalization for Some, Localization for Some Others', in: *Thesis Eleven* 54, 1998, pp. 37–49.

—— *Modernity and Ambivalence*, Polity Press, Cambridge 1991.

—— *In Search of Politics*, Polity Press, Cambridge 1999.

Beauftragte der Bundesregierung für Ausländerfragen, *Bericht über die Lage der Ausländer in der Bundesrepublik Deutschland*, Bonn 1997.

Beisheim, M., S. Dreher and G. Walter, *Im Zeitalter der Globalisierung? Thesen und Daten zur gesellschaftlichen und politischen Denationalisierung*, Nomos Verlag, Baden-Baden 1998.

Bellah, R. N., R. Madsen, W. M. Sullivan, A. Swidler and S. M. Tipton, *Habits of the Heart: Individualism and Commitment in American Life*, University of California Press, Berkeley, CA, 1985.

Bellamy, R., *Liberalism and Pluralism: Towards a Politics of Compromise*, Routledge, London/New York 1999.

Bellamy, R. and D. Castiglione, 'The Uses of Democracy: Reflections on the European Democratic Deficit', in: E. O. Eriksen and J. E. Fossum (eds.), *Democracy in the European Union*, Routledge, London/New York 1999, pp. 65–84.

Benhabib, S., *Situating the Self*, Routledge, London/New York 1992.

—— 'Toward a Deliberative Model of Democratic Legitimacy', in: S. Benhabib (ed.), *Democracy and Difference: Contesting the Boundaries of the Political*, Princeton University Press, Princeton 1996, pp. 67–97.

—— *Kulturelle Vielfalt und demokratische Gleichheit: Politische Partizipation im Zeitalter der Globalisierung*, Fischer Taschenbuch Verlag, Frankfurt am Main 1999.

Benhabib, S. (ed.), *Democracy and Difference: Contesting the Boundaries of the Political*, Princeton University Press, Princeton 1996.

Benjamin, W., *Über die Sprache überhaupt und über die Sprache des Menschen, Schriften II*, Suhrkamp Verlag, Frankfurt am Main 1955.

Berger, P. L. (ed.), *The Limits of Social Cohesion: Conflicts and Mediation in Pluralist Societies*,

Westview Press, Oxford 1998.

Berger, P. L. and T. Luckmann, *Die gesellschaftliche Konstruktion der Wirklichkeit: eine Theorie der Wissenssoziologie*, S. Fischer Verlag, Frankfurt am Main 1969.

Bernstein, R., *The New Constellation: The Ethical-Political Horizons of Modernity/Postmodernity*, Polity Press, Cambridge 1991.

Beyme, K. v., 'Mass Media and the Political Agenda of the Parliamentary System', in: F. Neidhardt (ed.), *Öffentlichkeit, öffentliche Meinung, soziale Bewegungen (Kölner Zeitschrift für Soziologie und Sozialpsychologie, Sonderheft 34)*, Westdeutscher Verlag, Opladen 1994, pp. 320–336

Bhabha, H. K., 'DissemiNation: Time, Narrative, and the Margins of the Modern Nation', in: H. K. Bhabha (ed.), *Nation and Narration*, Routledge, London/New York 1990, pp. 139–170.

Bielefeld, U., *Inländische Ausländer: Zum gesellschaftlichen Bewußtsein türkischer Jugendlicher in der Bundesrepublik*, Campus, Frankfurt am Main/New York 1988.

Billig, M., 'Socio-psychological Aspects of Nationalism: Imagining Ingroups, Others and the World of Nations', in: K. v. Benda-Beckmann and M. Verkuyten (eds.), *Nationalism, Ethnicity and Cultural Identity in Europe*, European Research Centre of Migration and Ethnic Relations (ERCOMER), Utrecht 1995, pp. 89–106.

Blau, P. M., *Exchange and Power in Social Life*, John Wiley & Sons, New York 1964.

Blumler, H., 'The Mass, the Public, and Public Opinion', in: B. Berelson and M. Janowitz (eds.), *Reader in Public Opinion and Communication*, Free Press, Glencoe, IL, 1953, pp. 43–49.

Bobbio, N., 'Gramsci and the Concept of Civil Society', in: J. Keane (ed.), *Civil Society and the State: New European Perspectives*, Verso, London 1988, pp. 73–99.

Bohman, J., *Public Deliberation: Pluralism, Complexity, and Democracy*, MIT Press, Cambridge, MA, 1996.

—— 'Constitution Making and Democratic Innovation: The European Union and Transnational Governance', in: *European Journal of Political Theory* 3:3, 2004, pp. 315–337.

Boltanski, L. and L. Thévenot, *De la justification: Les économies de la grandeur*, Gallimard, Paris 1991.

Bourdieu, P., *La distinction: Critique sociale du jugement*, Minuit, Paris 1979.

—— 'Epilogue: On the Possibility of a Field of World Sociology', in: P. Bourdieu and J. S. Coleman (eds.), *Social Theory for a Changing Society*, Westview Press, Boulder/San Francisco 1991, pp. 301–335.

—— (ed.), *La misère du monde*, Seuil, Paris 1993.

Bourdieu, P. and L. Wacquant, *An Invitation to Reflexive Sociology*, Chicago University Press, Chicago 1992.

Brandom, R., *Making Explicit: Reasoning, Representing, and Discursive Commitment*, Harvard University Press, Cambridge, MA, 1994.

—— *Articulating Reasons: An Introduction to Inferentialism*, Harvard University Press, Cambridge, MA, 2000.

—— 'Facts, Norms and Normative Facts: A Reply to Habermas', in: *European Journal of Philosophy* 8:3, 2000, pp. 356–374.

Brennan, T., 'Cosmopolitans and celebrities', in: *Race & Class* 31:1, 1989, pp. 1–20.

Brubaker, D., *Citizenship and Nationhood in France and Germany*, Harvard University Press, Cambridge, MA, 1992.

Brubaker, R. and F. Cooper, 'Beyond "Identity"', in: *Theory and Society* 29, 2000, pp. 1–47.

Bruner, J., *Actual Minds, Possible Worlds*, Harvard University Press, Cambridge, MA, 1986.

—— *Acts of Meaning*, Harvard University Press, Cambridge, MA, 1990.

Bruner, J. and A. Amsterdam, *Minding the Law*, Harvard University Press, Cambridge, MA, 2000.

Bruter, M., 'Civic and Cultural Components of a European Identity: A Pilot Model of Measurement of Citizens' Levels of European Identity', in: R. H. Herrmann, T. Risse and M.B. Brewer (eds.), *Transnational Identities: Becoming European in the EU*, Rowman & Littlefield, New York 2004, pp. 186–213.

Bryman, A. and R. G. Burgess (eds.), *Analyzing Qualitative Data*, Routledge, London/New York

1994.

Burns, T., C. Jaeger, A. Liberatore, Y. Mény and P. Nanz, 'European Parliamentary Governance: Transition and Challenge', in: *Green Paper for EU Parliaments*, 2000.

Calhoun, C., 'Introduction: Habermas and the Public Sphere', in: C. Calhoun (ed.), *Habermas and the Public Sphere*, MIT Press, Cambridge, MA, 1992, pp. 1–48.

—— 'Civil Society and the Public Sphere', in: *Public Culture* 5:2, 1993, pp. 267–280.

—— 'Social Theory and the Public Sphere', in: B. S. Turner (ed.), *The Blackwell Companion to Social Theory*, Blackwell, Oxford 1996, pp. 504–544.

—— 'Nationalism and the Public Sphere', in: J. Weintraub and K. Kumar (eds.), *Public and Private in Thought and Practice: Perspectives on a Grand Dichotomy*, Chicago University Press, Chicago 1997, pp. 75–102.

—— *Habermas and the Public Sphere*, MIT Press, Cambridge, MA, 1992.

Cavalli-Wordel, A., *Schicksale italienischer Migrantenkinder: Eine Fallstudie*, Beltzverlag, Weinheim 1989.

Celan, P., *Ausgewählte Gedichte*, Suhrkamp Verlag, Frankfurt am Main 1968.

Chartier, R., *Cultural History: Between Practices and Representations*, Polity Press, Cambridge 1988.

Chicago Cultural Studies Group, 'Critical Multiculturalism', in: D. T. Goldberg (ed.), *Multiculturalism: a Critical Reader*, Blackwell, Oxford 1994, pp. 114–139.

Chiellino, G., 'La nascita della memoria biculturale', in: G. Scimonello (ed.), *Cultura Tedesca/ Deutsche Kultur: Letteratura e immigrazione*, vol. 10, Donzelli Editore, Rome 1998, pp. 23–32.

Citrin, J. and J. Sides, 'More Than Just Nationals: How Identity Choice Matters in the New Europe', in: R. H. Herrmann, T. Risse and M. B. Brewer (eds.), *Transnational Identities: Becoming European in the EU*, Rowman & Littlefield, New York 2004, pp. 161–185.

Clifford, J., 'Identity in a Mashpee', in: J. Clifford, *The Predicament of Culture: Twentieth Century Ethnography, Literature and Art*, Cambridge University Press, Cambridge 1988, pp. 277–346.

Cohen, J. L., 'Democracy, Difference, and the Right of Privacy', in: S. Benhabib (ed.), *Democracy and Difference: Contesting the Boundaries of the Political*, Princeton University Press, Princeton 1996, pp. 187–217.

Cohen, J. and A. Arato, *Civil Society and Political Theory*, MIT Press, Cambridge, MA, 1992.

Cohen, J., 'An Epistemic Conception of Democracy', in: *Ethics* 97, 1986, pp. 26–38.

—— 'Deliberation and Democratic Legitimacy', in: A. Hamlin and P. Pettit (eds.), *The Good Polity: Normative Analysis of the State*, Blackwell, Oxford 1989, pp. 17–34.

—— 'Procedure and Substance in Deliberative Democracy', in: S. Benhabib (ed.), *Democracy and Difference: Contesting the Boundaries of the Political*, Princeton University Press, Princeton 1996, pp. 95–119.

Coulmas, F. (ed.), *A Language Policy for the European Community: Prospects and Quandaries*, Mouton de Gruyter, Berlin 1991.

Craib, I., *Experiencing Identity*, Sage, London 1998.

Dahl, R., *Democracy and its Critics*, Yale University Press, New Haven 1989.

Davidson, D., 'The Very Idea of a Conceptual Scheme', in: *Proceedings and Addresses of the American Philosophical Association* 47, 1974, pp. 5–20; reprinted in D. Davidson, *Inquiries into Truth and Interpretation*, Oxford University Press, Oxford 1984.

—— *Inquiries into Truth and Interpretation*, Oxford University Press, Oxford 1984, pp. 183–198.

—— 'Reality Without Reference', in: D. Davidson, *Inquiries into Truth and Interpretation*, Oxford University Press, Oxford 1984, pp. 215–225.

—— 'Radical Interpretation', in: D. Davidson, *Inquiries into Truth and Interpretation*, Oxford University Press, Oxford 1984, pp. 125–139.

—— 'The Method of Truth in Metaphysics', in: D. Davidson, *Inquiries into Truth and Interpretation*, Oxford University Press, Oxford 1984, pp. 199–214.

—— 'A Nice Derangement of Epitaphs', in: E. LePore (ed.), *Truth and Interpretation: Perspectives on the Philosophy of Donald Davidson*, Blackwell, Oxford 1986, pp. 433–446.

De Bùrca Gràinna, 'The Quest of Legitimacy in the European Union', in: *The Modern Law Review* 59:3, 1996, pp. 349–376.

Dean, J., *Solidarity with Strangers: Feminism after Identity Politics*, University of California Press, Berkeley, CA, 1996.

Delanty, G., 'The Frontier and Identities of Exclusion in European History', in: *History of European Ideas* 22:2, 1996, pp. 93–103.

—— 'What does it mean to be a "European"?', in: *Innovation* 18:1, 2005, pp. 11–22.

De la Porte, C. and P. Nanz, 'Open Method of Coordination – a Deliberative and Democratic Mode of Governance?', in: *Journal of European Public Policy* 11:2, 2004, pp. 267–288.

De Swann, A., *Words of the World: The Global Language System*, Polity Press, Cambridge 2001.

Deutsch, K. W., *Political Community and the North Atlantic Area*, Princeton University Press, Princeton 1957.

—— *Nationalism and Social Communication: An Inquiry into the Foundations of Nationality*, MIT Press, Cambridge, MA, 1966.

Deutsche Shell (ed.), *Jugend 2000*, vol. 2, Leske+Budrich, Opladen 2000.

Dewey, J., 'The Public and its Problems', in: J. Dewey, *Later Works: 1925–1927*, vol. 12, University of Southern Illinois Press, Carbondale 1988, pp. 238–327.

Duchesne, S., *Citoyenneté à la française*, Presses de sciences politiques, Paris 1997.

Dunne, M., 'Postscript: Multiculturalism on Europe and America', in: M. Dunne and T. Bonazzi (eds.), *Citizenship and Rights in Multicultural Societies*, Keele University Press, Keele 1995, pp. 265–281.

Duranti, A. and C. Goodwin, *Language as an Interactive Phenomenon*, Cambridge University Press, Cambridge 1992.

Eatwell, R. (ed.), *European Political Cultures: Conflict or Convergence?*, Routledge, London/New York 1997.

Eco, U., *The Search for the Perfect Language*, Blackwell, Oxford 1995.

Eder, K., K. U. Hellman and H. J. Trenz, 'Regieren in Europa jenseits öffentlicher Legitimation: Eine Untersuchung zur Rolle von politischer Öffentlichkeit in Europa', in: *Politische Vierteljahresschriften*, Sonderheft 39, 1998, pp. 321–344.

Ehlermann, C., Meny, Y. and H. Bribosia, *A Basic Treaty for the European Union: a Study of the Reorganisation of the Treatise*, European University Institute, Florence 2000.

Eichener, V., *Das Entscheidungssystem der Europäischen Union: Institutionelle Analyse und demokratietheoretische Bewertung*, Leske+Budrich, Opladen 2000.

Eley, G., 'Nations, Publics, and the Political Cultures: Placing Habermas in the Nineteenth Century', in: C. Calhoun (ed.), *Habermas and the Public Sphere*, MIT Press, Cambridge, MA, 1992, pp. 289–339.

Elster, J., *The Cement of Society: A Study of Social Order*, Cambridge University Press, Cambridge 1989.

Emerson, C., *The First Hundred Years of Mikhail Bakhtin*, Princeton University Press, Princeton 1997.

Emerson, C. and G. Morson, *Mikhail Bakhtin: Creation of Prosaics*, Stanford University Press, Stanford, CA, 1990.

Epstein, R., *Simple Rules for a Complex World*, Harvard University Press, Cambridge, MA, 1995.

Erikson, E., *Childhood and Society*, Norton Press, New York 1951.

Eurobarometer, 'The European Union: "A view from the top"', *Top Decision Makers Survey Summary Report*, Brussels 1996.

Fabbri, P., *Alla ricerca della propria identità*, Quaderno UDEB 81, Frankfurt am Main 1999.

Faist, T., 'International Migration and Transnational Spaces: Their Evolution, Significance and Future Prospects', in: *InIIS-Arbeitspapier (Universität Bremen)* 9, 1998.

Fanon, F., *The Wretched of the Earth*, Penguin, Harmondsworth 1967.

Favell, A., 'European Citizenship and the Incorporation of Migrants and Minorities in Europe: Emergence, Transformation and Effects of the New Political Field', in: *Paper of the European*

Forum *(European University Institute)*, 1997, pp. 1–57.

Fentress, J. and C. Wickham, *Social Memory: New Perspective on the Past*, Blackwell, Oxford 1992.

Ferree, M. Marx, W. Gamson, J. Gerhards and D. Rucht, 'Four Models of the Public Sphere in Modern Democracies', in: *Theory and Society* 31:3, 2002, pp. 289–324.

Ferejohn, J., 'Accountability and Authority: Toward a Theory of Political Accountability', in: A. Przeworski, S. C. Stokes and B. Manin (eds.), *Democracy, Accountability, and Representation*, Cambridge University Press, Cambridge 1999, pp. 131–153.

Ferry, J.-M., 'Identité et citoyenneté européennes', in: J. Lenoble and N. Dewandre (eds.), *L'Europe au soir du siècle: identité et démocratie*, Editions Esprit, Paris 1992, pp. 177–188.

—— *La Question de l'Etat européen*, Gallimard, Paris 2000.

Fischer-Rosenthal, W. and G. Rosenthal, 'Narrationsanalyse biographischer Selbstpräsentationen', in: R. Hitzler and A. Honer (eds.), *Sozialwissenschaftliche Hermeneutik*, Leske+Budrich, Opladen 1997, pp. 133–165.

Fishkin, J. S., *Democracy and Deliberation: New Directions in Democratic Reform*, Yale University, New Haven 1991.

—— *The Voice of the People: Public Opinion and Democracy*, Yale University Press, New Haven 1995.

Fleisher Feldman, C., 'American Narratives of National Identity: The Cowboy Story', talk and typescript presented at the Vygotsky Centennial, Geneva 1996.

Flichy, P., *Une histoire de la communication moderne: Espace public et vie privée*, La Découverte, Paris 1991.

Føllesdal, A., 'Democracy, legitimacy and majority rule in the European Union', in : A. Waele and M. Nentwich (eds.), *Political Theory and the European Union, Legitimacy, Constitutional Choice and Citizenship*, Routledge, London/New York 1998, pp. 34–48.

—— 'Union Citizenship: Unpacking the Beast of the Burden', in: *Law and Philosophy* 20:3, 2001, pp. 233–255.

Fraser, N., 'Rethinking the Public Sphere: A Contribution to the Critique of Actually Existing Democracy', in: C. Calhoun (ed.), *Habermas and the Public Sphere*, MIT Press, Cambridge, MA, 1992, pp. 109–142.

—— 'Politics, Culture, and the Public Sphere: Toward a Postmodern Conception', in: L. Nicholson and S. Seidman (eds.), *Social postmodernism: Beyond identity politics*, Cambridge University Press, Cambridge 1995, pp. 287–312.

—— 'Rethinking Recognition', in: *New Left Review* 3, 2000, pp. 107–120.

Freund, B., 'Frankfurt am Main und der Frankfurter Raum als Ziel qualifizierter Migranten', in: *Zeitschrift für Wirtschaftsgeographie* 42:2, 1998, pp. 57–81.

Fuchs, M., 'The Universality of Culture: Reflection, Interaction and the Logic of Identity', in: *Thesis Eleven* 60:1, 2000, pp. 11–22.

Fulbrook, M., 'Germany for the Germans? Citizenship and Nationality in a Divided Nation', in: D. Cesarani and M. Fulbrook (eds.), *Citizenship, Nationality and Migration in Europe*, Routledge, London/New York 1996, pp. 88–105.

Gabel, M. J., *Interests and Integration: Market Liberalization, Public Opinion, and European Union*, The University of Michigan Press, Ann Arbor 1998.

Gadamer, H.-G., *Wahrheit und Methode*, Mohr, Tübingen 1965.

Garcia, S., 'Europe's Fragmented Identities and the Frontiers of Citizenship', in: *RIIA Discussion Papers, The Royal Institute of International Affairs* 45, 1993.

Garnham, N., 'The Media and the Public Sphere', in: P. Golding, G. Murdock and P. Schlesinger (eds.), *Communicating Politics: Mass communication and the political process*, Holmes & Meier, New York 1986, pp. 37–53.

—— 'The Media and the Public Sphere', in: C. Calhoun (ed.), *Habermas and the Public Sphere*, MIT Press, Cambridge, MA, 1992, pp. 359–376.

Geertz, C., *The Interpretations of Cultures*, Basic Books, New York 1973.

Gellner, E., *Nations and Nationalism*, Cornell University Press, Ithaca 1983.

—— *Culture, Identity and Politics*, Cambridge University Press, Cambridge 1987.

Gerhards, J., 'Die Macht der Massenmedien und die Demokratie: Empirische Befunde', in: *Discussion Paper, Wissenschaftszentrum Berlin* FS III, 1991, pp. 91–101.

—— 'Westeuropäische Integration und die Schwierigkeit der Entstehung einer europäischen Öffentlichkeit', in: *Zeitschrift für Soziologie* 22:2, 1993, pp. 96–110.

—— 'Politische Öffentlichkeit. Ein system- und akteurtheoretischer Bestimmungsversuch', in: F. Neidhart (ed.), *Öffentlichkeit, öffentliche Meinung, soziale Bewegungen*, Westdeutscher Verlag, Opladen 1994, pp.77–105.

—— 'Europäisierung von Ökonomie und Politik und die Trägheit der Entstehung einer europäischen Öffentlichkeit', in: M. Bach (ed.), *Die Europäisierung nationaler Gesellschaften. Sonderheft 40 Kölner Zeitschrift für Soziologie und Sozialpsychologie*, Westdeutscher Verlag, Opladen 2000, pp. 277–305;

—— 'Das Öffentlichkeitsdefizit der EU im Horizont normativer Öffentlichkeitstheorien', in: Kälble H., M. Kirsch and A. Schmid-Gernig (eds.), *Transnationale Öffentlichkeiten und Identitäten im 20. Jahrhundert*, Campus Verlag, Frankfurt am Main/New York 2002, pp. 135–158.

Gerhards, J. and F. Neidhardt, 'Strukturen und Funktionen moderner Öffentlichkeit. Fragestellungen und Ansätze', in: *Discussion Paper, Wissenschaftszentrum Berlin* FS III, 1990, pp. 90–101.

Gerstenberg, O., 'Law's Polyarchy: A Comment on Cohen and Sabel', in: O. Gerstenberg and C. Joerges (eds.), *Private Governance, Democratic Constitutionalism and Supranationalism*, European Communities, Brussels 1998, pp. 31–48.

—— 'Private Ordering, Public Intervention and Social Pluralism', in: O. Gerstenberg and C. Joerges (eds.), *Private Governance, Democratic Constitutionalism and Supranationalism*, European Communities, Brussels 1998, pp. 205–218.

Gerstenberg, O. and C. Sabel, 'Directly-Deliberative Polyarchy: An Institutional Ideal for Europe?', in: R. Dehousse and C. Joerges (eds.), *Good Governance and Administration in Europe's Integrated Market (Collected Courses of the Academy of European Law, XI)*, Oxford University Press, Oxford 2002, pp. 289–341.

Gifreu, J., 'Linguistic order and spaces of communication in post-Maastricht Europe', in: *Media, Culture & Society* 18:1, 1996, pp. 127–139.

Gilroy, P., *The Black Atlantic: Modernity and Double Consciousness*, Harvard University Press, Cambridge, MA, 1993.

Girault, R. (sous la direction de), *Identité et conscience européennes au XX siècle*, Hachette, Paris 1994.

Goddard, V. A., J. R. Llobera and C. Shore (eds.), *The Anthropology of Europe: Identities and Boundaries in Conflict*, Berg, Oxford/Providence 1994.

Goffman, E., *Behavior in Public Places: Notes on the Social Organization of Gatherings*, The Free Press, New York 1963.

Grenz, W., 'Die Ausländer- und Asylpolitik der rot-grünen Bundesregierung', in: C. Butterwege and G. Hentges (eds.), *Zuwanderung im Zeichen der Globalisierung. Migrations-, Integrations- und Minderheitenpolitik*, Leske+Budrich, Opladen 2000, pp. 105–119.

Grimm, D., 'Braucht Europa eine Verfassung?', in: *Juristenzeitung* 50:12, 1995, pp. 581–591.

—— 'Does Europe need a Constitution?', in: *European Law Journal* 1:3, 1995, pp. 282–302.

Gutmann, A., 'Challenges of Multiculturalism in Democratic Education', in: R. K. Fullinwider (ed.), *Public Education in a Multicultural Society: Policy, Theory, Critique*, Cambridge University Press, Cambridge 1996, pp. 156–179.

Haas, E. B., *The Uniting of Europe: Political, Social and Economic Forces 1950–1957*, Stanford University Press, Stanford, CA, 1958.

Habermas, J., *Legitimationsprobleme im Spätkapitalismus*, Suhrkamp Verlag, Frankfurt am Main 1973.

—— 'The Public Sphere', in: *New German Critique*, 1974.

—— *Legitimation Crisis*, Beacon Press, Boston 1975.

—— *Theorie des kommunikativen Handelns*, 2 vols, Suhrkamp Verlag, Frankfurt am Main 1981.

—— 'The Normative Content of Modernity', in: J. Habermas, *The Philosophical Discourse of Modernity*, MIT Press, Cambridge, MA, 1987, pp. 336–367.

—— 'Motive nachmetaphysischen Denkens', J. Habermas, *Nachmetaphysisches Denken*, Suhrkamp Verlag, Frankfurt am Main 1988, pp. 35–60.

—— *The New Conservatism: Cultural Criticism and the Historians' Debate*, MIT Press, Cambridge 1989.

—— *The Structural Transformation of the Public Sphere*, MIT Press, Cambridge, MA, 1989.

—— *Strukturwandel der Öffentlichkeit: Untersuchungen zu einer Kategorie der bürgerlichen Gesellschaft*, Suhrkamp Verlag (new edition), Frankfurt am Main 1990.

—— *Theory of Communicative Action*, vol. 2, Polity Press (new edition), Cambridge 1991.

—— *Faktizität und Geltung: Beiträge zur Diskurstheorie des Rechts und des demokratischen Rechtsstaats*, Suhrkamp Verlag, Frankfurt am Main 1992.

—— 'Further Reflections on the Public Sphere', in: C. Calhoun (ed.), *Habermas and the Public Sphere*, MIT Press, Cambridge, MA, 1992, pp. 421–461.

—— 'Individuation through Socialization: On Mead's Theory of Subjectivity', in: J. Habermas, *Postmetaphysical Thinking: Philosophical Essays*, MIT Press, Cambridge, MA, 1992.

—— 'Anerkennungskämpfe im demokratischen Rechtsstaat', in: C. Taylor and A. Gutman (eds.), *Multikulturalismus und die Politik der Anerkennung*, S. Fischer Verlag, Frankfurt am Main 1993, pp. 147–196.

—— 'Struggles for Recognition in the Democratic Constitutional State', in: C. Taylor and A. Gutman (eds.), *Multiculturalism and the Politics of Recognition*, Princeton University Press, Princeton 1994, pp. 107–148.

—— 'On the Internal Relation between the Rule of Law and Democracy', in: *European Journal of Philosphy* 3:1, 1995, pp. 12–20.

—— 'Remarks on Dieter Grimm's "Does Europe need a Constitution?"', in: *European Law Journal* 1:3, 1995, pp. 303–307.

—— *Between Facts and Norms. Contributions to a Discourse Theory of Law and Democracy*, MIT Press, Cambridge, MA, 1996.

—— 'Braucht Europa eine Verfassung? Eine Bemerkung zu Dieter Grimm', in: J. Habermas, *Die Einbeziehung des Anderen*, Suhrkamp Verlag, Frankfurt am Main 1996, pp. 185–191.

—— 'Der europäische Nationalstaat – Zu Vergangenheit und Zukunft von Souveränität und Staaatsbürgerschaft', in: J. Habermas, *Die Einbeziehung des Anderen*, Suhrkamp Verlag, Frankfurt am Main 1996, pp. 128–153.

—— *The Inclusion of the Other*, MIT Press, Cambridge, MA, 1996.

—— 'Inklusion – Einbeziehen oder Einschließen? Zum Verhältnis von Nation, Rechtsstaat und Demokratie', in: J. Habermas, *Die Einbeziehung des Anderen*, Suhrkamp Verlag, Frankfurt am Main 1996, pp. 154–184.

—— 'Three Normative Models of Democracy', in: S. Benhabib (ed.), *Democracy and Difference. Contesting the Boundaries of the Political*, Princeton University Press, Princeton 1996, pp. 21–30.

—— 'The European Nation-State', in: J. Habermas, *The Inclusion of the Other*, MIT Press, Cambridge, MA, 1996, pp. 105–128.

—— 'The Nation, the Rule of Law, and Democracy', in: J. Habermas, *The Inclusion of the Other*, MIT Press, Cambridge, MA, 1996, pp. 129–153.

—— *On the Pragmatics of Communication*, MIT Press, Cambridge, MA, 1998.

—— 'Toward a critique of the Theory of Meaning', in: J. Habermas, *On the Pragmatics of Communication*, MIT Press, Cambridge, MA, 1998, pp. 277–306.

—— 'Hermeneutische und analytische Philosophie. Zwei komplementäre Spielarten der linguistischen Wende', in: J. Habermas, *Wahrheit und Rechtfertigung. Philosophische Aufsätze*, Suhrkamp Verlag, Frankfurt am Main 1999, pp. 65–101.

—— 'From Kant to Hegel: On Robert Brandom's Pragmatic Philosophy of Language', in: *European Journal of Philosophy* 8:3, 2000, pp. 322–355.

—— 'Werte und Normen. Ein Kommentar zu Hilary Putnams kantischem Pragmatismus', in: *Deutsche Zeitschrift für Philosophie* 48:4, 2000, pp. 547–564.

—— *Truth and Justification*, MIT Press, Cambridge, MA, 2003.

—— 'Hermeneutic and Analytic Philosophy: Two Complementary Versions of the Linguistic Turn', in J. Habermas, *Truth and* Justification, MIT Press, Cambridge, MA, 2003, pp. 51–81.

Hall, S., 'Who Needs "Identity"?', in: S. Hall and P. du Gay (eds.), *Questions of Cultural Identity*, Sage, London 1996, pp. 1–17.

Haltern, U., 'Pathos and Patina: The Failure of Constitutionalism in the European Union', in: *European Law Journal* 14:19, 2003, pp. 14–44.

Hampshire, S., *Justice is Conflict*, Princeton University Press, Princeton 2000.

Hannerz, U., *Transnational Connections: Culture, People, Places*, Routledge, London/New York 1996.

Harvey, D., *The Condition of Postmodernity: An Inquiry into the Origins of Cultural Change*, Blackwell, Oxford 1990.

—— *Justice, Nature & the Geography of Difference*, Blackwell, Oxford 1996.

Haug, S., 'Soziales Kapital: Migrationsentscheidungen und Kettenmigrationsprozesse am Beispiel der italienischen Migranten in Deutschland', Dissertation, Universität Mannheim 1999.

Heater, D., *What is Citizenship?*, Polity Press, Cambridge 1999.

Held, D., 'The Decline of the Nation-State', in: S. Hall and M. Jacques (eds.), *New Times*, Lawrence and Wishart, London 1989, pp. 191–204.

Heritier, A. and S. Schmidt, 'After Liberalization: Public-Interest Services and Employment in the Utilities', in: F. Scharpf and V. Schmidt (eds.), *Welfare and Work in the Open Economy*, vol. 2, Oxford University Press, Oxford 2000, pp. 554–596.

Herzfeld, M., 'Segmentation and Politics in the European Nation-State: Making Sense of Political Events', in: K. Hastrup (ed.), *Other Histories*, Routledge, London/New York 1992. pp. 62–81.

—— *Cultural Intimacy: Social Poetics in the Nation-State*, Routledge, London/New York 1997.

Hirschkop, K., *Mikhail Bakhtin: An Aesthetic for Democracy*, Oxford University Press, Oxford 1999.

—— 'It's Too Good to Talk: Myths and Dialogue in Bakhtin and Habermas', in: *New Formations* 2000:41, 2000, pp. 83–93.

Hirschman, A., *The Passions and the Interests: Political Arguments for Capitalism before its Triumph*, Princeton University Press, Princeton 1997.

Hobsbawm, E. and T. Ranger (eds.), *The Invention of Tradition*, Cambridge University Press, Cambridge 1983.

Holquist, M., *Dialogism: Bakhtin and his World*, Routledge, London/New York 1990.

Honig, B., *Political Theory and the Displacement of Politics*, Cornell University Press, Ithaca 1993.

—— 'Difference, Dilemmas, and the Politics of Home', in: S. Benhabib (ed.), *Democracy and Difference: Contesting the Boundaries of the Political*, Princeton University Press, Princeton 1996, pp. 257–277.

Hume, D., 'A Treatise of Human Nature', in: D. Hume, *The Philosophical Works*, vol. 2, Scientia Verlag, Aalen 1964.

—— *Enquiries concerning Human Understanding and concerning the Principles of Morals*, Clarendon Press, Oxford 1975.

Hymes, D., *Foundations in Sociolinguistics: An Ethnographical Approach*, Tavistock, London 1977.

Inglehart, R., *Cultural Shift*, Princeton University Press, Princeton 1990.

Joas, H., *Praktische Intersubjektivität: Die Entwicklung des Werkes von G.H. Mead*, Suhrkamp Verlag, Frankfurt am Main 1980.

Johnson, J., 'Is Talk Really Cheap? Prompting Conversation between Critical Theory and Rational Choice', in: *American Political Science Review* 87:1, 1993, pp. 74–86.

Kaelble, H., *Auf dem Weg zu einer europäischen Gesellschaft: Eine Sozialgeschichte Westeuropas*

1880–1980, Beck Verlag, München 1987.

—— 'Europäische Vielfalt und der Weg zu einer europäischen Gesellschaft', in: S. Hradil and Immerfall Stefan (eds.), *Die europäischen Gesellschaften im Vergleich*, Leske+Budrich, Opladen 1997, pp. 27–68.

Kantner, C., 'Öffentliche politische Kommunikation in der Europäischen Union: Eine hermeneutisch-pragmatische Perspektive', in: A. Klein and R. Koopmans (eds.), *Bürgerschaft, Öffentlichkeit und Demokratie in Europa*, Leske + Budrich, Opladen 2002, pp. 215–229.

Karpf, E., *'Und mache es denen hiernächst Ankommenden nicht so schwer': Kleine Geschichte der Zuwanderung in Frankfurt am Main*, Campus, Frankfurt am Main and New York 1993.

Katz, E. and P. Lazarsfeld, *Personal Influence: The Part Played by People in the Flow of Mass Communication*, Free Press, Glencoe, IL, 1955.

Kavanagh, D., *Political Culture*, Macmillan, London 1972.

Keane, J., *Public Life and Late Capitalism: Toward a Socialist Theory of Democracy*, Cambridge University Press, Cambridge 1984.

—— *Democracy and Civil Society*, Verso, London 1988.

—— *Civil Society: Old Images, New Visions*, Polity Press, Cambridge 1998.

—— *Global Civil Society?*, Cambridge University Press, Cambridge 2003.

Kielmansegg, P., 'Integration und Demokratie', in: M. Jachtenfuchs and B. Kohler-Koch (eds.), *Europäische Integration*, Leske+Budrich, Opladen 1996, pp. 47–71.

Kohli, M., 'The Battlegrounds of European Identity', in: *European Society* 2:2, 2000, pp. 113–137.

Koopmans, R.and H. Kriesi, 'Citizenship, National Identity and the Mobilisation of the Extreme Right: A Comparison of France, Germany, the Netherlands and Switzerland', in: *Wissenschaftszentrum Berlin für Sozialforschung*, 1997, pp. 1–37.

Koopmans, R. and P. Statham, 'Challenging the Liberal Nation-State? Postnationalism, Multiculturalism, and the Collective Claims-Making of Migrants and Ethnic Minorities in Britain and Germany', in: *Wissenschaftszentrum Berlin für Sozialforschung*, 1998, pp. 1–52.

Kopecký, P. and C. Mudde, 'Two Sides of Euroskepticism: Party Positions on European Integration in East Central Europe', in: *European Union Politics* 3:3, 2001, pp. 297–326.

Koslowski, R., *Migrants and Citizens: Demographic Change in the European State System*, Cornell University, Ithaca 2000.

Kostakopoulou, D., 'Is There an Alternative to Schengenland?', in: *Political Studies* 46, 1998, pp. 886–902.

Kriesi, H. et.al., *The Politics of the New Social Movements in Western Europe*, Minnesota University Press, Minneapolis 1995.

Kristeva, J., *Essays in Semiotics*, Mouton, Paris 1971.

Kumm, M., 'The Idea of a Thick Constitutional Patriotism and its Implications for the Role and the Structure of European Legal History', in: *German Law Journal* 6:2, 2005, pp. 319–354

Kymlicka, W., *Contemporary Political Philosophy: An Introduction*, Oxford University Press, Oxford 1990.

—— *Liberalism, Community, and Culture*, Clarendon Press, Oxford 1991.

—— *Multicultural Citizenship*, Oxford University Press, Oxford 1995.

—— *Politics in the Vernacular: Nationalism, Multiculturalism and Citizenship*, Oxford University Press, Oxford 2001.

Kymlicka W. and W. Norman (eds.), *Citizenship in Diverse Societies*, Oxford University Press, Oxford 2000.

Laborde, C., 'From Constitutional to Civic Patriotism', in: *British Journal of Political Science* 32, 2002, pp. 591–612.

Lacroix, J. 'For a European Constitutional Patriotism', in: *Political Studies* 50, 2002, pp. 944–958.

Ladmiral, J.-R. and E. M. Lipiansky, *La communication interculturelle*, Armand Colin Editeur, Paris 1989.

Research Centre on Migration and Ethnic Relations (ERCOMER), Utrecht 1995, pp. 71–88.

Negt, O.and A. Kluge, *Öffentlichkeit und Erfahrung*, Suhrkamp Verlag, Frankfurt am Main 1972.

Nicholson, L. and S. Seidman (eds.), *Social postmodernism: Beyond identity politics*, Cambridge University Press, Cambridge 1995.

Norman, W., 'Justice and Stability in multinational societies', in: A. Gagnon and J. Tully (eds.), *Multinational Democracies*, Cambridge University Press, Cambridge, 2001, pp. 90–109.

Norris Lance, M.and J. O'Leary Hawthorne, *The Grammar of Meaning: Normative and Semantic Discourse*, Cambridge University Press, Cambridge 1997.

Novi, L., 'Lebenswelten italienischer Migranten', in: J. Motte, R. Ohlinger and A. v. Oswald (eds.), *50 Jahre Bundesrepublik – 50 Jahre Einwanderung. Nachkriegsgeschichte als Migrationsgeschichte*, Campus, Frankfurt/New York 1999, pp. 243–258.

Offe, C., 'Challenging the Boundaries of Institutional Politics: Social Movements Since the 1960s', in: C. S. Maier (Ed.), *Changing Boundaries of the Poltical: Essays on the Evolving Balance Between the State and Society, Public and Private in Europe*, Cambridge University Press, Cambridge 1987.

—— 'Demokratie und Wohlfahrtsstaat: Eine europäische Regimeform unter dem Stress der europäischen Integration?', in: W. Streek (ed.), *Internationale Wirtschaft, nationale Demokratie: Herausforderungen für die Demokratietheorie*, Campus Verlag, Frankfurt/New York 1998, pp. 99–136.

—— '"Homogeneity" and Constitutional Democracy: Coping with Identity Conflicts through Group Rights', in: *The Journal of Political Philosophy* 6:2, 1998, pp. 113–141.

Ong, A., *Flexible Citizenship: The Cultural Logics of Transnationality*, Duke University Press, Durham 1999.

Oommen, T. K., *Citizenship, Nationality and Ethnicity*, Polity Press, Cambridge 1997.

Page, B., *Who Deliberates? Mass Media in Modern Democracy*, University of Chicago Press, Chicago 1996.

Pahl, R. E., 'The Search for Social Cohesion: from Durkheim to the European Commission', in: *Archives Européennes de Sociologie* 32:2, 1991, pp. 345–360.

Paillart, I. (ed.), *L'espace public et l'emprise de la communication*, Ellug, Grenoble 1995.

Papastergiadis, N., 'Tracing Hybridity in Theory', in: P. Werbner and T. Modood (eds.), *Debating Cultural Hybridity: Multi-cultural Identity and the Politics of Anti-racism*, Zed Books, London 1997, pp. 257–281.

Parekh, B., 'Dilemmas of a Multicultural Theory of Citizenship', in: *Constellations* 4:1, 1997, pp. 54–62.

—— *Rethinking Multiculturalism: Cultural Diversity and Political Theory*, Macmillan, London 2000.

—— *The Future of Multi-Ethnic Britain: Report of the Commission on the Future of Multi-Ethnic Britain*, Profile Books, London 2000.

Park, R. (ed.), *The University Studies in Urban Sociology*, Chicago University Press, Chicago 1925.

Passerini, L., *Europe in Love, Love in Europe*, I.B. Tauris Publishers, London 1998.

Peiss, K., 'Going Public: Women in Nineteenth Century Cultural History', in: *American Literary History* 3:4, 1991, pp. 817–828.

Peters, B., 'Der Sinn von Öffentlichkeit', in: F. Neidhart (ed.), *Öffentlichkeit, öffentliche Meinung, soziale Bewegungen (Kölner Zeitschrift für Soziologie und Sozialpsychologie, Sonderheft 3)*, Westdeutscher Verlag, Opladen 1994, pp. 42–76.

—— 'On Public Deliberation and Public Culture: Reflections on the Public Sphere', in: *InIIS-Arbeitspapier (Universität Bremen)* 7, 1997.

—— 'Nationale und transnationale Öffentlichkeit: Eine Problemskizze', in: C. Honegger, S. Hradil and F. Traxler (eds.), *Grenzenlose Gesellschaft?*, Leske+Budrich, Opladen 1999, pp. 661–673.

—— 'Deliberative Öffentlichkeit', in: L. Wingert and K. Günther (eds.), *Die Öffentlichkeit der Vernunft und die Vernunft der Öffentlichkeit: Festschrift für Jürgen Habermas*, Suhrkamp Verlag,

Frankfurt am Main 2001, pp. 655–677.

Peters B., S. Sifft, A. Wimmel, M. Brüggemann and K. Kleinen-Von Königslöw, 'National and Transnational Public Spheres: The Case of the EU', in: *European Review* 13:1, 2005, pp. 139–160.

Petersmann, E. U., 'Constitutionalism, Constitutional Law and European Integration', in E. U. Petersmann (ed.), *Constitutional Problems of European Integration*, Special Issue 46, Aussenwirtschaft, 1991, pp. 247–280.

Philipper, I., *Biographische Dimension der Migration: Zur Lebensgeschichte von Italienerinnen in Deutschland*, Beltzverlag, Weinheim 1997.

Phillips, A., *Democracy and Difference*, Polity Press, Cambridge 1993.

Picht, R., 'Interkulturelles Lernen und internationale Qualifikation', in: I. Gogolin et al. (eds.), *Kultur- und Sprachenvielfalt in Europa*, Waxmann Verlag, Münster 1991, pp. 176–187.

Pizzorno, A., 'Politics Unbound', in: C. S. Maier (ed.), *Changing Boundaries of the Political: Essays on the Evolving Balance Between the State and Society, Public and Private in Europe*, Cambridge University Press, Cambridge 1987, pp. 27–62.

Preuss, U. K., 'Problems of the Concept of European Citizenship', in: *European Law Journal* 1:3, 1995, pp. 267–281.

—— 'Citizenship in the European Union: a Paradigm for Transnational Democracy?', in: D. Archibugi, D. Held and M. Köhler (eds.), *Re-imagining Political Community. Studies in Cosmopolitan Democracy*, Polity Press, Cambridge 1998, pp. 138–151.

—— 'The Relevance of the Concept of Citizenship for the Political and Constitutional Development of the EU', in: U. K. Preuss and F. Requejo (eds.), *European Citizenship, Multiculturalism, and the State*, Nomos Verlag, Baden-Baden 1998, pp. 11–28.

—— 'Citizenship and Democracy in Europe: Foundations and Challenges', paper presented at the Conference on European Citizenship at Columbia University, 21 November 2003 [on file with the author].

Pries, L. (ed.), *Transnationale Migration, Soziale Welt, Sonderband 12*, Nomos Verlag, Baden-Baden 1997.

Projekt zur Förderung des Schulerfolgs italienischer Kinder in Deutschland e.V., *Informationsblätter*, Frankfurt am Main 1998.

Pugliese, E., 'Italy Between Emigration and Immigration and the Problem of Citizenship', in: D. Cesarani and M. Fulbrook (eds.), *Citizenship, Nationality and Migration in Europe*, Routledge, London/New York 1996, pp. 106–121.

Putnam, H., 'Analyticity and Apriority: Beyond Wittgenstein and Quine', in: H. Putnam, *Reason, Truth and History*, Cambridge University Press, Cambridge 1981, pp. 115–138.

—— *Reason, Truth and History*, Cambridge University Press, Cambridge 1981.

—— 'Philosophers and Human Understanding', in: H. Putnam, *Realism and Reason: Philosophical Papers, III*, Cambridge University Press, Cambridge 1983, pp. 184–204.

—— *Realism and Reason: Philosophical Papers, III*, Cambridge University Press, Cambridge 1983.

—— 'Vagueness and Alternative Logic', in: H. Putnam, *Realism and Reason: Philosophical Papers, III*, Cambridge University Press, Cambridge 1983, pp. 271–286.

—— 'Why Reason can't be naturalized', in: H. Putnam, *Realism and Reason. Philosophical Papers, III*, Cambridge University Press, Cambridge 1983, pp. 229–247.

—— 'The Science-Ethic Distinction', in: M. Nussbaum and A. Sen (eds.), *The Quality of Life*, Oxford University Press, Oxford 1993, pp. 143–157.

—— 'The Question of Realism', in: H. Putnam, *Words and Life*, Cambridge University Press, Cambridge 1994.

Putnam, R., *Making Democracy Work: Civic Traditions in Modern Italy*, Princeton University Press, Princeton 1993.

Quine, W. V., *World and Object*, Harvard University Press, Cambridge, MA, 1960.

Rawls, J., 'The Domain of the Political and Overlapping Consensus', in: *New York Law Review* 64:2, 1989, pp. 233–255.

—— *Die Idee des politischen Liberalismus: Aufsätze 1978–1989*, Suhrkamp Verlag, Frankfurt am Main 1992.

—— *Political Liberalism*, Columbia University Press, New York 1993.

Raz, J., 'Liberalism, Skepticism and Democracy', in: *Iowa Law Review* 74:4, 1989, pp. 761–786.

—— 'Multiculturalism: A liberal Perspective', in: *Dissent* 1, 1994, pp. 67–79.

Réau, E. de, *L'idée d'Europe au XXe siècle: Des mythes aux réalités*, Editions complexe, Paris 1996.

Renan, E., 'Qu'est-ce qu'une nation?', in: E. Renan, *Oeuvres complètes*, vol. 1, Calmann Lévy, Paris 1947.

Reynié, D., *Le triomphe de l'opinion publique: L'espace public français du XVIe au XXe siècle*, Editions Odile Jacob, Paris 1998.

Ricoeur, P., *Hermeneutics and the Human Sciences: Essays on Language, Action and Interpretation*, Cambridge University Press, Cambridge 1981.

—— 'Imagination in Discourse and in Action', in: P. Ricoeur, *From Text to Action: Essays in Hermeneutics, II*, Athlone Press, London 1991, pp. 169–187.

Risse, T., 'European Institutions and Identity Change', in: R. H. Herrmann, T. Risse and M. B. Brewer (eds.), *Transnational Identities: Becoming European in the EU*, Rowman & Littlefield, New York 2004.

Robbins, B., *Secular Vocations: Intellectuals, Professionalism, Culture*, Verso, London 1993.

Roche, M. and R. van Berkel (eds.), *European Citizenship and Social Exclusion*, Ashgate, Aldershot 1997.

Rosanvallon, P., *La démocratie inachevée: Histoire de la souveraineté du peuple en France*, Gallimard, Paris 2000.

Rubin, H. and I. Rubin, *Qualitative Interviewing: The Art of Hearing Data*, Sage, London 1995.

Sabel, C. and J. Cohen, 'Directly-Deliberative Polyarchy', in: O. Gerstenberg and C. Joerges (eds.), *Private Governance, Democratic Constitutionalism and Supranationalism*, European Communities, Brussels 1998, pp. 1–30.

—— 'Sovereignty and Solidarity in the EU: A Working Paper Where We Face Some Facts', in: *Reconfiguring Work and Welfare in the New Economy: A Transatlantic Dialogue*, A Conference at the European Union Center, UW-Madison, 2001.

Sabel, C., S. Helfer and J. P. MacDuffie, 'Pragmatic Collaborations: Advancing Knowledge While Controlling Opportunism', in: *Industrial and Corporate Change* 9:3, 2000, pp. 443–487.

Sahlins, P., *Boundaries. The Making of France and Spain in the Pyrenees*, University of California Press, Berkeley, CA, 1989.

Sandel, M., *Liberalism and the Limits of Justice*, Cambridge University Press, Cambridge 1982.

Sassatelli, M., 'Imagined Europe: The Shaping of a European Cultural Identity through EU Cultural Policy', in: *European Journal of Social Theory* 5:4, 2002, pp. 435–451.

Sassen, S., *Cities of a World Economy*, Pine Forge Press, Thousand Oaks 1994.

Saussure, F. de, *Cours de linguistique générale*, Payot, Paris 1922.

Sauter, S., *Wir sind 'Frankfurter Türken': Adoleszente Ablösungsprozesse in der deutschen Einwanderungsgesellschaft*, Brandes & Apsel, Frankfurt am Main 2000.

Scharpf, F., 'Democratic Policy in Europe', in: *European Law Journal* 2:2, 1996, pp. 136–155.

—— 'Negative and Positive Integration in the Political Economy of European Welfare State', in: G. Marks, F. Scharpf, P. C. Schmitter and W. Streek, *Governance in the European Union*, Sage, London 1996, pp. 15–39.

—— *Games Real Actors Play: Actor-Centered Institutionalism in Policy Research*, Westview Press, New York 1997.

—— 'Demokratie in der transnationalen Politik', in: W. Streek (ed.), *Internationale Wirtschaft, nationale Demokratie: Herausforderungen für die Demokratietheorie*, Campus Verlag, Frankfurt am Main/New York 1998, pp. 151–174.

—— *Governing in Europe: Effective and Democratic?*, Oxford University Press, Oxford 1999.

—— 'European Governance: Common Concerns vs. The Challenge of Diversity', MPIfG Working Papers 01/6, Cologne 2001.

Schlesinger, P. C., '"Europeanness" – A New Cultural Battlefield?', in: *Innovation in Social Sciences* 5:2, 1992, pp. 11–22.

—— 'Europeanisation and the Media: National Identity and the Public Sphere', in: *Working Paper No. 7, Oslo: ARENA*, 1995, pp. 1–33.

—— 'From Cultural Defense to Political Culture: Media, Politics snd Collective Identity in the European Union', in: *Media, Culture & Society* 19:3, 1997, pp. 369–391.

—— 'The Babel of Europe? An Essay on Networks and Communicative Spaces', in D. Castiglione and C. Longman (eds.), *Public Discources of Law and Politics in Multicultural Societies*, Hart Publishing, Oxford, forthcoming.

Schmitter, P., 'Representation and the Future Euro-Polity', in: *Staatswissenschaften und Staatspraxis* 3:3, 1992, pp. 379–405.

—— 'Alternatives for the Future European Polity: Is Federalism the Only Answer?', in: M. Telò (ed.), *Démocratie et construction européenne*, Presses de l'Université de Bruxelles, Brussels 1995.

—— 'Imagining the Future of the Euro-Polity with the Help of New Concepts', in: G. Marks, F. Scharpf and P. C. Schmitter and W. Streek (eds.), *Governance in the European Union*, Sage, London 1996.

—— 'If the Nation-State Were to Wither away in Europe, What Might Replace it?', in: S. Gustavsson and L. Lewin (eds.), *The Future of the Nation State*, Nerenius & Santerus, Stockholm 1996, pp. 211–245.

—— 'Is it Really Possible to Democratize the Euro-Polity?', in: A. Føllesdal and P. Koslowski (eds.), *Democracy and the European Union*, Springer, Berlin 1997, pp. 13–36.

—— *How to Democratize the European Union … and Why Bother?*, Rowman & Littlefield, Lanham 2000.

—— 'The Scope of Citizenship in a Democratized European Union: From Economic to Political to Social and Cultural?', in: K. Eder and B. Giesen, *European Citizenship between National Legacies and Postnational Projects*, Oxford University Press, Oxford 2000.

—— 'What is There to Legitimate in the European Union … and How Might this be Accomplished', in: forthcoming.

—— 'Needs, Interests, Concerns, Actions, Associations and Modes of Intermediation: Toward a Theory of Interest Politics in Contemporary Society', (unpublished manuscript).

Schmitter, P. C. and W. Streeck, 'From National Corporatism to Transnational Pluralism: Organized Interests in the Single European Market', in: *Politics & Society* 19:2, 1991, pp. 133–164.

—— 'Organized Interests and the Europe of 1992', in: N. J. Ornstein and M. Perlman (eds.), *Political Power and Social Change: The United States Faces the United Europe*, AEI Press, Washington, DC 1991, pp. 46–67.

Schönwälder, K., 'Migration, Refugees and Ethnic Plurality as Issues of Public and Political Debates in (West) Germany', in: D. Cesarani and M. Fulbrook (eds.), *Citizenship, Nationality and Migration in Europe*, Routledge, London/New York 1996, pp. 157–187.

Schultze, G., 'The importance of associations and clubs for the identities of young Turks in Germany', in: J. Rex and B. Drury (eds.), *Ethnic Mobilisation in a Multi-cultural Europe*, Avebury, London 1994, pp. 135–142.

Schütze, F., 'Biographieforschung und narratives Interview', in: *Neue Praxis: Zeitschrift für Sozialarbeit, Sozialpädagogik und Sozialpolitik* 13:3, 1973, pp. 283–293.

Seligman, A. B., *The Idea of Civil Society*, Princeton University Press, Princeton 1992.

—— 'The Fragile Ethical Vision of Civil Society', in: B. S. Turner (ed.), *Citizenship and Social Theory*, Sage, London 1993, pp. 139–161.

Sennett, R., *The Fall of Public Man*, Knopf, New York 1974.

Shklar, J., *American Citizenship: The Quest for Inclusion*, Harvard University Press, Cambridge, MA, 1991.

Shohat, E. and R. Stam, *Unthinking Eurocentrism: Multiculturalism and the Media*, Routledge, London/New York 1994.

Shore, C., 'Inventing the "People's Europe": Critical Approaches to European Community "Cultural Policy"', in: *Man* 28:4, 1993, pp. 779–800.

—— 'Usurpers or pioneers? European Commission bureaucrats and the question of "European consciousness"', in: A. Cohen and N. Rapport (eds.), *Questions of Consiousness*, Routledge, London/New York 1995, pp. 217–236.

—— 'Governing Europe: European Union audiovisual policy and the politics of identity', in: C. Shore and S. Wright (eds.), *Anthropology of Policy: Critical Perspectives on Governance and Power*, Routledge, London/New York 1997, pp. 165–192.

—— *Building Europe: The Cultural Politics of European Integration*, Routledge, London/New York 2000.

Shore, C. and A. Black, 'Citizen's Europe and the Construction of European Identity', in: V. A. Goddard, J. R. Llobera and C. Shore (eds.), *The Anthropology of Europe: Identity and Boundaries in Conflict*, Berg, Oxford 1994.

Shotter, J., 'Psychology and Citizenship: Identity and Belonging', in: B. S. Turner (ed.), *Citizenship and Social Theory*, Sage, London 1993, pp. 115–148.

Sintomer, Y., *La démocratie impossible? Politique et modernité chez Weber et Habermas*, La Découverte, Paris 1999.

Sintomer, Y. and M.-H. Bacqué, 'L'espace public dans les quartiers populaires d'habitat social', in: C. Neveu (ed.), *Espace publique et engagement politique: Enjeu et logique de la citoyenneté locale*, L'Harmattan, Paris 1999, pp. 115–148.

Smith, A. D., 'Towards a Global Culture?', in: *Theory, Culture & Society* 7:2–3, 1990, pp. 171–191.

—— 'National identities and the idea of European unity', in: *International Affairs* 68:1, 1992, pp. 55–76.

Somers, M. R., 'Citizenship and the Place of the Public Sphere: Law, Community, and Political Culture in the Transition to Democracy', in: *American Sociological Review* 58:5, 1993, pp. 587–620.

—— 'Narrating and Naturalizing Civil Society and Citizenship Theory: The Place of Political Culture and the Public Sphere', in: *Sociological Theory* 13:3, 1995, pp. 229–274.

—— 'What's Political or Cultural about Political Culture and the Public Sphere? Toward an Historical Sociology of Concept Formation', in: *Sociological Theory* 13:2, 1995, pp. 113–144.

Soysal, Y., *Limits of Citizenship: Migrants and Postnational Membership in Europe*, University of Chicago Press, Chicago 1994.

—— 'Changing Citizenship in Europe. Remarks on postnational membership and the national state', in: D. Cesarani and M. Fulbrook (eds.), *Citizenship, Nationality and Migration in Europe*, Routledge, London/New York 1996, pp. 17–29.

—— 'Changing Parameters of Citizenship and Claim-making: Organized Islam in European Public Spheres', in: *Theory and Society* 26:4, 1997, pp. 509–527.

Spradley, J., *The Ethnographic Interview*, Harcourt Brace, Orlando, FL, 1997.

Stolcke, V., 'New Boundaries, New Rhetorics of Exclusion in Europe', in: *Current Anthropology* 36:1, 1995, pp. 1–24.

Strauss, A. and J. Corbin, *Basics of Qualitative Research: Grounded Theory, Procedures and Techniques*, Sage, London 1990.

Stråth, B. (ed.), *Europe and the Other, and Europe as the Other*, Peter Lang Verlag, Brussels 2000.

Streek, W., 'Einleitung: Internationale Wirtschaft, nationale Demokratie?', in: W. Streek (ed.), *Internationale Wirtschaft, nationale Demokratie: Herausforderungen für die Demokratietheorie*, Campus Verlag, Frankfurt am Main/New York 1998, pp. 7–58.

Street, J., *Politics and Popular Culture*, Polity Press, Cambridge 1997.

Swidler, A., 'Culture in Action: Symbol and Strategies', in: *American Sociological Review* 51, 1986, pp. 273–286.

Taggart, P., 'A Touchstone of Dissent: Euroscepticism in Contemporary Western European Party Systems', in: *European Journal of Political Research* 33, 1998, pp. 363–388.

Tajfel, H. (ed.), *Human Groups and Social Categories*, Cambridge University Press, Cambridge

1981.

Tarrow, S., 'Building a Composite Polity: Popular Contentions in the European Union', in: *Working Paper (Institute for European Studies, Cornell University)* 3, 1998.

Taylor, C., 'Atomism', in: C. Taylor, *Philosophy and the Human Sciences: Philosophical Papers*, vol. 2, Cambridge University Press, Cambridge 1985, pp. 187–210.

—— *Sources of the Self: The Making of Modern Identity*, Harvard University Press, Cambridge, MA, 1989.

—— 'Modes of Civil Society', in: *Public Culture* 3:1, 1990, pp. 95–118.

—— *The Ethics of Authenticity*, Harvard University Press, Cambridge, MA, 1992.

—— 'The Politics of Recognition', in: C. Taylor and A. Gutman (eds.), *Multiculturalism and the Politics of Recognition*, Princeton University Press, Princeton 1992, pp. 25–73.

—— 'Liberal Politics and the Public Sphere', in: C. Taylor, *Philosophical Arguments*, Harvard University Press, Cambridge, MA, 1995, pp. 257–287.

—— 'Nationalism and Modernity', in: R. McKim and J. McMahan (eds.), *The Morality of Nationalism*, Oxford University Press, Oxford 1997, pp. 31–55.

Taylor, C. and A. Gutman (eds.), *Multiculturalism and the Politics of Recognition*, Princeton University Press, Princeton 1994.

Taylor, P., *The European Union in the 1990s*, Oxford University Press, Oxford 1996.

Tertilt, H., *Turkish Power Boys. Ethnographie einer Jugendbande*, Suhrkamp Verlag, Frankfurt am Main 1996.

Therborn, G., *European Modernity and Beyond: The Trajectory of European Societies 1945–2000*, Sage, London 1995.

Thomas, A., 'Psychologische Grundlagen interkultureller Kommunikation und interkulturellen Lernens im Zusammenhang mit Jugendaustausch', in: I. Gogolin et al. (eds.), *Kultur- und Sprachenvielfalt in Europa*, Waxmann Verlag, Münster 1991, pp. 188–202.

Thompson, J. B., *The Media and Modernity: A Social Theory of the Media*, Polity Press, Cambridge 1995.

Tietze, N., *Islamische Identitäten: Formen muslimischer Religiosität junger Männer in Deutschland und Frankreich*, Hamburger Edition, Hamburg 2001.

Todorov, T., *Mikhail Bakhtine, le principe dialogique*, Le Seuil, Paris 1981.

Touraine, A., 'European Sociologists Between Economic Globalization and Cultural Fragmentation', in: T. Boje, B. van Steenbergen and S. Walby (eds.), *European Societies: Fusion or Fiction?*, Routledge, London/New York 1999, pp. 249–262.

Trenz, H.-J., 'Mobilising Collective Identities: the Public Discourse on Immigration in Portugal and Germany', Dissertation, European University Institute, Florence 1999.

Tully, J., *Strange Multiplicity: Constitutionalism in an Age of Diversity*, Cambridge University Press, Cambridge 1995.

Turner, B. S., 'Contemporary Problems in the Theory of Citizenship', in: B. S. Turner (ed.), *Citizenship and Social Theory*, Sage, London 1993, pp. 1–18.

Turner, T., 'Anthropology and Multiculturalism: What is Anthropology that Multiculturalists Should be Mindful of It?', in: *Cultural Anthropology* 8:4, 1993, pp. 411–429.

van de Steeg, M., Bedingungen für die Entstehungen von Öffentlichkeit in der EU', in: A. Klein and R. Koopmans (eds.), *Bürgerschaft, Öffentlichkeit und Demokratie in Europa*, Leske+Budrich, Opladen 2002, pp. 169–190.

van den Brink, B., *The Tragedy of Liberalism: An Alternative Defense of a Political Tradition*, SUNY Press, Albany, NY, 2000.

Vološinov, V., *Marxismus und Sprachphilosophie*, Ullstein Verlag, Frankfurt/Berlin 1975.

—— *Marxism and the Philosophy of Language*, Harvard University Press, Cambridge, MA, 1986.

von Humboldt, W., *Werke*, vol. III, *Schriften zur Sprachphilosophie*, Wissenschaftliche Buchgesellschaft, Darmstadt 1963.

—— *On Language: On the Diversity of Human Language Construction and its Influence on the Mental Development of the Human species*, M. Losonsky (ed.), trans. P. Heath, Cambridge University Press, Cambridge 1999.

Wagner, P., *Soziologie der Moderne*, Campus Verlag, Frankfurt am Main/New York 1995.

—— 'Fest-Stellungen, Beobachtungen zur sozialwissenschaftlichen Diskussion über Identität', in: A. Assmann and H. Friese (eds.), *Identitäten: Erinnerung, Geschichte, Identität*, 3, Suhrkamp Verlag, Frankfurt am Main 1998, pp. 44–72.

Wagner, P. and H. Friese, 'Not All that is Solid Melts into Air: Modernity and Contingency', in: M. Featherstone and S. Lash (eds.), *Spaces of Culture: City, Nation, World*, Sage, London 1999, pp. 101–115.

Waldron, J., 'Minority Cultures and the Cosmopolitan Alternative', in: T. v. Willigenburg, F. Heeger and W. v. d. Burg (eds.), *Nation, State and Coexistence of Different Communities*, Kok Pharos, Kampen 1995, pp. 105–151.

—— 'Multiculturalism and Mélange', in: R. Fullinwider (ed.), *Public Education in a Multicultural Society: Policy, Theory, Critique*, Cambridge University Press, Cambridge 1996. pp. 93–118.

—— *Law and Disagreement*, Oxford University Press, Oxford 1999.

—— 'Cultural Identity and Civic Responsibility', in: W. Kymlicka and W. Norman (eds.), *Citizenship in Diverse Societies*, Oxford University Press, Oxford 2000, pp. 155–176.

Wallerstein, I., 'Culture as the Ideological Battleground of the Modern World-System', in: *Theory, Culture & Society* 7:2–3, 1990, pp. 31–55.

—— 'Eurocentrism and its Avatars: The Dilemmas of Social Science', in: *New Left Review* I:226, 1997, pp. 93–107.

Walzer, M., *Spheres of Justice*, Basic Books, New York 1983.

—— 'The Idea of Civil Society: A Path to Social Reconstruction', in: *Dissent* 38, 1991, pp. 293–304.

—— 'The Politics of Difference: Statehood and Toleration in a Multicultural World', in: R. McKim and J. McMahan (eds.), *The Morality of Nationalism*, Oxford University Press, Oxford 1997, pp. 245–257.

Warner, M., 'The Mass Public and the Mass Subject', in: C. Calhoun (ed.), *Habermas and the Public Sphere*, MIT Press, Cambridge, MA, 1992, pp. 377–401.

Weber, E., *Peasants into Frenchmen*, Stanford University Press, Stanford, CA, 1976.

Weiler, J., 'The Transformation of Europe', in: *The Yale Law Journal* 100, 1991, pp. 2403–2483.

—— 'Does Europe Need a Constitution? Demos, Telos and the German Maastricht Decision', in: *European Law Journal* 1:3, 1995, pp. 219–258.

—— 'Europe: The Case against the Case for Statehood', in: *European Law Journal* 4:1, 1998, pp. 43–62.

—— *The Constitution of Europe: "Do the New Clothes Have an Emperor" and Other Essays on European Integration*, Cambridge University Press, Cambridge 1999.

Weiss, R., *Learning from Strangers: The Art and Method of Qualitative Interview Studies*, Free Press, New York 1994.

Wellmer, A., 'Conditions of a Democratic Culture', in: A. Wellmer, *Endgames*, MIT Press, Cambridge, MA, 1998, pp. 39–62.

Werbner, P., *The Migration Process: Capital, Gifts and Offerings among British Pakistanis*, Berg Publishing, Oxford 1990.

—— 'Introduction: The Dialectics of Cultural Hybridity', in: P. Werbner and T. Modood (eds.), *Debating Cultural Hybridity: Multicultural Identities and the Politics of Anti-Racism*, Zed Books, London 1997.

Werbner, P. and T. Modood (eds.), *Debating Cultural Hybridity: Multi-cultural Identities and the Politics of Anti-Racism*, Zed Books, London 1997.

—— (eds.), *The Politics of Multiculturalism in the New Europe: Racism, Identity and Community*, Zed Books, London 1997.

Wiener, A., 'Making sense of the new geography of citizenship: Fragmented citizenship in the European Union', in: *Theory and Society* 26:4, 1997, pp. 529–560.

Williams, B., *Problems of the Self: Philosophical Papers 1956–1972*, Cambridge University Press, Cambridge 1973.

Williams, R., *Culture and Society 1780–1950*, Chatto & Windus, London 1958.

Wittgenstein, L., *Philosophical Investigations*, Blackwell, Oxford 1967.
—— 'Philosophische Untersuchungen', in: L. Wittgenstein, *Werkausgabe, Bd.1*, Suhrkamp Verlag, Frankfurt am Main 1995, pp. 224–458.
Wolton, D., *La dernière utopie: Naissance de l'Europe démocratique*, Flammarion, Paris 1993.
Young, I. M., *Justice and the Politics of Difference*, Princeton University Press, Princeton 1990.
—— 'Communication and the Other: Beyond Deliberative Democracy', in: S. Benhabib (ed.), *Democracy and Difference: Contesting the Boundaries of the Political*, Princeton University Press, Princeton 1996, pp. 120–135.
—— *Inclusion and Democracy*, Oxford University Press, Oxford 2000.
Zabusky, S. E., *Launching Europe: An Ethnography of European Cooperation in Space Science*, Princeton University Press, Princeton 1995.
Zizek, S., 'Multiculturalism, or, the Cultural Logic of Multinational Capitalism', in: *New Left Review* I:225, 1997, pp. 28–51.
Zürn, M., *Regieren jenseits des Nationalstaats*, Suhrkamp Verlag, Frankfurt am Main 1998.
—— 'Democratic Governance Beyond the Nation State: The EU and Other International Institutions', in: *European Journal of International Relations* 6:2, 2000, pp. 183–222.

Index